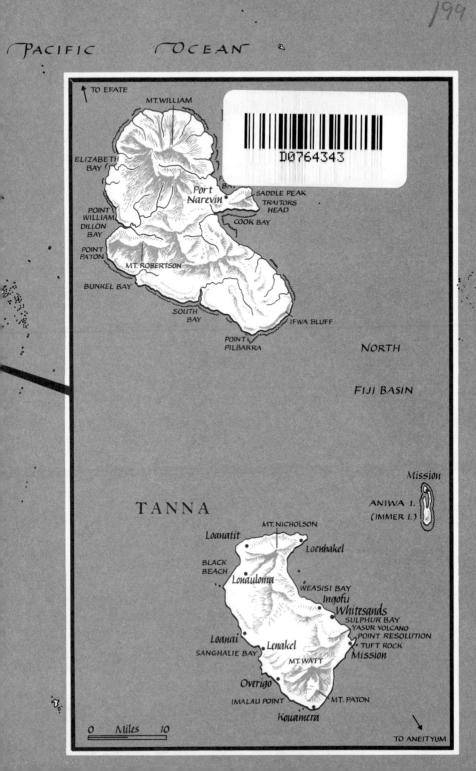

199

PACIFIC OCEAN

TO EFATE

MT. WILLIAM

D0764343

ELIZABETH
BAY

Port
Narevin

SADDLE PEAK
TRAITORS
HEAD

POINT
WILLIAM
DILLON
BAY

COOK BAY

POINT
PATON

MT. ROBERTSON

BUNKEL BAY

SOUTH
BAY

IFWA BLUFF

POINT
PILBARRA

NORTH

FIJI BASIN

Mission

ANIWA I.
(IMMER I.)

TANNA

MT. NICHOLSON

Loanatit

Loenbakel

BLACK
BEACH

Lonauloma

WEASISI BAY

Ingofu
Whitesands
SULPHUR BAY
YASUR VOLCANO
POINT RESOLUTION
TUFT ROCK
Mission

Loanai

Lenakel

SANGHALIE BAY

MT. WATT

Overigo

MT. PATON

IMALAU POINT

Kouamera

0   Miles   10

TO ANEITYUM

By Edward Rice

*A Polemical Work
about a Black Tragedy*

DOUBLEDAY & COMPANY, INC.
GARDEN CITY, NEW YORK
1974

JOHN FRUM
HE COME

EDWARD RICE

ISBN: 0-385-00523-7
Library of Congress Catalog Card Number 73-79704
Copyright © 1974 by Edward Rice
All Rights Reserved
Printed in the United States of America
First Edition

The ornament on the title page is a reproduction of a New Hebridean sand drawing of a palm leaf.

To all the people of the world,
of whatever race or color,
who pass their lives
with some bastard's foot
on their faces.

That fella he messiah bilong black island
bring Cargo bilong him long America
Book long John Frum
two joe captain cockle shell
Captain Honest, Captain World
Kalbapen, Karaperamum
Man-Tanna
Tom Navy, Mr Nabnab
Jake, Joe, Sam, Henry
Noah, Isac, Gladys
He got friends all right
He all tok-tok
bout Cargo he come America
It is true all right

john the great
my brother here is joe: my name
  is karaperamum
every thing is near me
see us two joe captain cockle shell

JOHN FRUM
in a letter

[Mellis, a John Frum leader at Sulphur Bay] By what authority has this man come? Who is he? I was seventeen years in prison and sixteen years here, thirty-three years in all, and still people ask me about John. I am tired of answering damn fool questions.

What is this man's authority? Who sent him?

[John Kalate, from Green Point] John is his authority. This man has already told you that he was sitting in a very small place and reading a very small piece of paper when he saw the name John Frum. His authority comes from John. It was John who brought him here. That is his authority, from John.

CONTENTS

ILLUSTRATIONS

9. Lauhman Teni
10. John Kalate
11. Sam Tacuma
12. Mellis, John Frum leader at Sulphur Bay
13. Sulphur Bay
14. Tom Hiwa
15. Tom Navy
16. A John Frum cross

INTRODUCTION

This is a book about "Cargo" and a cargo messiah named John Frum. This enigmatic person appeared shortly before World War II on an obscure island in the South Pacific—Tanna in the New Hebrides—coming to lead the Tannese out of the bondage of the white man. Freedom was the first stage in John's message; the second was the proclamation of Cargo.

John—variously described as a Tannese, or as a white, or as a man who could take any form—was seen by a number of Tannese over a period of several years, first on Tanna and later over a hundred miles away on the island of Efate, in Port Vila, where several dozen Tannese had been imprisoned for believing in him. After the War John went away, though from time to time he would speak through certain leaders who would then pass his messages on to the people. Even today Chief Mellis (or Mailes) at Sulphur Bay on Tanna claims he sees John still.

Cargo on Tanna follows the tradition of other Melanesian islands. Loosely defined, Cargo is the belief that someday the people of this or that place—the locale is most often the South Pacific—will be given certain material goods now possessed by whites and denied to the black and brown man by white selfishness. Belief in Cargo first arose in the nineteenth century, when Europeans began to appear in number in the South Pacific. Cargo-type movements appeared among the Maori of New Zealand, the Hawaiians and the Fijians, to name but a few; they were also noticed among the American Indians, and in Africa, Siberia and China and other areas which felt the sudden pressure of white expansion. South Pacific Cargo received its greatest impetus during World War II, after the arrival of American troops, who landed on dozens of islands with unlimited types of western goods, from war materials to washing machines, movie theaters, Nissen huts, eating utensils, canned foods, candy bars and chewing gum, cigarettes, beer and whiskey and other luxuries undreamed of by people scarcely out of the Stone Age. The people of these islands, commonly called Kanakas,[1] had had little or no contact with whites in the past, and now they made the natural assumption that such goods were the product of magic, for no one had seen them being made. And since many of the American troops were black, the Kanaka realized that there were black men who shared in this white magic. From this followed the assumption that with his own magic the Kanaka could have similar goods. But these movements were not leaderless. Various messiahs arose everywhere, promising both the coming of Cargo by ship or plane (or even by rocket in one area of New Guinea) and an end to white domination. Few of these messiahs lasted more than a short time, a few months or a few years being the normal course of their leadership. When Cargo did not come as promised, their followers lost faith and turned to other leaders or gave up the idea of Cargo. Some groups reverted to their subservient colonial role, passive and inward-turning. Others, maturing from the experience, saw the solution in political action or in labor organizations, co-operatives and national parties. All too often the authorities (usually British) sought to stop Cargo by arresting leaders, an action that elevated them to the status of martyrs, or at least helped prolong that particular movement because its members could now believe that the whites were trying to prevent them from discovering the "secret" of Cargo which had so long been hidden.

On Tanna, a quite isolated island at the bottom of the New Hebrides chain, the messianic cult of John Frum has survived since the period before World War II. John, according to the Tannese, may have appeared as early as 1937, and one leader—Lauhman Teni—dates John's first manifestation about 1930. The cult was firmly established—and "John Frum" and his chief followers arrested—well before the time the American forces landed in Port Vila, the capital town of the islands, in mid-1942. What is remarkable, considering the extreme volatility of other cargo cults, is that the John Frum movement has survived so long and so persistently. It has endured seventeen years of mass arrests, deportation, exile and imprisonment of Frumist leaders and followers by the British, and now carries on in the expectation that John will return, with Cargo and with a better life for the people of Tanna, their white rulers being expelled. And Tanna, once the center of the universe, will again be eminent, sharing its role with its equal, America, which is expected to aid in the restoration of the island to its former glory. With John's Second Coming among the Tannese, as he told them in a dramatic meeting at Green Point, they will enter a land of "milk and honey."

The question of Cargo

For most whites the idea of Cargo is one of complete disbelief, bordering on ridicule. "Baloney" and "bullshit" are some of the least obnoxious phrases I have heard whites use in reference to Cargo. The inability of the unsophisticated native to understand the white man's means and methods of production and the expectation that white-produced goods will be given or will come freely to him seems to many whites humorous rather than tragic. For the white man's mind is unable to grasp the simple fact that not everyone in the world knows how western products are manufactured or where they come from. The white himself is taught from infancy about western products, and the native's failure to know their origin automatically gives the white a feeling of superiority; his fixed belief in his own better intelligence is once again confirmed. Some whites, more understanding, wonder at the black man's naïveté and express a certain sympathy for his ignorance. But no matter what attitude the white may have, few try to see Cargo from the viewpoint of the Kanaka.

Cargo has engaged the attention of a number of anthropologists and sociologists, primarily the movements in New Guinea and Papua, where the beliefs run wild and in profusion: docks have been built for the coming ships and airstrips hacked out of the jungles for planes with Cargo; in some instances the people even built decoy planes of bamboo and wood to attract the jets they can see and hear flying overhead. Cargo is also believed to be buried in the earth. The arrival, or discovery, of Cargo depends on learning the white man's secrets for obtaining it.

Cargo beliefs, in all their variations and shadings, have been profusely examined and written about by whites, so that today the scholarly literature runs into hundreds of essays, theses and studies, though complete books barely number half a dozen (I have listed the latter in the notes). In my own random reading I have found these works, short or long, to be scholarly and objective, as indeed they should be, but most of them share one great fault in common: they speak of Cargo as the white man sees it. In a word, their "neutrality" and "objectivity" are pro-white. Is the Kanaka's view of Cargo ever given? How does the black man, speaking as a *black man,* feel about Cargo?

There is another aspect. Lawrence[2] complains that many of the published works, while they "provide stimulating hypotheses," are "handicapped by the authors' lack of firsthand knowledge of actual cults." Worsley[3] adds another serious complaint: since research depends so much on the reports of District Agents, missionaries and other whites, "nearly all our material comes from sources hostile to the movements."

John Frum He Come tries to rectify these biases in its own rather special, biased way. *John Frum He Come* approaches Cargo from the black man's side, subjectively, emotionally, even "irrationally," though many whites' views of Cargo are included. But here the black man will speak in his own words. The book is empathetic and sympathetic to certain beliefs (primarily those of blacks) and hostile to others (whites'). For the book speaks insofar as possible with the voice of the black people of Melanesia, people of harsh, lush, ravaged lands, in voices of hope, anger, frustration, rage—voices that have been hurt yet remain trustful. How many whites could continue to express such yearnings in the face of what the black man has suffered?

You will find that *John Frum He Come* is not scientific in the accepted sense, that is, as an objective study. There can be nothing objective for me in writing about people who have been virtually destroyed by my fellow whites. So the book might be described at best as taking a poetic, mythic view of Cargo and its followers, because it is not only literal but universal. It is "factual," in the sense that the facts have been gathered from known sources, or are facts *believed* to be true and accepted as such in the minds of the people who present them, whether black or white.

*

Westerners must try to accept Cargo on its own terms, not theirs, for Cargo is a reality, even though their western-conditioned minds tell them it is impossible. What they are actually saying is that other people's Cargo is ridiculous and their own is real and true. For no matter how much whites may believe themselves superior and free of superstition, Cargo enters into everyone's life and hopes, whether white, black, brown, yellow or red. For, in a sense, any expectation of a reward or a return, gratuitously given by some other "force," physical or intangible, might be described as Cargo. As the late Thomas Merton said, we have in the primitive selves we often try to bury, something which is "alien, hostile and strange," which is continually trying to assert itself. We yearn for the mysterious, the ineffable, the irrational, and accept them against reason.

Within our own world, such expectations as winnings from sweepstakes, numbers, lotteries and sports pools, or foundation grants, welfare, marrying an heiress or a Rockefeller, a meteoric rise in some exotic career (being discovered by a movie or TV talent scout), or even in ordinary business, the discovery of a new miracle stock (a new IBM or Xerox), the reliance on cult works like I Ching or on astrology—these are all notably crass expressions of white Cargo yearnings. The fact that certain gratuitous rewards are bestowed from time to time (a few people do win sweepstake lotteries, or refrigerators on "The Price Is Right") serves to confirm such hopes for western Cargo. Religion easily becomes a form of Cargo: people pray before a statue of the Holy Infant of Prague for success in business, and there are numerous other devotions among Christians of all sects which will bring health, wealth and happiness. To say nothing of the gypsy, who *knows*. Even in the New Hebrides a kind of *white* Cargo runs rampant. The white occupation forces have gone all out for tourism in two centers (Vila and Santo), despite the fact that ordinary services such as electricity, water, sewerage, hotel space and telephones are in extremely short supply and cannot even meet the current demand. This kind of white man's "Cargo" expectation runs throughout many parts of the world. The subject will be discussed in more detail in a later chapter. Thus virtually any "unrealistic," almost magical, hope of bettering one's mundane life fits into the broad concept of Cargo.

*

I approach this book with a built-in bias. I have traveled in various parts of the "undeveloped" world—Latin America, India, the Middle East, Southeast Asia, East Africa, and know of the struggles of blacks and browns in the slums of American cities and red men on their "reservations"—and have a strong antipathy to the activities of the white man. Mr. Charlie is no kind, old, generous uncle, but a murderous son of a bitch. It is now a cliché that white civilization is in one bad way, but of course few whites do more than deplore it, meanwhile going about their business of being White, that is, exploitative, fascistic and murderous, forcing their ways upon others and robbing the rest of the world of land, resources, cultural objects and even soul-force. "Western civilization is disintegrating," remarked Mahatma Gandhi in a passage I am quoting from memory, "yet you have the arrogance to offer it as the cure for our own problems."

I am neither an anthropologist nor a sociologist. I have not researched cross-cousin relationships, upward mobility, comparative linguistics or comparative religions among the people of the New Hebrides, or any of the other scholarly subjects that are usually reserved for Ph.D. theses. What I have tried to do is present, first, a general picture of the white man's attack on the South Pacific, and then to detail one black island's cry of anguish under the white man's smothering presence. The cry is literal, but it is also symbolic, mythic, and it speaks not only for the people of Tanna but for all men anywhere, black, brown, yellow, red (and white) who are being destroyed—murdered! —by a superior force which can be seen and sometimes comprehended by the victims (and even emulated in an attempt to profit by, control or divert its obscene powers), a force which is always threatening and murderous. I use the word "murder" deliberately, for murder is the only description of what is happening to people whose way of life, history, religion, self-esteem, dignity, honor, tradition, custom, livelihood, soul, spirit, mind, art and culture are being destroyed by the whites of Europe and America. Everything of value, developed or accumulated over vast periods of time, often quite painfully and with much anguish and search, is now being eroded—stoved-in, chipped away, crushed—by the West. Transistor radios, the Latin alphabet, pidgin English, motion pictures, concrete-block houses, tin roofs, broken-down buses (have you ever ridden the public transportation in a Third World country?[4]), jobs in mines, factories and hotels, on roads, docks and plantations (working for whites of course), and all the other junk the West dumps on these poor people (with the possible exception of medical care) are no reward for the looting of their resources and the extinction of their lives. Families, clans, tribes, nations are destroyed, and no matter how cruel certain aspects of other people's lives may seem (and practices like child marriage, child labor, slavery, arranged marriages, and of course head-hunting and cannibalism, which are nearly extinct now, are objectionable to whites), the West should not arrogate to itself the privilege and the fun of tampering with them.

I know that I am taking an extreme and unpopular point of view—the white, no matter how liberal or radical, still thinks it is right to help the "unfortunates" of the world—and one which cannot be always defended (Mead makes a good case for western progress among the peoples of Peri, in the Manus Islands[5]), but my bias is one that I want to state in this book. I cannot be objective as a professional anthropologist or sociologist might be in covering the same ground. There is still a small hope for a kind of ecological movement to halt the contamination of people like those of Tanna—the majority of the human race, actually. Not only is time running short to save the world's natural resources, earth, air and sea, but her people as well, a point we are all vaguely conscious of. Man's primordial innocence is being destroyed by his primordial stupidity, greed, vanity and ignorance.

*

The book is the result of several years of reading in Cargo and related subjects, followed by a visit among the John Frum people. During the time I was on Tanna I spent most of my days among John's followers. We seemed to have established a good rapport with each other and a mutual trust. I say this not to boast (it is a commonplace that writers like to prove how In they are in obscure worlds) but merely to emphasize that the material in this book is, in my opinion, accurate and reflective of the thoughts and wishes of the movement. I had expected to pass several months before I would meet any of the Frum members and to be able to talk with them openly, but I was fortunate in making contact immediately upon my arrival in Tanna. I am still in touch with certain men in the movement.

On Tanna I lived in a "native-style" bungalow owned by a local planter several miles from other whites; the bungalow was about a three-mile walk from the trading post, and about two from one of the central John Frum villages; half a mile away was another small center, and of course all around me were hamlets with members of the cult. I spent day after day with various Frum people, crossing the island to other centers or going by boat. There are white colonials on Tanna, some English-speaking, the remainder French, and while I talked to a few of them and received good insights into their view of the movement, I found the whites in the New Hebrides, with a few rare exceptions, all too typical of what is known as the colonial mind.

The Tannese told me things they said had not been told to other whites. These "secrets" are printed here, because they want the rest of the world not only to know about John but to find out something of what it is like to live under a colonial regime. To the best of my knowledge, the only other white man who spent any length of time talking about John Frum on a person-to-person basis was the French anthropologist Jean Guiart, who had visited Tanna twenty years earlier.[6] There have been other whites who have looked into John, one of them a documentary film maker whose film is not highly regarded on Tanna (it was shown in the Presbyterian mission), and various journalists who pick up their views from the Australian trader who also runs one-day tours from Port Vila. As far as I know, only *John Frum He Come* gives an extensive Tannese view of John in the words of Man-Tanna.

Why did I go to Tanna to investigate John Frum? I can give no rational answer. Before I went to the island I thought of Cargo and John Frum from the outside, as "interesting" subjects, as the material for a book or for magazine articles. I looked at the faraway Tannese as interested whites invariably do, as a curious "native" anthropological and sociological subject, such as we educated, book-literate whites have been doing for the last century throughout the world. We make wonderful clumps of words, as books, articles, reports, theses, studies. We may get some money or a degree or some fame. Meanwhile the subject of the study goes on being poor and underprivileged. On Tanna I became increasingly drawn into the movement, and my view changed from "objective" to subjective. A white who had come down from Vila to salvage the wreckage of a plane that had crashed during my stay there said to me, "I bet you crack up when they tell you those stories about John." I replied that, on the contrary, when the people would tell me about John—"He stood this close to me" (and they would reach out and touch me on the arm) "and he smoked a cigarette and he said such and such"—I believed them; he was completely real, and I couldn't make fun of them as the colonials did. Still, why did I go to Tanna to search out John Frum? Still, no rational answer. I am a writer and photographer by profession and I must have subjects. But why John Frum? The Tannese thought that John had brought me to Tanna, to learn about him and to present him to America. It is possible. Tanna is an out-of-the-way place, in an obscure chain of undeveloped islands with a bad climate and worse living conditions, no matter how much the Port Vila Chamber of Commerce may try to glamorize it as a tourist resort. It is expensive to get to and to live in. Obviously, there is some inexplicable reason for my going to Tanna, and that I am willing to accept.

My first two days with the John Frum people were passed in listening to a long monologue by Lauhman Teni, one of the island's elders, in which he dictated both his personal history and the account of John's appearances on Tanna, along with some general information about Tanna and the past, and the conditions which led to John's coming. We sat under a great spreading banyan tree high on a hill by Sydney village (the proper name is Isitni), overlooking Lenakel Bay. We were surrounded by other men from the village, about twenty to thirty of them, and a number of children. The men habitually carry machetes or bush knives and enjoy the pastime of whacking the ground with them during conversations. Whack, whack, whack. A most unnerving experience at the time. Since I was a stranger to the Tannese, and I knew that in the past the appearance of a white man often meant trouble, I prefaced my first meeting with an account of my background: how I had seen a "story" of John in *The New York Times* (which they did not know of), had clipped out the story and put it away, and months later had found it again, reread it and was impressed by the figure of John. I had found some other references to John, all of which I suspected were not very accurate. I finally decided to come to Tanna to learn more about him. I stressed that I was not English, Australian or French, nor a government official nor a missionary. I said that I am an American but was not bringing "Cargo." I could not make promises. I did not have friends in the American Government I could ask to send Cargo to Tanna. I came, merely, as one man interested in John, to talk to other men who knew John. I showed an airline map tracing my flight from New York to Honolulu to Pago Pago to Apia to Suva to Vila to Lenakel. I am not sure they understood the map, though a few of

On a Pacific Island, They Wait For the G.I. Who Became a God

Special to The New York Times

TANNA, New Hebrides, April 11—The west Pacfic is dotted with crude wooden crosses painted red in honor of the G.I. who became a god in the influential "cargo cult" known as the John Frum Movement.

Who John Frum really was, if he ever existed at all, is not known. But one branch of the widespread cult reveres, as a sacred relic of the mysterious white messiah, an old United States Army field jacket with sergeants stripes and the red cross of the Medical Corps on the sleeves. Members of the cult believe the jacket was worn by John Frum back when the New Hebrides were a way stop on the road to Guadalcanal.

The red wooden crosses found on the beaches and in the jungles, with little fences around them, signify the faith of the believers that John Frum will return some day in an airplane loaded with good things for all, as he is said to have promised long ago.

On at least two occasions followers have hacked clearings in the jungle to make landing strip for John Frum's plane. Bamboo sheds have been constructed to hold the cargo that he is expected to bring. Imitations of wartime field radio stations, with ropes instead of wires attached to bamboo masts and tin cans for earphones, have been built to receive John Frum's messages.

'We Can Wait Awhile'

"People have waited nearly

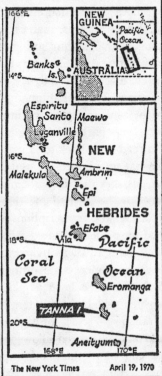

The New York Times   April 19, 1970

an expert on island affairs in the British section of the dual government at Vila, on Efate Island, said in a recent interview.

Seeing the white man's wealth of consumer goods, made of materials unknown in the stone age culture of the jungle villages, and not understanding the processes of a cash economy, the primitive Melanesians conclude that these luxuries must flow from some supernatural source he said.

them had worked as sailors and had been as far away as Australia, and some had gone to other New Hebridean islands or to New Caledonia for jobs. I talked about my children and my travels in other parts of the world. I showed two magazine articles I had written, one about the people of Calcutta, the other about geothermal energy in Turkey (one of the Tannese, Tom, I think it was, made some comments about the possible tapping of the sulphur springs at Port Resolution, on the other side of Tanna). While I was talking a jeep with two white men came roaring up the hill; the men gave me a curious look and went away. While Lauhman Teni spoke, I wrote down every word he said, though sometimes his words seemed obscure and his sentences garbled. At the end of the second session he asked me to read it all back to him. I was surprised at the request and somewhat uncomfortable. But I read out every word, including those passages that had not made sense (I questioned their accuracy but he assured me that I had taken them down quite correctly). My transcription was perfect, and the village accepted me as being honest, reliable and friendly and not there to subvert John, so I was invited to drink kava.

My acceptance came primarily because I am an American, and the Tannese have a gilded view of America, the reasons for which will be seen later. However, if I had been English, Australian or French, or a government official or a missionary, I would not have been allowed in the villages nor would people have said more than a few polite words to me. "American" brings certain privileges in parts of Melanesia, though from my own viewpoint America's practices as a colonial power are virtually as bad as those of Britain and France. But I had privileges I believe not given other whites, and I respect them.

After those first two days I was openly accepted by most Tannese, though I may have been thought somewhat eccentric. The local Europeans seem to have another opinion, as you might guess, of a white man who associates with natives. Anyway, John was there, to speak through the person of his people.

*

John Frum is a mystery, and as such we must approach him. We cannot take him at one gulp. So John is revealed layer by layer. One man's John is not another's. There is no official John, though various areas may claim that their own view is the correct one and the only one. Green Point (where John first appeared), Lenakel, White Sands/Sulphur Bay and Green Hill each vie for authority. Which is Rome and which Avignon no man can say.

But John reveals himself as he wishes. We see the thesis stated. Incorrectly at first, for it is whites who speak, in various colorful, exaggerated, romantic, untrue statements written to proclaim the naïveté of the black mind. Then the white attack comes in earnest. John is a fake, a hoax, a mirage, a fantasy. Of course he is. No white man can accept a black, brown, yellow or red point of view. (White man he bosman, he superior.) But in the end we find John in all his glory, his mystery, his hope, his chiliasm, and we wonder if we can accept him. Most of us dare not. But John will be there waiting, someday to bridge us with our brothers, leaping across the Law, to unite us in faith, charity and love.

A further note

The material in *John Frum He Come* is derived from many sources. I have made an effort to keep it simple, to present central themes, to float with the main streams that wash the Pacific's black islands. One can be swamped with source material and the accompanying footnotes, references and citations. Published works have been consulted and drawn upon when necessary, but much of this material has been changed or reworked to present alternative points of view. Such sources include not only the usual scholarly material in book, essay, quarterly or thesis form, but newspapers and magazine articles, government papers, mission reports and letters. Legend, myth and tradition have been used. In many cases, in working from written material (all of which is White), great license has been taken in rearrangement, presentation and interpretation, for we are entering an area of myth-dream. Here mundane factual statement loses its solidity in the vision and the hurt of the black man. That a white steals a thousand acres from a Melanesian is a fact about a business operation; for the black man it is not only a fact of another sort but a loss of part of his soul, his life force.

The final sections of *John Frum He Come* are based upon firsthand interviews with people—Melanesians—who experience John and the hope of Cargo as everyday parts of their lives, who have been nourished over the years in the expectation of John's Second Coming, have gained sustenance from it. Some of the men who speak have been born into John Frum and know no other influence. The words are those of real people—as I said, black people—speaking for themselves, speaking as *men* and not as "informants" or research sources. In certain instances the names of some Tannese have been changed to protect them from white power in their own land. Since many black people in the Pacific may take a simple name—Sam, Tom, John, Robert, Joe, Henry, Jimmy, and so on, to make it easier for Europeans to identify them—any such single name may be a pseudonym (or may not), but a full name, like John Kalate or Sam Tacuma, is always real. The whites have not been identified except in general terms, for I have no wish to get into arguments with rascals (and two or three thoroughly nice people) who spoke to me (openly) as "one white to another," separating "us" from "them."

   *

The word "native" is an unfortunate one. It is commonly used, but it has a more or less derogatory sound. *The Pacific Islands Monthly,* the trade journal of white exploitation of the South Seas, has discussed the problem without finding a solution, but in the end one tends to use it as the simplest means of handling a complex description. What alternatives are there?—ethnic, indigene? The white colonials use the word "boy" for any islander, no matter what his age or stature.

Boy.

   *

The geography of the South Pacific may seem complicated to a reader whose orientation is toward Europe or Latin America, but the end paper maps will make the area clear. Money is given in terms of Australian dollars unless otherwise noted. The Australian dollar is equivalent to $1.42 American, or conversely, the American dollar is worth only $.70 Australian and may slide further.

*

John Frum may also be spelled Jonfrum. Europeans pronounce Frum to rhyme with Come, but among themselves the Tannese pronounce it to rhyme with Broom.

*

Many people are to be thanked for aid and information, among them John Kalate, Lauhman Teni, Joe Johnson Hiopel, Sam Tacuma, Tom Hiwa, Henry Weiwai, Mellis and Poita; and, Tom, Joe, Jimmy, Ben, Sam, George, Alan and Fred, variously of Tanna, Fortuna, Erromanga and Malekula. Also, William L. Coop, R. U. Paul, Albert Sacco, Stanley Osee, Gordon Norris, Joe Mulders, Thomas D. Beatty, Elizabeth J. LeBus, Captain Midnight and the usual many others "too numerous to name." The late Thomas Merton deserves mention for several invaluable conversations about Cargo shortly before he left on the trip that brought him to his death. Also, the young artist-poet Ted Rice for several insights into the role of spirit forces.

JESUS CHRIST HE NO COME

Jesus Christ He no come

Back at the end of the century we heard that Jesus Christ was
   coming.[1]
Would lead the Christians to heaven.
Pagans would be consumed by fire.
Along with Tanna.
Fire all around.
The Bible say, Come Lord Jesus!
Just about the last words in the Bible.
Jesus never come.
Then Isac appeared, sometime 1930s, thereabouts.
Isac promised John and disappeared. We never saw Isac again.
John came and spoke to us.
John he speak in many ways, many times, full of wisdom.
We will have a cataclysm, Yasur will erupt. Tanna will be
   leveled, the mountains flattened, the earth will rise. All the
   islands Tanna Aneityum Aniwa Erromanga will be merged.
One land one people.
John will return to bring us an era of peace and joy.
The whites will leave.
We will regain our youth.
No more death.
There will be no illness.
Kava drinking as before.
Dancing, circumcision.
Custom will return.
John's messengers, the ropes of Frum, spread the message
   throughout Tanna, taking with them a shell of kava from
   village to village. In each village the kava is drunk and new
   kava is prepared. Only two men, both Roman Catholics,
   refuse to drink kava as a sign of accepting John and his
   message.
We threaten them with death but they are adamant.

John told us:

Spend your foreign money, throw it into the sea.

Which we did.

Don't go to the Presbyterians. No more Church!

We stopped.

Take you children out of school.

We removed our children.

Dance all night!

We danced all night and into the day.

The British District Agent, Mr. Nicol, arrested "John," that is, he arrested a certain Manehevi.

There is a trial, and Manehevi is tied to a tree to show us that he is an imposter.

Of course! Manehevi is not John.

We tell that to Mr. Nicol.

Mr. Nicol arrests this man and that man. He arrests Joe Nalpin and Lauhman Teni, Robert Somo and Sam Nako. There is no end to the arrests. Everybody gets sent to the calaboos in Vila. Eleven men this time, nine men that time, three men, ten men, like that. All to the calaboos in Vila.

Every day, after work, John appears to these men. He talks to them and smokes cigarettes with them.

He tells them many wondrous things.

The Americans are coming.

The Americans come.

They give us presents: meats, rice, tobacco, cloth, dishes, clothes, apples, knives, aspirins, blankets.

John has spoken Truth.

A fresh start in the J.F. affair

"Strange happenings at a place called Green Point," reports the Rev. J. Bell later to his Synod. "Roughly twelve months ago [late 1940] meetings were called secretly and took place in a clearing cut out of the bush, with a huge banyan tree over all to shut out the light from the sky. They took place at night and no light was allowed, not even the glow of a cigarette or a pipe. Chiefs and elders and others were given positions befitting their rank, near to Jon Frum. A few bold spirits tried to peer into his face, but his face was well hidden by a big hat. When he spoke it was in a falsetto voice and he said little. He was said to have told the chiefs they were fools to work for the Government for nothing.

"Wonder tales spread like wildfire . . . He lived before Noah but ascended above the clouds during the flood and has never known death. He too served God and was sent by him. Jon Frum was said to have visited the Government Agent, and punched his nose, drunk beer at a trader's and driven a golden car to another."

In his reports Mr. Nicol, the District Agent, notes that there is a certain "John Frum" at Green Point who has drawn crowds with promises of gourds full of shillings. Nicol remarks tartly: "It is of course the usual idea that Tanna natives could run Tanna better than I can." Kava, a narcotic, hallucinogenic drink, long banned by the Presbyterian mission, is openly drunk; dancing, also banned, is now done publicly. Natives buy knives. John's early messages are innocuous (he encourages communal work and condemns laziness).

Goats are killed to feed the dancers.

Meanwhile Nicol has sent two assessors—native assistants—to Green Point to investigate. They return "ardent followers" of John. A party of three assessors sent to correct the mistakes of the first two also go over to John. Panic among the whites.

Cattle and pigs are sacrificed for the dances, which are now being held nightly in different villages. John promises new schools, houses like white men's, a new and true religion, a new government.

There is a run on the trading posts, all owned by either whites or Chinese. Over a thousand pounds are spent, despite the depression caused by the low price of copra. Bell: "The idea was to buy out the stores and so get rid of the white man's money." Money is also thrown into the sea. The natives want Tanna "as it was before the white man came." A most commendable idea! By May of 1941 church attendance is nil.

Some natives are arrested with the aid of Chief Koukare, a pro-mission Tannese. But it is rumored that John Frum has promised to deliver the prisoners. One of the arrested men, Karua, says that John is "pure spirit," but Kohu implicates one Manehevi as Frum. After twenty-four hours of questioning, Manehevi breaks down and admits he is Frum. He is tied to a tree as an example for another twenty-four hours, then sent to Port Vila along with ten others.

Police from Vila arrive and burn down a Green Point village.

Apparent end of the Frum business. It is now July 1941.

A month later. It seems that Manehevi is only a scapegoat to protect the real "culprit"—the word is European—and John Frum continues. New information is afloat: John Frum is king of America; he will send his son to America to seek the King, who is Rusefel; John Frum and Rusefel are cousins. Almost immediately John's three sons, Isac, Jacob and Lastuan, land by plane at Lake Siwi, at the foot of Yasur, the volcano. John's sons are half-castes (but there is no mention of their presumably white mother). They have black hair, are dressed in long robes with pockets; no, they wear lava-lavas; they wear khaki shorts, like white men.

At Sulphur Bay, near Siwi, they appear under a banyan tree and give orders to Gladys, eleven-year-old daughter of Nambas. Only Gladys, who is accompanied by Dorothi and Mersi, can translate their mysterious words. A sack of magic stones is laid under a banyan tree to ensure the coming of the Divine Children.

Isac is to be king of southeast Tanna; his brothers will be kings too.

John's children occupy much of Mr. Nicol's official reports for the next eight or nine months.

Fearful rumors circulate among the whites. The boys and girls are dedicated to new gods. They are living in communal houses. There is communal bathing. Licentious behavior is feared.

Kava drinking and dancing continue.

John's "ropes" or messengers have gone out all over the island with his word. Rope is an important term, for it is the same as the word for vine, which is *nul*. The Ropes of John.

Mr. Nicol arrests Isac, AKA Siaka and sends him and others to prison in Port Vila; sentences are imposed for "incest" and "adultery." Isac/Siaka dies in prison a year later.

Mid-1942. Americans land in Port Vila and Santo, just as John had promised.

Word comes that many of the Americans are black.

Kava drinking and dancing abound.

Missions still boycotted.

1943: Mr. Nicol goes on holiday and Mr. Rentoul ("I can say that I have never shaken the hand of a native") takes over for a few months.

Mr. R. notes a feeling of tension. He gives a native three months in prison for reporting that Mount Tukesmeru (height 1,084 meters) is full of soldiers, will open on the Day to fight for John; another report says that Americans will come ashore at Sulphur Bay.

October 11. Mr. N. returns. In the North, in the Green Hill area, Neloig is now revealed as the true John Frum, King of America and of Tanna. Though illiterate, King Neloig has begun a school system for the children in his domain. He has also organized a labor force of some two hundred men, plus armed guards, who are hard at work constructing an airstrip for the arrival of American planes bringing goods from the States from John Frum's father. Rusefel will send a white woman for each of John's soldiers. Liberator planes will bring the cargo. Nicol is warned that if he comes armed, he will be killed. It is the first time the gov't is threatened. "Position getting out of hand," Nicol informs Vila, asking for one hundred reinforcements. Police and militia soon arrive, accompanied by two U.S. officers, one a Major Patton (or Patten).

Natives are disarmed.

Patton speaks to natives, "trying to persuade them of their folly." And: "This was backed up by a demonstration of the power of a tommy gun turned on a John Frum poster pinned on a nearby tree."

Natives run like hell!

Good ole U.S. know-how shows natives stupidity of their ignorant ways.

Mr. Nicol has a John Frum hut burned down and sends forty-six prisoners off to Vila. Two years for King Neloig (later certified insane), a year each for ten others.

Neloig soon escapes into the bush. (Three years later he is captured, put into the crazy house; you think crazy house for natives is fun place?)

Mr. Nicol offers a pearl of wisdom: "It is quite evident that we may expect sporadic attempts to renew the John Frum movements every time some mad coon gets it into his head he is John Frum. And that there also is a very strong feeling in favour of anyone who raises the standard." (Shortly after this observation, Mr. N. runs his jeep into a road barrier in Vila and is killed. The date is December 1944.)

Exiles all over the New Hebrides, here and there. Wives are sent to them, a most humane action. But the missionaries fear the breakdown of native morals if husbands and wives are separated.

13 September 1946. Acting District Agent to British Resident Commissioner, Vila: "Report on situation in Tanna. Orgiastic dancing, excessive kava drinking, breakdown of custom, scattering of communal life and deterioration of sanitation and hygiene, even in villages of close European contact."

April 1947. Prices rise. Natives raid Bannister's store in White Sands, tear off price tickets, but otherwise do no damage, steal nothing and retire. Whites mystified by odd native act. What do the bastards want?

"On the orders of John Frum, sir. John Frum like black now white."

Whatever that means.

Iokayae is John Frum, it appears, all the previous John Frums not being John Frum *at all!* Iokayae receives orders from a certain Isac who speaks before sunset on Thursdays in the bush.

Isac abhors the colors red, blue and yellow, the common dyes of the women's pandanus leaf skirts, for to Isac red is blood, blue sickness and yellow death, these being negatives that are now abolished. Only black and white are tolerated.

Iokayae and two other men are arrested and get five-year sentences; twelve men get two years in prison each plus five years of exile.

Late in 1947 the affair of the coconuts erupts. From the exiles on the distant island of Malekula come four coconuts. Panic among the whites. What do the coconuts mean? The people at Sulphur Bay plant the coconuts but the whites dig them up. Meanwhile—the date is completely vague—the people at Lenakel, having learned a lesson, plant at least one coconut on the beach and by the seventies the tree is fully grown. It is authoritatively known that this is the place where John will come ashore "to form up the ants" to go to Leminuh, the most sacred spot on Tanna, long barred to the Tannese by the missionaries.

Early 1952. Charley Numwanyan, a member of the police force attached to the British residency at Isangel, remarks to his father that the new District Agent, a Mr. Bristow, is an avatar of Noah or perhaps is his son. Noah is also none other than John. Meanwhile it is rumored that Noah's brother Mwan, held prisoner in America, will return on a warship. The entire population of Tanna will be welcomed by Noah/Bristow, assisted by the gods Itotengteng, Mwayamawaya and Nakenkëp, after which all the Europeans on Tanna will leave.

Later in the year civil disturbances are reported around Lenakel. Many arrests are made.

In February 1954, Captain World appears in the Green Point area. He is a silent figure who wears bright-red clothing. This tall, mysterious stranger appears frequently, much to the annoyance of the District Agent. A native named Nakomaha, who is constantly in trouble (assault, bigamy, cheek) and has been in and out of prison, is suspected of having some connection with Captain World. "Offence could not . . . be laid at NAKO-MAHA's door though all evidence pointed to him and he appeared to be intent on subversive activities. [Consequently] he is banished to Vila for a further 2 years."

Nakomaha's prison terms are extended a few months at a time for various offenses, real or imaginary and it is not until January, 1957, that he is returned to Tanna. A month later: "Red flags hoisted on tall trees and est. 2,000 natives visited Sulphur Bay hoping to see J.F. NAKOMAHA maintained flags were to become symbols of Tannese aspirations etc. (They subsequently turned out to be old American flags.) Wild rumors prevalent re ships, submarines etc. . . . However, *natives were friendly and no breaking of law took place*. Government's new policy of non-intervention appeared to have good effect and take a certain amount of wind out the sails of the ringleaders." Thus the British District Agent to his superior in Port Vila.

A final word, dated April 17, 1957. "Visit of American ship *Yankee* to Tanna. Speech by Commander pointing out that in America people had to work for what they had, not wait for it to appear by other less certain means!"

WHITE SHADOWS ON
THE SOUTH SEAS

Some of us don't talk to our mothers-in-law.
Others don't talk to our brothers' wives.
Just as among white people, I hear.

*

Women may not go near the kava grounds.
Or other sacred sites.
The sexes are separated.
Women are born to serve men.
You can tell an important man by the number of his wives.
He also has the most pigs.
A wife costs plenty pigs. Plenty!
Certain clans may not associate with each other.
Spirits roam the forests, the glades, the mountainsides.
God lives in the volcanoes.
We call ourselves *man*.
Other people, on other islands, even in other villages, are not
    man.
In the past, we used to eat other men, other people. If they were
    brave we got a part of their braveness from their flesh.
A most commendable idea, which the white man stopped.
(He thinks!)
We often ate people because we were hungry. Protein
    deficiency. Have you ever roasted and eaten a succulent
    young child?
The white man used to shell hell out of us for this and for that.
We turned our backsides to him.
More shells.

*

There is a certain ambience in the South Pacific we must try to
capture, a certain feeling about the area. Not that every island is
the same, or that every village on an island is identical to its
neighbors. Some are more so than others. In general, life has been

very primitive, and in general, it is still so for most people. The West has come with a heavy hand, to change what it could by robbery and conversion, but in remote valleys and mountainsides, on distant islands, life continues on a primitive level. One cannot say that Tanna is like New Georgia, that Fiji is like Arnhem Land, but certain traits float about, binding this vast area with an invisible web of custom, legend and tradition, history and mood. Life has been guided by certain rigid and rarely yielding principles, of family structure, clan, tribe or totem; taboos rule, and spirits range the land outside. Parents may love their children or not, or their relatives, but an air of cruelty and disregard for other people is rampant. Head-hunting and cannibalism were certainly facts of life; knowledgeable people today say that they are still practiced, but secretly, in order not to arouse the white officials. Magic is a ruling force; little is accomplished without it, whether for good or evil. One rarely grows a crop, or faces the fury of the weather, or wishes the death of an enemy, without magic. But wetman, he no see magic. Wetman make fun of magic.

So much the worse for him.

In the area comprising Melanesia—the Black Islands—and the black continent of Australia (now virtually lily white with Aussies) savagery has ruled. The blacks were plenty savage, which is a reason we whites felt free to be as savage, or more so. We didn't do anything to them that they weren't doing to themselves. They had minds and spirits as black as their bodies, let me tell you. Black skin, black heart. They lived like animals. Wrote Mrs. Mary Ann Robson Paton, gentle wife of a prominent missionary on Tanna and dead of a post-parturient fever 3 March 1859: "One can have no idea of the dark and degraded state of these poor Heathen," words we can still echo over a century later. Mary Ann was a lady; she knew a Heathen when she saw one.

The Southern Pacific covers some forty million square miles, the land area of all the islands except for that of New Guinea, barely more than that of a smaller American state. Nothing but water! Melanesia runs from the shores of eastern Australia and bird-shaped New Guinea across the Solomons, the New Hebrides, New Caledonia and the Loyalties to Fiji, the rough dividing line between blacks and browns; to the North, across the Equator, is Micronesia, also brown. The Polynesian browns reached as far as Easter Island in their fabulous canoe voyages; various groups returned westward in new searches, or were driven back by storms, so you now find small groups of Polynesians in the Solomons (Ontong Java) and the New Hebrides (Futuna and Omba) and in other places where they seem somewhat out of context, people a little lighter in skin color, with different features, and their languages definitely Polynesian in structure. The blacks are negroid and negrito, so closely resembling African and American blacks in appearance that only an anthropologist can tell the differences. An eerie experience, to step out of the bushplane on a New Hebridean jungle landing strip and find you are on a rolling African savannah.

Into this black-brown watery world the whites intruded. Those in small groups and the loners (missionaries, traders, adventurers) stood nearly 100 per cent chance of being killed, beheaded, roasted and eaten. Not even a martyr's grave awaited them but the rumbling of a hundred thousand stomachs. Gastric juices, arise!

We will take a brief look at some of these whites, a general view, a sort of albatross survey of this and that white man as he paddles into lagoons, bays and harbors in search of water, food, gold, slaves and souls, a good lay, for it was the white who transformed violence into Violence.

Spaniards learn Patagonians not easy targets

Fernando Magellan, Portuguese navigator, sailing a fleet of five Spanish ships, 290 men, setting off 1519 around Cape Horn on the way to the Pacific, stops for the winter at Patagonia. He is impressed by the huge size of the natives; giants they are. On account of their novelty, Magellan orders his arquebusiers to shoot a few to take home. One of the Spaniards, who kept a chronicle of the voyage, complains that they "could not hit one of those giants, because they did not stand still in one place, but leaped hither and thither." I mention this incident not only to show that Europeans considered natives (anywhere) less than human, but also to point out that the early guns were clumsy and unwieldy weapons. A man had to be a dead shot before he could get a dead native, a fact that spared many an islander in the Pacific in the years to come.[1]

It is Magellan who, after circumnavigating the tip of South America, discovers the Pacific in this voyage of great daring (a rebellion of officers is crushed, ships get lost, water and stocks are depleted, crew ill with scurvy, men die). Magellan finds the Mariannas group, plunders the natives of food, and dies in a native war in the Philippines 27 April 1521, age forty-one. The survivors sail on home: one ship, eighteen men all that remain of the magnificent courageous pageant that had set out. It is the first voyage around the world. The Philippines are to become an important Spanish colony, though one that is a financial burden.

Mendaña takes off

Forty years later the Spaniards in Peru pick up information from their conquered peoples about a "rich" land far out in the ocean to the West. Some torture helps get the news aired. But a question of semantics is involved, so much being lost in the translation. To the Peruvians, "rich" means a land well-favored with trees, fruit and water. To the Spaniards, "rich" means gold, their great obsession. The unknown lands, with their tantalizing promise, are called the Isles of Solomon by the Spaniards, though what the Peruvians have been talking about is probably Tahiti.

Preparatory to further exploration of the Pacific, the Spaniards occupy several promising ports in the Philippines in 1565 and build bases. There is (on their imaginative charts) a huge missing continent still to be discovered, according to certain "secret" maps passed down from the ancients. This is the legendary Terra Australia Incognita speculated upon by Pomponius Mela

JOHN FRUM HE COME

(A.D. 50) and later by Marco Polo. Untold riches are expected, not only material wealth but millions of souls to be added to the spiritual coffers of the Holy Roman Catholic Apostolic Church (H.Q. Rome, Avignon and elsewhere).

Meanwhile another expedition is taking shape in Peru, this under Alvaro de Mendaña y Neyra, nephew of the Spanish viceroy. Mendaña sets out in 1567 on a more southerly route than those taken by other fleets. His first major landfall is the island (now called) Ontong Java, one of the "western" islands the Spanish eventually decide are the Isles of Solomon. Mendaña next discovers Santa Isabel and Guadalcanal. The Cross is planted on appropriate sites. Naked savages are found everywhere, but none of the gold or silver or other riches the Spaniards seek.

Back to Peru they go, the expedition admittedly a failure. For the present, the viceroy is not interested in another search, the Spaniards' energies being concentrated on the fantastic wealth at hand in the Americas. In fact, twenty-seven years, a lifetime for many men, are to pass before Mendaña sails again. In 1595 he sets out to colonize the Isles of Solomon in what seems like a practical combination of search and settlement. He has four ships—the *San Geronimo,* the *Santa Isabel, Santa Catalina,* and *San Felipe*—with some four hundred men, some of them married soldiers with families. The year before, the viceroy had written the Spanish king that he was (now) encouraging Mendaña to colonize the Solomons, which, it was becoming obvious, could be an important link between the growing Spanish settlements in the Philippines and those in Latin America. Also, there is a high number of vagrants and other wastrels in Peru; the solution: dump them in the South Pacific.

So off they go, Mendaña hopeful, with his parcel of married soldiers and discontents, and before long they are low on water. Trouble seems to be building up, but on seventh September the Spaniards see smoke ahead and the next day they land, unfortunately having lost the *Santa Isabel,* an important ship of the almiranta class, on the way. The ship is never seen again, despite a search.[2]

Mendaña has discovered the Santa Cruz islands with this

landing. Later they are charted as lying between the eastern and
southerly tip of the Solomons and the northern New Hebrides.
The men of Santa Cruz, soon to be feared as the most savage
and ruthless in all the Pacific (we will hear of them again),
give the Spaniards a hard time. Two thirds of the surviving
members of the expedition are unable to establish bases on shore.
The others live in a stockade under twenty-four-hour-a-day
siege. Though Mendaña has ordered a peaceful approach
toward the natives, his men prefer a hard line, and several islanders are killed. However, one chief, a man named Malope,
seems friendly and gives the invaders food. Now fighting breaks
out among the whites. To crush the incipient rebellion Mendaña
comes ashore one morning and murders the rebel leaders, de-
capitating them and putting the heads on poles atop the stockade. Meanwhile, while Spaniards are killing each other, some of
the rebels are off in the jungle giving Malope his due. One more
dead native. Bad show all around.

But the tragedy is near an end. Mendaña dies (old age, despair, fever?) and his chief pilot, a Portuguese, name of Fernão
de Queiroz, takes over. The Spanish records list him as Quiros,
and by that name we will follow him. The attempt at settlement
is abandoned, and the ships depart the islands, one to Manila, the
other two to Peru.

The South Pacific has become an obsession with Quiros, but
the government by now has had its fill of sending men and ships
off into the whirlpool. Quiros' life is consumed by the hope of
one more voyage. Objections confront him: no one is really interested. He approaches the Viceroy of Mexico, who directs him
to Spain. It is 1605 before Quiros has a boat and crew; the King
is dilatory about sending off still another expedition to disaster.
At Guadalupe, on the way to Peru, sixty of his crew are killed
by natives, a frightful massacre. A storm tosses his ships onto
rocks. A new boat is built out of the wreckage, and at last, after
suffering reduced rations, the expedition reaches Panama. Finally the Viceroy of Peru gives him two ships and a launch, with
one hundred and thirty men and six Franciscan monks. Off they
go. Four months later they land among a group of islands, later

called the New Hebrides by Commander James Cook, an Englishman. But Quiros gives the islands saints' names as he sails among them. At Virgen Maria they finally land. Quiros estimates that there are two hundred thousand people on the island. He has instructed his men to act as "fathers to children" in dealing with the natives, but the command is also, "Chiefs and other natives who appear to be of consequence should be kept in the ship as hostages," a practice which this expedition and others are to observe scrupulously. A typical incident after capturing two natives: "At dawn, the Captain, pretending he had quarrelled with all [his crew] for putting them in the stocks, let them out. He then ordered the barber to shave off their beards and hair, except one tuft on the side of their heads. He also ordered their fingernails and toenails to be cut with scissors, the use of which they admired. He caused them to be dressed in silks of various colors, gave them hats with plumes, tinsel and other ornaments, knives, and a mirror, into which they looked with caution. Arrived at the beach, they were told to jump out, which they could hardly believe."

Up until the capture of their men the islanders have been friendly, giving the Spaniards food. Now they shower the whites with arrows. The Spaniards fire their arquebuses at them, wounding three. Admiral Torres, the second in command of the Spaniards' ships, writes in his journal, "They are a people that never miss an opportunity to do mischief."

So the stage for the unending conflict is set, in a scenario that is to be repeated over and over again, the friendly, helpful whites trying to civilize the natives, the natives returning good will with arrows, and the whites firing their arquebuses (later rapid-fire rifles and cannon) in return. Will those savages ever learn?

Never.

More of the same, as the expedition goes from island to island, offering friendship and presents, capturing and dressing up a few natives, and receiving showers of arrows and spears in answer. Some thanks!

Finally Quiros comes across a great land, obviously (to him) the continent he has been searching for. Here are huge mountains and adequate water, forests and rich land. A fine bay—called Big Bay—gives anchorage. Quiros names the "continent" Terra Australis del Espiritu Santo, the Farthest Land of the Holy Spirit. The Spaniards go ashore, the natives seem friendly, but one of the crew shoots a man. A Moorish soldier cuts off the native's head, and the body is hung by one foot from a tree. Fighting breaks out. The whites set ambushes and kill off a few natives, including one who is obviously a chief. The Spaniards now begin a settlement on shore, with much pageantry and a Mass, naming it Nouva Jerusalema and calling the river on which it is situated the Jordan. It is a scene of great beauty. The Spaniards are impressed by the riches before them: black earth, an abundance of fruit and vegetables, numerous houses, large herds of pigs, handsome, clear-eyed, sociable natives, and, most encouraging, a metallic stone suspected of bearing silver. Herons, ducks and wild pigeons inhabit the river edges. A beautiful spot, no doubt about it.

But it is the same old pattern. New Jerusalem lasts five weeks and two days, the natives being first friendly, then recalcitrant and then hostile and warring. No food is brought after the first few days. The Spaniards now must forage. With their unwieldy arquebuses they fire upon a native ceremony. The natives flee, and the Spaniards seize pigs and other foods. One Spaniard wrote, "Our people took from a single house they entered fourteen pigs." A man's entire fortune, and one near-sacred, for pigs are not only wealth but a divine food, eaten only upon ceremonial occasions.

Quarrels among the Spaniards, illnesses and depression, fish poisoning. Their morale sinks. On the eighth of June Quiros and Torres hoist anchor, each in a separate ship, and set off. They are separated in bad weather and never meet, Torres heading West and discovering more islands before landing in the Philippines, Quiros, the expedition a shambles, hopes dashed, expectations vanished, sails to Peru, believing until his death that he had indeed discovered the lost continent in his Terra Australis del

Espiritu Santo. No continent that, but one of the major islands of the New Hebrides.

*

A decent period of time spares the Solomons and the New Hebrides from Europeans, though Spanish ships, bearing bullion from the port of Acapulco in Mexico, make the northern run to Manila regularly, the Philippines being without the riches of the Americas and requiring a subsidy. In 1642–43 the Dutch explorer Abel Tasman reaches Ontong Java, which he names, but otherwise Europeans confine themselves to the regular spice trade in India and Southeast Asia.

Silence in the South Pacific.

The cannibals kill, roast and eat, heads are taken, wars fought on gentlemanly terms according to established rules, pigs traded, tusks pulled, wives bought. The good life continues.

Stone is the vehicle of choice. Weapons, tools, totems. The stone is magic, and magic is the stone. Someday the stone will disappear except for magic, a use that iron, steel and plastic can never replace.

The eighteenth century. Now the invasion begins in earnest. Commodore John Byron, grandfather of the poet (thus his claim to fame!), and otherwise known as Foul-Weather Jack for his many misadventures, sails to the Pacific, is rewarded with his name on a pinpoint island in the Gilbert area. Then, in 1767, comes Carteret, in a voyage we can ignore (inadequate provisions, a rebellious crew—same old story). The next year provides us with one of the Greats. This is Louis-Antoine de Bougainville, to whom Tahiti in all its lush grandeur is revealed. Bougainville finds and charts many of the New Hebridean islands, and then the Solomons. He shows that Quiros' Terra Australis del Espiritu Santo is merely an island. Careful navigation and precise map-making are taking over at last. Bougainville is the second white man here after Quiros, one hundred and sixty-two years later. But the natives haven't changed. On the first encounter a shower of stones mixed with arrows hits French landing parties. "A few rifle shots soon put a check on their boldness." But

Bougainville soon sees white power in a different way. When natives again draw French fire, Bougainville reprimands his men and says, "I took steps to avoid the dishonor of any further abuse of the superiority of our forces." At another time he says: "We were so strong that we could not punish them." He sounds like a rare type, intelligent, understanding, daring. His voyage is marked by his having unwittingly brought aboard the first European woman to reach the New Hebrides, twenty-six-year-old "Jean" Baret, who had come on the cruise as the (male) assistant to the ship's botanist. Though officers and crew see Mlle Baret every day, no one realizes her sex until a Tahitian, with a mere glance discovers the secret and reveals it with an offhand comment. Bougainville returns home to much acclaim, but certain French intellectuals attack him for "spoiling" the simple savage by his white presence, this being an age when Natural Man is honored.

Captain God among the ape-men

Meanwhile Commander James Cook (on his last voyage promoted to captain) is exploring the South Pacific. Cook, the son of an English farmer, makes three voyages, starting in 1768, opening up areas previously unknown; his discoveries include the fair islands of New Zealand. Cook is curious, tolerant, eager to observe native life as lived, on one occasion attending a human sacrifice in Tahiti, on another allowing a cannibal feast aboard his ship. On his second voyage (1772–75), after circumnavigating the Antarctic and finding and naming New Caledonia, he roams through the New Hebrides from North to South and gives the chain the name they now bear. Cook states that the islands are as beautiful as Tahiti, but: the natives are another picture, "the most ugly, ill-proportioned people they ever saw," reports an account of the voyage based on his observations, with "a very dark-coloured and rather diminutive race, with long heads, flat faces and monkey countenances." And in another passage, "ape-like." Wherever he is, Cook has no hesitation about going ashore and trying to establish peaceful meetings with the chiefs—he has an unerring eye for the top man—but somehow circumstances constantly intervene. Thus we see a trail of dead natives following the shower of arrows that follow some white gaucherie or other.

Cook sails South. At Erromango there is a misunderstanding with the people, arrows being fired by one side and muskets by the other, climaxed by a four-pound shot at a group that has stolen oars from a longboat. At Tanna, where Cook enters a fine harbor (which he names Port Resolution in honor of his ship), the natives seem at first "hospitible, civil and good-natured," but—"suddenly their behaviour was insolent and daring." More bullets and a four-pounder. Here events swing back and forth. The whites never know if the blacks will be friendly or not. In one incident, when a native offers a club in exchange for some beads, then paddles off without giving up the club, Cook gives the fellow a few rounds of musket shot. "This transaction, however, seemed to make little or no impression on the people; on the contrary, they began to halloo and make a sport of it. One fellow showed us his backside in a manner which plainly conveyed his meaning." Ashore, Cook, in his usual manner, points to the ground to learn the native name for the island. Native thinks he wants to know word for earth, says, "Tanna," that being earth in their lingo. So, Tanna it is forever.[3]

The Tannese are intermittently friendly, bringing food or throwing stones as the mood strikes them. There is no major incident on Tanna until one native approaches a line the English have drawn on the beach as a boundary in the usual custom of whites staking out other peoples' territory as their own. The sentry raises his musket, pulls the trigger. Cook writes: "I was astonished beyond measure when the sentry fired, for I saw not the least cause." The wounded man is carried away by his friends. Cook and his surgeon follow to give aid, but arrive in time only to see the man die. In panic, some natives bring coconuts and fruit to Cook and lay them at his feet in supplication. "So soon were these daring people humbled," says the Commander. But he stays no longer than necessary. Tanna's first contact with the whites is a great loss of innocence. Worse is to come. From top to bottom the entire chain is now open to the whites. The European flood is upon the New Hebrides, as upon so many islands in the Pacific, lapping at the beaches but leaving the interior to the natives. The beachcomber will soon appear, along with the missionary and other do-gooders, the trader, planter, sandalwooder, and not far behind the rapacious foreign government, the administrator, teacher, hotelier, tourist and land developer. It is anyone's guess who is the worst.

On his last voyage (1776–79) Cook discovers Hawaii, naming it the Sandwich Islands after a distinguished friend, goes off to search a northwest passage in Alaska, returns to the Sandwiches. At Kealakekua Bay, previously untouched, he is taken to be the god Lona, long awaited by the natives, who expected him to return on a "floating island." Lona, a deified chief, is the god of peace and light. None of this is known to Cook at the time, the information coming from later researchers. Cook's crew rapidly depletes the native resources of food, and the expedition sails off amidst the sullen anger of the islanders. But a storm drives it back to the same beach and Cook goes ashore, though he knows the danger. The whites are attacked. No stupids these natives, having observed how the muskets work. After Cook's men have fired a volley in warning, the whites are rushed as they try to reload. Cook and four marines are killed.

God is dead, 14 February 1779.

The biggest feast ever

Big drama coming up. In 1788, French explorer Jean-François Galaud de la Pérouse, with two ships, *La Boussole* and *L'Astrolabe*, sets out from Australia's Port Jackson (later Sydney) for the Solomons. Mission includes secret report British activities Australia, consider possibilities French colonization New Zealand, and finally, see if Bougainville's islands same Mendaña called Isles of Solomon. It was a no-nonsense expedition, the

JOHN FRUM HE COME

French having learned how to treat natives from the failure of others. La Pérouse has already reported home:

"We punish by force the slightest thefts and the least injustice: we show the natives the use of our firearms that flight will not save them from our resentment; we refuse them permission to come on board and we threaten to punish with death those who come too close to us. This method is a hundred times preferable to our earlier moderation; and if we have any regret it is that we came among these people with principles of kindness and patience."

That's telling them!

La Pérouse disappears. Both ships gone. Not a trace. French efforts to find the expedition fail. Twenty-five years later, Peter Dillon, an Irishman operating out of India, drops three people on the remote and lonely island of Tikopia east of the Santa Cruzes. They are a German, his Fijian wife and an Indian. God knows what they thought they were doing! In 1826, Dillon anchors off Tikopia and learns that the trio is still alive. The Indian offers to sell the silver sheath of a European sword which the Tikopians claim has come from Vanikolo 140 miles to the West. Local legend is that years back two European ships had been wrecked there. Old men, then boys, know the story.

Dillon writes (1829): "I immediately came to the conclusion that the two ships must have been those under the command of the far-famed and lamented Count de la Pérouse, as no other two European ships were lost or missing at so remote a period." But it is not until 1830 that Dillon can visit Vanikolo. His supposition is correct, as he learns from talking to the old men. Meanwhile another Frenchie has also visited Vanikolo and heard the same story.

Both of La Pérouse's ships had run aground on a reef off Vanikolo, but the wrecks happened some distance apart and the survivors were rescued by two different tribes, luckily for one, not so for another, the latter being killed and eaten. The first group, including the captain himself, got ashore, built a stockade for defense, and out of the wrecked ship constructed a smaller one in which they sailed off, leaving behind two men who had either deserted or were being punished or may have been captured by the islanders. Now La Pérouse vanishes for once and for all, though island rumors put his arrival at Ponape in the Carolines. Here the Frenchies' luck runs out and the natives have one big feast of long pig. The two men left behind survive natives, storms and boredom and live, according to the people on Vanikolo, to their natural deaths. So much for the explorers. Now the adventurers, missionaries, etc., move into the picture. Not a pretty one, though, as we will see. Native, watch out, white man he gonna getcha.

End of eighteenth century, beginning nineteenth. American whalers all over Pacific. See Herman Melville, etc., for exciting literature on subject. Not our province. Also other later writers like Pierre Loti and Robert Louis Stevenson for Pacific ambiance.

In 1803 sandalwood, big Chinese item (incense, furniture inlay, fans, prayer beads, disinfectant, etc.) is discovered in Fiji, transforming island life. Previously sandalwood has been a major export item from western New Guinea, a Dutch monopoly. Now the (British) East India Company moves in, with a complicated series of trades, exchanges and currency manipulation, involving Chinese tea and silver and Indian opium. Letters of credit in London, high finances, big stakes. Fortunes are made, a few lost. By 1813 Fiji is virtually denuded of sandalwood. In 1825 Peter Dillon notes that there is sandalwood in the New Hebrides, mainly on Tanna and Erromanga, some on Vaté. So attention turns to the lower islands of the chain. The sandalwood captains are whites (British from New South Wales, a few Americans), but their crews are brown (Polynesians from Tonga, Tahiti and Hawaii). Iron is bartered with the chiefs on Tanna and Erromanga. It seems that the chiefs do not understand what the captains are about. The trees have a certain soul-substance just like people, for some clans are descended from trees. In the eyes of the New Hebrideans the foreigners are not only stealing their trees but worse, hurting their soul-substance. The whites, no fools, send the browns ashore to deal with the blacks. The work is hard, the climate bad. Malaria affects the Polynesians and they die—"like flies," says one writer. In 1830, in one great sandalwood expedition from Tahiti, two thirds of the Polynesian crew dies within a few days while fighting ashore to gain possession of the sandalwood trees. Somewhere between one thousand and twelve hundred browns go to their deaths. Such figures are hard to believe, but they are reported by the white captain, Jacques Moerenhout, who noted that the islanders "have obstinately refused all communication with strangers; and if some disembark from their ships they kill all those whom they are able to surprise."

The whites are called traders, but what do they trade?

"The mists of heathenism will gradually give way"

The year 1848. Revolutions all over Europe. The place is a mess. Now the missionaries are running a parallel invasion in the Pacific. The twenty-two-ton schooner *Undine* makes an exploratory visit to New Caledonia, "at her helm, the almost incredibly handsome Englishman, forty years old, with curly light brown hair, sensitive features, penetrating blue eyes, a debonair manner." Personality radiates calm, confidence, friendliness and leadership. A brilliant linguist, the reputation of being "the most intrepid skipper in the Pacific." Our hero is George Augustus Selwyn, Bishop of New Zealand. Missionary, but with a new approach. Instead of founding a residential mission on each island, he will, with their parents' permission, take selected upright boys to school in New Zealand for the summer and the following year return them home, where they will be able to pass on some of what they have learned. A most heavenly, or a most diabolical, plan, depending on your point of view. But the good Bishop has stipulated that "In taking to them the religion of Englishmen he would in no way force upon them English methods and ways of life, except in so far as they are part of morality." Fat chance!

After New Caledonia and the Loyalty Islands in 1848, comes a visit August 1849 to the New Hebrides, starting with Aneityum, the southernmost. The way has already been cleared—by sandalwooders. A later historian of the Mission's work wrote (1900) that the traders were "but a source of danger to those who followed them, for upon them the natives avenged the blood shed by their predecessors. On the first expedition the Bishop would never allow anyone to share with him the peril of landing on unknown shores, but caused the *Undine* to stand off while he swam ashore with such presents as he could carry in his hat to propitiate the chief, and to testify to his peaceable intent. The magic charm of his presence and absolute fearlessness was at once apparent."

The Bishop stated his mission quite succinctly:

"The first impression produced upon one of these lads, newly brought from a heathen island, is that of wonder at the new and strange persons and practices in his learning—his dormant intellect will have enough to do in taking in the wonders which he sees around him. Order and discipline, steadiness and regularity, make his life different from anything he has known before: he contrasts law with lawlessness. Having arrived at this point, it is probable that he returns to his own country. He finds that he is conscious of a want which he never knew before; he will wish to return again to New Zealand. Then his mind will enlarge— some great truth will present itself to him, the first ray of dawn in the darkness; and then, little by little, when once this truth is grasped, the mists of heathenism will gradually give way before it. To watch this process—to know by the brightening eye, the look of intelligence, the changing expression, that the heart is expanding and the mind awakening to the love of God and man—this is the blessing not seldom granted to those whose happy lot it is to live with the natives of the Melanesian Islands."

Selwyn makes a point of not interfering with island customs except those like cannibalism and head-hunting, remarking, "When the people become Christians they will decide for themselves which customs are evil and must be given up." In four years he visits over fifty islands, picking up forty boys speaking ten different tongues. In 1851, near Port Sandwich, Malekula, one of the larger of the New Hebrides, an attempt is made upon the Bishop and his crew as they are returning from collecting fresh water. But trouble is rare, considering the experiences of other whites.

Selwyn returns to London briefly in 1854, where he takes on as his assistant and chaplain John Coleridge Patteson, a man equally remarkable. In 1856 Selwyn and Patteson visit San Cristobal in the Solomons.

Bad scene, that, the Solomons. Only eleven years earlier a French R.C. mission, under Bishop Jean-Baptiste Epalle, with eight priests and four brothers disembark at San Cristobel to begin their mission. The Bishop, seeing his soldiers for Christ firmly established, now goes off to Santa Isobel to establish a second post. He barely has his foot ashore on the sands when he is killed. End of attempt. At the first base the missionaries hold on until 1852, with three killed and eaten by cannibals, one dead of "other" causes, and the survivors weakened and prostrated by malaria. So much for the Frenchies! On neighboring Guadalcanal in 1848, one Benjamin Boyd, a sheepherder from New South Wales, comes ashore with the grandiose scheme of employing cannibals as shepherds (presumably to scare off other sheepherders?). At any rate, Mr. Boyd falls victim to his own imaginative plan and is cooked and eaten in 1851.

Bad scene, the Solomons, everyone agrees. So it is now the turn of the English Bishop to swim ashore, hat stuffed with goodies, to visit chief Iri on San Cristobel. Selwyn and company explore Iri's domain. The whites "examined his boat-house, and beautiful canoes, all inlaid with mother-of-pearl, and passed on to his house—the council-hall—a long low building of wattles, with twenty-eight skulls on the ridge pole, two of which had been so recently added that they were not darkened with smoke," wrote the Mission's historian. The Bishop ("rather as if he were having a discussion at his club in London") gives the Church line on native wars and skull houses (a No No!). No response from the chief at this display of bad manners, but he consents to five boys going off with the Bishop.

Various stops along the way, the major one being at the islands of Nukupa and Ndende in the Santa Cruzes. Selwyn writes, "Sea and river alike fringed with the richest foliage, birds flying, fish leaping in the perfectly still water. Such exquisite scenery! Canoes coming off, and people on shore sitting under their coconuts." They are "all very shy of the white man, whom they evidently had cause to dread," wrote the historian, because "they saw few people, though they gathered from the cultivation that there must be a large population driven inland by the attacks on the coastal settlements," white captains being the culprits. On Vanikolo, the missionaries find no one when they land, but a "horrible odor" draws them inland. The scene: sixty European skulls (the crew of one of the La Pérouse ships) in a skull house, and outside a stone-lined oven; in the ground a new feast a-cooking.

Progress is made (conversions, more students). Then in 1861 Patteson is consecrated the first Bishop of Melanesia. A linguist like Selwyn, Patteson is also "urbane, broad-minded, tolerant, perceptive, artistic, a scholar and a man of action." Patteson visits the New Hebrides and writes that it is evident that he "could walk where I please, or row about in the little two-oared boat of the *Undine*, with that intuitive feeling of security, which is never felt, I believe, without good reason."

The Mission marches on, though not without a few casualties (some of the visiting scholars succumb to the climate of New Zealand; the school is moved to Norfolk Island, a milder place). Patteson takes over for Selwyn. At Omba in the New Hebrides in 1864 he is almost killed by a native hoping to avenge a murder committed by an English trader. The assassin's hand stops in midair. The Bishop is spared. An act of God? Later at Ndende, where he had previously made a peaceful landing, he and his party receive a shower of arrows from four hundred men on the beach. The islanders pursue by canoe. Two young white missionaries, descendants of the mutineers of the *Bounty,* are to die from their wounds.

So far no luck in the Santa Cruzes. The Bishop sets off for another try. On 20 September 1871, Patteson's ship is anchored off Nukupu, "a palm-covered fleck of sand." The island is considered rather friendly; the Bishop speaks the language and plans on going ashore to ferret out information on conditions at Ndende. But unknown to the missionaries, Nukupu has just been visited by a blackbirder, the captain disguised in episcopal robes in order to gain the natives' acceptance. Five men have been carried off to Fiji. Tragedy looms.

Patteson sets out in his longboat, transfers outside the island's reef to a native canoe. Ashore he is invited to the meeting house, a cool, thatched building about twenty feet square. The conversation is friendly. As Patteson rises to leave, he is struck from behind on the right side of the skull; the bone is shattered. Then comes a second blow on the head and a third on his body. A "savage yelling" resounds. Natives in canoes by the reef shower arrows on the longboat. In the village the Bishop's body is stripped by the women (but they leave his shoes on). Two further wounds are made. Is the symbolism clear?—a wound for each man kidnaped. The corpse is wrapped in a palm-fiber net and placed in a canoe, which is now towed by two women in another canoe out to the reef. The canoe with the Bishop's body is cut loose, the women paddle swiftly back to shore, and the ship's boat cautiously picks up the drifting canoe with its tragic cargo.

On the shore a great piercing yell swells forth.
Those fellas send big message to Queen bilong Bishop:
That message he say: LEAVE US ALONE!
That Queen Toria he got message.
Two months later ship bilong him bombard island.[4]
You should have seen the bastards run!

    *

Those fool English never learn nothing: 12 August 1875
    Captain James Graham Goodenough, Commodore of the
    Australian naval squadron, he make good will visit to Nukupu
    (crazy man!) and he get himself struck down by bone-tipped
    arrows. Eight days later that man he dead!
LEAVE US ALONE GODDAM IT
    LEAVE US
        ALONE!

WHITE SHADOWS ON THE SOUTH SEAS   31

Australia: the smell of the white man is killing us[5]

"The belief of the Bibbulmun that the first white man were the
returned spirits of their own dead relatives led to friendly
feelings towards the 'spirits' from their first encounter."

*

What a surprise!
   the fences, sheep, horses, cattle
   with their boundaries
the telegraph line with its magical messages
swifter and truer than smoke signals
ships in the estuaries, jetties, wharves

*

"Who shall say what vague despair and unrest entered these
primitive minds as the natives behold one after another of their
cherished homing spots ruthlessly swept away in the restless
march of civilisation, and the winding tracks to their various
food grounds obliterated by houses and streets? On their own
country they were trespassers."

*

Jangga meenya bomunggur. The smell of the white man is killing us.

*

Year 1846. Bishop Salvado, O.S.B., founds New Norcia among
the dingo-totem tribes of Victoria Plain, eighty miles N. of
Perth.

He camps with natives at waterholes to win their confidence.

Establishes (with financial aid of Queen of Spain) church
and monastery, "a seat of the arts and sciences with its colleges of
secular and religious education, rail-way town of considerable
importance with its far-flung and prosperous agricultural estates,
a jewel of the south-west."

Don Salvado feeds and clothes the natives, builds a tiny

JOHN FRUM HE COME

Spanish village of stone houses, tidy streets, pays the natives a tidy wage to live in his exemplary homes. An allotment of land for each native for farming and gardening. Money in the bank for the native. Handicrafts, stock work, telegraphy, accountancy, music, languages.

Squalor develops. Dingo-totem people sleep on beds but are unhappy. They wear clothing and develop chest complaints and fevers. They cannot learn cleanliness.

Dingo-totems want to go walkabout but fear the Bishop.

Dingo-totems die and are carried away to neat little picturesque cemetery for burial with full rites R. C. Church.

More dingo-totems are rounded up and put in the houses of the now dead. Superstitious people with a fear of the dead, they die too. The good Bishop, rosary in his fingers, counts the first year 250 members of his little experiment, coming & coming, living &.

Dying.

Kindness kills.

Don Salvado selects five promising young dingo-totem boys and takes them to Rome to the Benedictine seminary to study for the priesthood. The order of Melchesidec. Four die.

The survivor, "returned to New Norcia, promptly flung away his habit and made for the bush and died there."

Please, *do* leave us alone, Your Grace.

Native he speak

Frankly, we didn't know what to make of the white man in
　　the beginning. Some of us thought he was an ancestor coming
　　back (we got that crazy legend of the dead being white-faced),
　　or a god. Pleased hell out of him, to think he was a god. He
　　made the most of it for a while, but we caught on. He was
　　just as dead as anybody else when we put a few arrows in him.
We were puzzled by his feet. Tried eating the damned thing.
　　Tough as leather.
Of course it was his shoe. But the first time he took his shoe off

in our presence, that bishop fella [Patteson] had red feet and
no toes. We had to learn about socks too.

Well, the white man got our lands. Took our women (even
though we gave them a good beating, before and after),
arrested our chiefs and disgraced them, brought us diseases,
measles, V.D., the usual.

We were afraid those early years. He had guns and plenty of
power. But by the time we got over our fear it was too late.
His power was greater than our power.

Bout the only area where he is afraid of us is sex. White man
thinks all the native does is fuck. Thinks we got bigger penises
than his. All the time fucking. "Native sensuality must be
stopped," he says in his euphemistic manner. We go on
fucking. We can see his fury over this.

We're not going to disillusion him.

We got BIG ones!

Confrontation

[*Burridge in Mambu*][6] Tangu are men. They have their own
conventions for proving their manhood, for establishing their
integrity as men. In their own villages and among their own
kind Tangu are able to be men; and they wear their manhood
with dignity. In a European environment they cannot but feel
themselves to be something rather less. The fact is that [in a
quarrel] when Tangu face a European, eye to blazing eye,
within arm's length, the sap runs dry. Tangu submit. And they
know that they do so. But they would like it to be otherwise.
"Are we dogs?" they cry in impassioned fury. "Are we not men
as they are?"

*

"The first rule in dealing with a native is never to allow him to
disobey the orders of a white man, and we have given an order.
It must be carried out. Once more we command them to move
the barang [baggage], stepping closer to the middle chief, who

seems to be in authority. He refuses for them all. The time for action has come. He receives a forceful blow on the point of his jaw; without a sound he goes down. His six-foot body stretches out full-length on the sand, lies quiet for the moment; then, his senses slowly returning, he rises painfully and, cowering before us, goes to the pile of barang, selects the lightest of the pieces, carries it to a spot we designate, and deposits it there. Then he turns to the others and calls to them to come and assist him with the work.[7]

*

"There have been brutal whites in the islands and they have done no end of harm. A native came at me not long ago with a drawn knife. I turned just in time to see the fellow coming. I gave him a good kick in the stomach. And while he was reeling from that, I hit him one in the jaw and shut him straight up. He will be a good boy for a long time."[8]

Confrontation II

Eastward & earlier in the Marquesas, the dying Paul Gauguin, defending islanders in court against unfair and trumped-up charges, had ascribed the abuses to the absurdity of trying to govern primitive and unlettered South Seas people with European laws and regulations. The scene is French, but it could be German, British or American. Wrote Gauguin: "At the inquiry the accused is interrogated through an interpreter who is unfamiliar with the nuances of the language, especially judicial language, which is very difficult to translate into the primitive native tongue, except perhaps by means of paraphrases . . . The natives are very much reserved in the presence of Europeans, who seem to them so much superior and better informed. They also remember the cannons of the past, and have been intimidated by the police, other magistrates, etc., even before they appear in court. Therefore they prefer to

confess even when innocent, knowing that to deny the offence
is to incur a bigger penalty. In short, it is terrorism."[9]

I ate the *whole* thing

Australian justice of the Papua New Guinea Supreme Court
he rule that seven men from cannibal tribe
who eat friend killed in battle
no commit crime by their standards
Case dismissed
"Considered an enlightened decision," comments The New York
Times.
Year is 1971.

*

We all know that the peoples of the South Pacific practiced cannibalism and head-hunting in the past. They also engaged in the
live burial of the elderly and the killing of widows of chiefs and
other important people.

There are several myths surrounding the folklore of cannibalism. First, that of the big black pot. Bodies were roasted over a
fire or perhaps baked. Second, cannibalism was not merely a
ritual, in which the eater partook of some spiritual quality of
the eaten, such as his soul or his bravery or his prowess in war,
though ritualistic aspects do form part of the practice, and some
peoples would not eat a woman for fear of becoming feminized.
Cannibalism was sometimes a part of good nutrition, there being
a shortage of protein foods in many areas. Since pigs form a
good part of a man's wealth, they were not often eaten except
on ceremonial occasions, when dozens would be killed (and still
are). Birds are hunted, fowl is sometimes eaten. Cattle, sheep
and goats have been introduced by whites, but they rarely form
part of the native's diet. Fish are eaten by coastal peoples, but
with care, for many of them are poisonous. So human flesh—
long pig—formed part of the diet in the South Pacific and Australia because people were hungry and liked a good feast; one
longed for proteins without knowing what proteins were. Today

in the areas where cannibalism is (apparently) banned by the white powers, the native peoples are suffering from various types of malnutrition. WHO is quite concerned.

Robert Louis Stevenson, in one of the many excellent articles he wrote for the New York *Sun* during his voyages in the Pacific in 1888, 1889 and 1890, devoted some space to the subject of cannibalism. In one article he wrote:

"Nothing more strongly arouses our disgust than cannibalism, nothing so surely unmortars a society; nothing, we might plausibly argue, degrades the minds of those that practise it. And yet we ourselves make much the same appearance in the eyes of the Buddhist and the vegetarian. We consume the carcasses of creatures of like appetites, passions, and organs with ourselves; we feed on babes, though not our own; and the slaughter-house resounds daily with screams of pain and fear." He points out that "Many islanders live with their pigs as we do with our dogs; both crowd around the hearth with equal freedom; and the island pig is a fellow of activity, enterprise, and sense. He husks his own cocoa-nuts, and (I am told) rolls them into the sun to burst."

About the island's cannibals (the island is not specified): "They were not cruel; apart from this custom, they are a race of the most kindly; rightly speaking, to cut a man's flesh after he is dead is far less hateful than to oppress him whilst he lives; and even the victims of their appetite were gently used in life and suddenly and painlessly despatched at last. In island circles of refinement it was doubtless thought bad taste to expiate on what was ugly in the practise."

*

The final myth to be discarded is that cannibals eschew white flesh as being too salty or smelling badly. Plenty of white flesh was chewed, with relish or without. In fact, whites were consumed as voraciously as blacks and browns. Virtually any white man who was killed (and Chinese, too) was roasted and eaten. Waste not want not.

The subject of cannibalism (and other forms of antisocial behavior) is treated extensively in the older literature about the

South Seas, especially those works published before World War I, when it was quite common and easily attested to. I have been told within the last few months by a missionary who works in the Pacific that, in his belief, cannibalism is still being practiced on various islands. But since the white authorities have better means of getting about and better communications, cannibalism is done in secret. One doesn't admit it in the presence of whites. I mentioned this to my travel agent. She replied, "Nonsense, how could they practice cannibalism when they're trying to build up their tourist industry?" A beautiful *non sequitur*.

The cannibal area ran from Malaya, Borneo, the Indies, Australia and New Zealand, across New Guinea and Papua and other parts of Melanesia into Fiji, Tahiti and Hawaii, give or take a few islands. When the nineteenth century brought about a severe and rapid change in island life, with slavery, depopulation, epidemics, white exploitation and so on, cannibalism and other forms of violence increased, facts testified to by both natives and whites. W. Lawry (*Visit to the Friendly and Feejee Islands*, London, 1850) writes that an old chief told him that "all the old people, and especially his own father, used to tell him that these bloody wars, and this eating of one another upon the present enlarged scale, sprang up in their days, and did not obtain to such an extent in the generation before them." Romilly, writing of the same period, says, "The civilizing process which the Solomon Islanders have received at the hands of the white man since that time [the 1850s] has made terrible savages of them." He also wrote: "In those days it is almost certain that the natives were not so hostile to the white men as they have now become."

Cannibalism took many forms. To start with the beginning, the eating of children. Daisy Bates, the extraordinary, eccentric, courageous Englishwoman who spent her life among the Australian aborigines, records numerous instances of cannibalism among them. The subject, passim, throughout her written works, upset her. One account is typical of the many she quotes: "The women quite frankly admitted to me that they had killed and eaten some of their children—they liked 'baby meat.'" And: "Baby cannibalism was rife among these central-western peoples, as it is west of the border in Central Australia. In one group, east of the Murchison and Gascoyne Rivers, every woman who had a baby had killed and eaten it, dividing it with her sisters, who, in turn, killed their children at birth and returned the gift of food, so that the group had not preserved a single living child for some years. When the frightful hunger for baby meat overcame the mother before or at the birth of the baby, it was killed and cooked regardless of sex."

Osa Johnson, writing in the 1920s about the New Hebrides, describes an incident on Malekula. "One group of men and little girls attracted our attention. The men acted as though they were bargaining with each other. One of them was showing off a little girl to another, who finally gave him two boar's tusks, took the little girl and walked away with her.

" 'Martin, is he buying her for a wife?' I whispered, aghast.

"Martin and our head boy were talking in low tones.

" 'It's worse than that,' said Martin. 'Atree says she is for kai-kai.' "

Later in the day the Johnsons visit an Australian missionary couple who have two little Malekulan girls as servants; the children have been rescued from the meat market. The wife says, "Some of the Malekulans actually fatten their girl children like pigs and sell them to other tribes for food. We rescued these two. My husband paid for them in trade stuff and we brought them home. Nobody has ever asked whether we ate them." Etc.

Of course adults were killed everywhere, not only in wars but in ceremonial rites, accidents, and just for food. Mrs. Bates writes: "Everyone of the central nations was a cannibal. Human meat had always been their favorite food, and there were killing vendettas from time immemorial. Victims were shared according to the law. The older men ate the soft and virile parts, and the brain; swift runners were given the thighs; hands, arms or shoulders went to the best spear-throwers, and so on." Romilly had the fortune of witnessing a tribal battle on an island off New Ireland in which six men were killed. He then describes the cannibal preparations in detail, how the bodies were prepared for cooking, the roasting, and finally the eating, with various comments on the entire process, which attracted him as much as it disgusted. One small sample, out of thousands of words of detail: "When taken out of the ovens, the method of eating [human flesh] is as follows. The head of the eater is thrown back, somewhat after the manner of an Italian eating macaroni. The leaf is opened at one end, and the contents are pressed into the mouth till they are finished." The Deputy Commissioner then discusses various aspects of cannibalism. In some places, he remarks, human flesh is a food, in others a ritual, and in others one assumes some of the characteristics of the victim—hence some people will not eat a woman. But others will eat "anything." He observes that in the New Hebrides human flesh is usually dried in the sun, or jerked, and it "seems to be looked on more as an article of food than in most places." He adds: "In New Ireland, human flesh was eaten in the most open matter-of-course way, by young and old, women and children and it was spoken of as delicious food, far superior to pork." He estimates that a third of the people of New Guinea are cannibals, two thirds of those of the New Hebrides and of the Solomons, and all of the peoples of Santa Cruz, the Admiralties, Hermits, Louisades, Engineers and D'Entrecasteaux. In conclusion: "I believe Captain S——— and I are the only two white men in the Pacific who have ever witnessed either a large native battle or a cannibal feast. Both are of the greatest interest to look back upon."

Much later Puxley wrote: "A doctor whose acquaintance I made, told me of an experience he had lately in the New Hebrides; for, having to go inland, he was forced to pass the night in a cannibal village, and he was a little disturbed when several of the men who had been consulting together at a little distance came up and began to feel him, evidently to see if he were worth eating; he therefore calmly assured them he knew what they intended to do and on his part he intended to shoot the first man who approached him henceforth until he left in the morning; and finding that their intentions were known, they left him alone. But the well-known missionary—Mr. Chalmers of New Guinea—was not so fortunate; for trusting to his knowledge of the natives, he ventured too far inland, and the next thing the whites on the coast heard was that he and his companions had been speared to death. As Mr. Chalmers was much loved, an expedition was sent to recover the bodies and, if possible, catch the actual murderers; but all that could be recovered of the 'Livingstone of New Guinea' was his head, the rest of his body having been eaten by his murderers." Puxley adds: "One old cannibal told a friend of mine that they did not care much for whites, 'they were too salt.' Chows [Chinamen] are far better, being 'plenty too much sweet.' Still, in spite of the salt taste, a white trader was killed and eaten only last year in the New Hebrides." (Apparently he was referring to the murder of one Mr. Clappcott, whom we will meet again.)

We are heading, sooner or later, in the direction of Tanna, and cannibalism on Tanna was a privilege of certain people, and not an aberration. It was enjoyed by notables, chiefs and other dignitaries of various hereditary lines. The body of an enemy would be (would be?—perhaps *is!*) sent along traditional routes from the sacred kava grounds of one village to another, swinging from a pole like a pig. At the kava ground it was received by the inhabitants of the village and hung by the feet for the night at a special tree. A "glabrous" pig and kava were given in exchange to the carriers of the body. The next day the body was carried on to the next kava ground, with the customary exchange of gifts, continuing from place to place, to the ground where the body was to be roasted and eaten, a decision made partially by the fact that decomposition had set in and the skin was beginning to burst from the gases. The acceptance of the body implied the obligation to return the favor sooner or later, and when possible the corpse of a vanquished enemy (or some other unfortunate) would be sent back down the line, with the proper exchange of glabrous pigs and kava. The cooking and eating of the body was done not only by the men of privilege but also by certain women. The brains were a special delicacy, much appreciated; the skull was placed in the crotch of a banyan tree for all to admire and to recollect the delicacies it represented. Sometimes there was more than these ritualistic gourmet feasts. Guiart records (in 1954) the case of one Numwanyan of the village of Lètapu who was not satisfied with the flesh he was given at a feast, and so killed and ate a woman from Lenakel, and was about to kill her daughter when he suddenly felt that he was glutted.

On Tanna, turtles served as a kind of parallel sacrifice. They were sent along the same ceremonial routes as were human corpses and were eaten, in somewhat the same kind of ritual, by people of the turtle line. Turtles, more so than birds (from whom many clans are descended), were in their original form quite human. But turtles were rarer than human flesh. And their heads were something even more appreciated than humans'.

*

I have a vegetarian friend who believes that one should not eat anything one has not killed oneself. That was the supreme test of the carnivore, if he would do his own slaughtering. It is certainly a test the South Pacific cannibal would pass.

Anyway, human flesh is generally known as "long pig," as distinguished from ordinary pig, which plays the central role in the great celebrations of the islands, when they are slaughtered by the dozens, and everyone has a great stomach-bursting feast, stomachs, thighs and genitals, all over the penis-wrapper and falling on the ground, until we are so satiated we fall asleep in a stupor resembling drunkenness. We love to wallow in our pig fat and blood! Can you think of anything more sensual?

The missionaries come

We came as friends to dispel the black clouds of their minds, to bring the Word of our sacred Saviour Jesus of Nazareth. But instead they met us with bows and arrows, spears, stones, curses. Despite our best efforts they reverted again and again into the black ignorance of their savagery. Our country's warships shelled their villages. We stood aside from retaliatory acts but we realize that a show of peaceful strength brings them into the Light. We came as peacemongers, but until we proved the power of our love they remained in ignorance.

You have no idea of the incredible hardships we faced and the sacrifices we made, leaving behind families, loved ones, warm hearths, our green and lovely island, our motherland for hostile savage shores. But it was all for the love of Our Lord and God. We put an end to their barbaric ways. We forbid dancing, kava drinking, circumcision, polygamy, sensuality, magic, cannibalism, head-hunting, feasting, weaving, singing, drumming. We toppled their barbaric figures to the ground and burned every pagan idol we could find. We destroyed their savage artifacts and forbade any further production. Thus, stripped of their savage civilization, naked in the Lord, they could be clothed with the ways of the West and be led gracefully into the True Light.

We established laws, courts, stocks, prisons and fines to proclaim to Mr. Naked Savage that European ways are superior. We clothed the naked and cut their hair and shaved their faces. We forbade ornaments and paint, feathers and jewelry. We overcame their resistance with Her Majesty's shot and shell. We deposed their chiefs and replaced them with men more congenial to our Christian desires. They lacked authority with the natives but they had our powers behind them.

Eventually, after much trial, many sorrows, we were able to say, "Savagery is ended and our little Darkies are now the servants of the Lord." But the price was terrible. On Erromanga the Reverend John Williams was struck down on 20th November 1839 along with Mr. Harris. On the same island on 20th May 1861 the Gordons were savagely murdered by their own wards. Our Teachers from Futuna, Iona and Vasa were killed on Tanna in 1843. On Efate, Sipi, a Teacher from Samoa, was killed while ill with fever, 1845. On Efate nine years later four Teachers with wives and children were killed and eaten. Others dead of fever, fled in terror, work abandoned. But thus the Lord Jesus saved the naked painted savages of Melanesia.

Painted savages
Naked
Living in grass huts
Eating roots

Dancing
Singing
Killing pigs in a bloody melee
Indulging in sensual excesses
Feasting
Ignorant of the Lord's Day
  His work
  His Name!
Drunk on kava
Black minds in black bodies!

    *

The sweat blinded us
The water made us ill
The food disgusted us
The jungle was a foul breath
Foetid airless prison
Sun burning skull, skin, heart, mind
Rain falling like a lake overturned
Clothes, books, furniture rotting in the damp
Even our souls rotted
All for Jesus!

    *

The good Reverend will pass among you with his collection
basket (which you will note is made of the finest native work!).
He has recently returned from the Savage Isles. Please be
generous. Save a soul for Jesus!

    *

Such the missionary mind. Evangelists to the South Seas, iron
men, facing incredible hardships, willing to die for Jesus—and
often dying as martyrs (missionary jokes: iron pots, painted
feathered savages dancing). Who would have had it otherwise?
Robert Louis Stevenson, dying himself on a savage island (on
Upulu, Samoa, of consumption, 1884), writes: "With all their
gross blots, with all their deficiency of candour, humour and
common sense, the missionaries are the best and most useful

whites in the Pacific." Harrisson[10] adds: "I go further. I say that if the missionaries had come to the islands and done nothing, just sat down and drawn salaries until they died or were murdered, they would still be the best people in the Pacific. For everyone else was doing worse than nothing."

The man who set the tone of mission work in the New Hebrides (and later effected their joint annexation by Britain and France) was John G. Paton, a Scot and a Presbyterian. He said that he was not a fatalist though a Calvinist. After giving up a successful ministry in Glasgow (to tears, implorings, offers of a better living), he turned to the black minds of black-hearted black savages, serving for fifty years in the mission field, first on Tanna, and then, after he had fled for his life, for a short term on neighboring Aniwa, smaller population, more docile people, easier to threaten, bully and convert. Mr. Paton's departure from Tanna was quickly followed by *H.M.S. Curaçao* under Commander Sir William Wiseman, who "had thought it his duty to inflict punishment on the Natives for murder and robbery of Traders and others," starting with Tanna. Unfortunately for Paton's reputation, he and two other missionaries had gone along as "interpreters." The incident raised a real storm among antimissionaries in Australia and England, and the press had a ball, reporting that "The Tannese warriors were being blown to pieces by shot and shell, and lay in heaps on the bloody coast. And the Missionaries were represented as safe in the lee of the Man-of-war [in a mission ship, the *Dayspring*], directing the onslaught, and gloating over the carnage." Denials from the Reverend. But what went on in the recesses of *his* black mind? Nothing but pity for the infidels, you can count on that. After the *Curaçao* picnic, Tanna was occupied by the Reverend Watt, who had better nerves and a more successful reign, climaxed by *Twenty-five years of Mission life on Tanna,* by Mrs. Watt, Larlane Paisley, London, 1896; books came easily to the Tanna missionaries; others followed. Nice to let people at home know how you gave your all for Lord Jesus, while they (as Mr. Paton complained) have barely a thought for the laborers in the tropical vineyard.

Conditions were rough, no doubt about that. Mr. Paton's own book, *Missionary in the New Hebrides* (two volumes, 1889, Fleming H. Revell) was a classic in its field at a time when the native was getting his lumps from all sides. The following few passages, freely selected and arranged, give some flavor of life on Tanna in the mid-nineteenth century, and also show the even more special flavor of white thinking. Mr. Paton's words may seem like a parody, but they are his own, with a few additions for clarity or transition.

The Presbyterians have two mission posts on Tanna, one at Port Resolution, where Cook had landed, the other further South.

Read on.

Man-Tanna meets the Jesus freaks

What I write here is for the glory of God. I continually heard the wail of the perishing Heathen in the South Seas; and I saw that few were caring for them. I saw them perishing for lack of the true God and His Son Jesus. But Jesus called. With Mr. Copeland we set off for Tanna, an island of cannibals, where we feared we would all of us be cooked and eaten, two devoted men set apart to preach the Gospel to those dark and bloody naked Savages. My salary was £120 per annum.

When I first beheld these Natives in their paint and nakedness, and misery, my heart was as full of horror as of pity. My heart bleeds for the Heathen, and I long to see a Teacher [that is, a Christianized native from some other island such as Samoa or Tonga] for every tribe and a Missionary for every island of the New Hebrides. We found ourselves face to face with blank Heathenism. They were but children and full of superstition.

The first visible difference betwixt a Heathen and a Christian is—that the Christian wears some clothing, the Heathen wears none. When these poor creatures began to wear a bit of calico or a kilt, it was an outward sign of a change, though yet far from

JOHN FRUM HE COME

civilization. Concerning my former flock in Glasgow, though chiefly working girls and lads in trades and mills, their deep interest led them to unite their pence and sixpences and to buy web after web of calico, print and woollen stuffs, which they themselves shaped and sewed into dresses for the women, and kilts and pants for the men, in the New Hebrides. This continued to be repeated year after year, long after I had left them.

[Now, after various adventures on the way, Mr. Paton, Mrs. Paton (they had recently been married) and a Mr. Copeland are taken to Tanna, "an island of Cannibals," where he fears "our goods would have been plundered and all of us cooked and eaten." But a Dr. and Mrs. Inglis are already established ashore. Here come the whities.]

Missi, this is a dark land

We found the natives in a very excited and unsettled state. Threatened wars kept them in constant terror—war betwixt distant tribes, or adjoining villages, or nearest neighbours. The Chiefs, at both Stations, willingly sold sites for houses and appeared to desire Missionaries to live amongst them; but perhaps it was with an eye to the axes, knives, fishhooks, blankets, and clothing, which they got in payment, or hoped for in plunder, rather than from any thirst for the Gospel, as they were all savages and cannibals. They warily declined to promise protection to the Mission families and the Teachers; but they said they would not themselves do them any harm, though they could not say what the Inland people might do—not a bad specimen of diplomacy, leaving an open door for any future emergency, and neither better nor worse than the methods by which the civilized European nations make and break their treaties in peace and in war! Such promises meant and were intended to mean nothing. The Natives, both on Tanna, and on my second home at Aniwa, believed they had kept their promise, if they inflicted no injury with their own hands, even though they had hired others to do so. No Heathen there could be trusted one step beyond what appeared to be his own self-interest for the nonce; and nothing conceivable was too base or cruel to be done; if only it served his turn. The depths of Satan, outlined in the first chapter of the Romans, were uncovered there before our eyes in the daily life of the people, without veil and without excuse.

My first impressions drove me to the verge of utter dismay. On beholding these Natives in their paint and nakedness and misery, my heart was as full of horror as of pity. Had I given up my much-beloved work and my dear people in Glasgow, with so many delightful associations, to consecrate my life to these degraded creatures? Was it possible to teach them right and wrong? But that was only a passing feeling! I soon got as deeply interested in them, and in all that tended to advance them, and to lead them to the knowledge and love of Jesus, as ever had been my work at Glasgow.

To the Tannese, Dr. Inglis and I were objects of curiosity and fear; they came crowding to gaze at our wooden and lime-plastered house, they chattered incessantly with each other, and left the scene day after day with undisguised and increasing wonderment. Possibly they thought us rather mad than wise.

Party after party of armed men, going and coming in a state of great excitement, we were informed that war was on foot; but our Aneityumese Teachers were told to assure us that the Harbour people would only act on the defensive, and that no one would molest us at our work. One day two hostile tribes met near our station; high words arose, and old feuds were revived. The Inland people withdrew; but the Harbour people, false to their promises, flew to arms and rushed past us in pursuit of their enemies. The discharge of muskets in the adjoining bush, and the horrid yells of the savages, soon informed us that they were engaged in deadly fights. Excitement and terror were on every countenance; armed men rushed about in every direction, with feathers in their twisted hair—with faces painted red, black, and white, and some, one cheek black, the other red, others, the brow white, the chin blue—in fact, any colour and on any part—the

more grotesque and savage-looking, the higher the art! Some of
the women ran with their children to places of safety; but even
then we saw other girls and women, on the shore close by,
chewing sugar-cane and chaffering and laughing, as if their
fathers and brothers had been engaged in a country dance,
instead of a bloody conflict. In the afternoon, as the sounds of
the muskets and the yelling of the warriors, came unpleasantly
near to us, Dr. Inglis, leaning against a post for a while in silent
prayer, looked on us and said—

"The walls of Jerusalem were built in troublous times, and
why not the Mission House on Tanna? But let us rest for this
day, and pray for these poor Heathen."

We retired to a native house that had been temporarily
granted to us for rest, and there pled before God for them all.
The noise and the discharge of muskets gradually receded, as if
the Inland people were retiring; and towards evening the people
around us returned to their villages. We were afterwards
informed that five or six men had been shot dead; that their
bodies had been carried by the conquerors from the field of
battle, and cooked and eaten that very night by the savages at a
boiling spring near the head of the bay, less than a mile from the
spot where my house was being built. We also had a more
graphic illustration of the surroundings into which we had come,
through Dr. Inglis's Aneityum boy, who accompanied us as
cook. When our tea was wanted that evening, the boy could not
be found. After a while of great anxiety on our part, he returned,
saying—

"Missi, this is a dark land. The people of this land do dark
works. At the boiling spring they have cooked and feasted upon
the slain. They have washed the blood into the stream; they
have bathed there till all the waters are red. I cannot get water
to make your tea. What shall I do?"

Dr. Inglis told him that he must try for water elsewhere, till
the rains came and cleansed the polluted stream; and that,
meanwhile, instead of tea, we would drink from the cocoa-nut,
as they had often done before. The lad was quite relieved. It not
a little astonished us, however, to see that his mind regarded

their killing and eating each other as a thing scarcely to be noticed, but that it was horrible that they should spoil the water! How much are even our deepest instincts the creatures of mere circumstances! I, if trained like him, would probably have felt like him.

Next evening, as we sat talking about the people and the dark scenes around us, the quiet of the night was broken by a wild wailing cry from the villages around, long-continued and unearthly. We were informed that one of the wounded men, carried home from the battle, had just died; and they had strangled his widow to death, that her spirit might accompany him to the other world, and be his servant there, as she had been here. Now their dead bodies were laid side by side, ready to be buried in the sea. Our hearts sank to think of all this happening within ear-shot, and that we knew it not! every new scene, every fresh incident, set more clearly before us the benighted condition and shocking cruelties of these heathen people, and we longed to be able to speak to them of Jesus and the love of God. We eagerly tried to pick up their own tongue, to unfold to them the knowledge of the true God, and the salvation from all these sins through Jesus Christ.

Dr. Inglis and I, with the help of the Natives from Aneityum, having accomplished all that could be done for lack of lime and sawn wood to finish the new Mission House on Tanna, made an agreement with the Natives for knives, calico, and axes, to burn lime and prepare other things for our return. We then hastened back to Aneityum, that we might, if possible, get ready for settling on Tanna before the Rainy Season set in. That was rapidly approaching, and it brings with it discomfort and unhealthiness to Europeans throughout all these Pacific Isles.

*

[The missionaries are finally settled on Tanna, Mr. and Mrs. Mathieson at Umairarekar, on the south side of the island, and Mr. Copeland, Dr. and Mrs. Paton at Port Resolution. The missionaries begin to learn the language by pointing and asking questions, but—"they so often deceived us." Then the missionaries turn to the question of native beliefs, which they will hardly dignify with the name of religion.]

The Tannese had hosts of stone idols, charms and sacred objects, which they abjectly feared, and in which they devoutly believed. They were given up to countless superstitions, and firmly glued to their dark heathen practices. Their worship was entirely a service of fear, its aim being to propitiate this or that Evil Spirit, to prevent calamity or to secure revenge. They deified their chiefs, like the Romans of old, so that every village or tribe had its own sacred man, and some of them had money. They exercised an extraordinary influence for evil, these village or tribal priests, and were believed to have the disposal of life and death, through their sacred ceremonies, not only in their own tribe, but over all the Islands. Sacred men and women, wizards and witches, received presents regularly to influence the gods, and to remove sickness, or to cause it by the Nahak, i.e., incantation over remains of food, or the skin of fruit, such as bananas, which the person has eaten, on whom they wish to operate. They also worshipped the spirits of departed ancestors and heroes, through their material idols of wood and stone, but chiefly of stone. They feared these spirits and sought their aid; especially seeking to propitiate those who presided over war and peace, famine and plenty, health and sickness, destruction and prosperity, life and death. Their whole worship was one of slavish fear; and, so far as ever I could learn, they had no idea of a God of mercy or grace.

Let me here give my testimony on a matter of some importance—that among these Islands, if anywhere, men might be found destitute of the faculty of worship, men absolutely without idols, if such men exist under the face of the sky. Everything seemed to favor such a discovery; but the New Hebrides, on the contrary, are full of gods. The Natives, destitute of the knowledge of the true God, are ceaselessly groping after Him, if perchance they may find Him. Not finding Him, and not being able to live without some sort of god, they have made idols of almost everything; trees and groves, rocks and stones, springs and streams, insects and other beasts, men and departed

spirits, relics such as hair and fingernails, the heavenly bodies
and the volcanoes; in fact, every being and everything within the
range of vision or of knowledge has been appealed to by them as
God—clearly proving that the instincts of Humanity, however
degraded, prompt man to worship and lean upon some Being or
Power outside himself, and greater than himself, in whom he
lives and moves and has his being and without the knowledge of
whom his soul cannot find its true rest or its eternal life.
Imperfect acquaintance with the language and customs of
certain tribes may easily lead early discoverers to proclaim that
they have no sense of worship and no idols, because nothing of
the kind is visible on the surface; but there is a sort of
freemasonry in Heathen Religions; they have mysterious customs
and symbols, which none, even amongst themselves, understand,
except the priests and sacred men. It pays these men to keep
their devotees in the dark—and how much more to deceive a
passing inquirer! Nor need we hold up our hands in surprise at
this. It pays also nearer home, to pretend and to perpetuate a
mystery about beads and crucifixes, holy water and relics
[Catholicism!]—a state of mind not so very far removed from
that of the South Sea islander, not disapproving but rather
strongly proving that, whether savage or civilized, man must
either know the True God, or must find an idol to put in His
place.

Further, these very facts—that they did worship, that they
believed in spirits of ancestors and heroes, and that they cherished many legends regarding those whom they had never seen,
and handed these down to their children—and the fact that
they had ideas about the invisible world and its inhabitants,
made it not so hard as some might suppose to convey to their
minds, once their language and modes of thought were understood, some clear idea of Jehovah God as the great uncreated
Spirit Father, Who Himself created and sustains all that is. But
it could not be done offhand, or by a few airy lessons. The whole
heart and soul and life had to be put into the enterprise. The
idea that man disobeyed God, and was a fallen and sinful
creature—the idea that God, as a Father, so loved man that He

sent His only Son Jesus to this earth to seek and to save him—
the idea that this Jesus so lived and died and rose from the dead
as to take away man's sin, and make it possible for men to return
to God, and to be made into the very likeness of His Son Jesus—
and the idea that this Jesus will at death receive to the mansions
of Glory every creature under heaven that loves and tries to
follow Him—these ideas had to be woven into their spiritual
consciousness, had to become the very warp and woof of their
religion. But it could be done—that we believed because they
were men, not beasts. Our hearts rose to the task with a
quenchless hope!

A personal tragedy

My dear young wife, Mary Ann Robson, and I [had] landed on
Tanna on the 5th November, 1858, in excellent health and full
of all tender and holy hopes. On the 12th February, 1859, she
was confined of a son; for two days or so both mother and child
seemed to prosper, and our island-exile thrilled with joy! But
the greatest of sorrows was treading hard upon the heels of that
joy! My darling's strength showed no signs of rallying. She had
an attack of ague and fever a few days before her confinement;
on the third day or so thereafter, it returned, and attacked her
every second day with increasing severity for a fortnight.
Diarrhoea ensued, and symptoms of pneumonia, with slight
delirium at intervals; and then in a moment, altogether
unexpectedly, she died on 3rd March. To crown my sorrows,
and complete my loneliness, the dear baby boy, whom we had
named after her father, Peter Robert Robson, was taken from me
after one week's sickness, on the 20th March. Let those who
have ever passed through any similar darkness as of midnight
feel for me; as for all others it would be more than vain to try to
paint my sorrows!

Stunned by that dreadful loss, in entering upon this field of
labour to which the Lord Himself so evidently led me, my reason
seemed for a time almost to give way. Ague and fever, too,

laid a depressing and weakening hand upon me, continuously recurring and reaching oftentimes the very height of its worst burning stages. But I was never altogether forsaken. The ever-merciful Lord sustained me, to lay the precious dust of my beloved Ones in the same quiet grave, dug for them close by at the end of the house; in all of which last offices my own hands, despite breaking heart, had to take the principal share! I built the grave round and round with coral blocks, and covered the top with beautiful white coral, broken small as gravel; and that spot became my sacred and much-frequented shrine, during all the following months and years when I laboured on for the salvation of these savage Islanders amidst difficulties, dangers, and deaths. Whensoever Tanna turns to the Lord, and is won for Christ, men in after-days will find the memory of that spot still green—where with ceaseless prayers and tears I claimed that land for God in which I had "buried my dead" with faith and hope. But for Jesus, and the fellowship He vouchsafed me there, I must have gone mad and died beside that lonely grave.

"No one can take your place"

A strange presentment possessed my heart
ever since the day of our marriage
(cloudless and happy)—
that which was so precious and blessed
was about to be withdrawn
   I felt her loss
beyond all conception or description
in that dark land.

The sandalwooders

[*From a letter from Mr. Copeland and the Reverend Paton*]
"We found the Tannese to be painted Savages, enveloped in all the superstition and wickedness of heathenism. All the men and

children go in a state of nudity. The older women wear grass skirts, and the young women and girls, grass or leaf aprons like Eve in Eden. They are exceedingly ignorant, vicious and bigoted, and almost void of natural affection. Instead of the inhabitants of Port Resolution being improved by coming in contact with white men, they are rendered much worse; for they have learned all their vices, but none of their virtues—if such are possessed by the pioneer traders among such races! The sandalwood traders are as a class the most godless of men, whose cruelty and wickedness make us ashamed to own them as our countrymen. By them the poor, defenceless Natives are oppressed and robbed on every hand; and if they offer the slightest resistance, they are ruthlessly silenced by the musket or revolver. Few months here pass without some of them being so shot, and, instead of their murderers feeling ashamed, they boast of how they despatch them. Such treatment keeps the Natives always burning under a desire for revenge, so that it is a wonder any white man is allowed to come among them. Indeed, all Traders here are able to maintain their position only by revolvers and rifles; but we hope a better state of affairs is at hand for Tanna."

*

The sandalwood trade had a great share in the guilt of breaking up and ruining our Mission. Thousands upon thousands were made by it yearly, so long as it lasted; but it was a trade steeped in human blood and indescribable vice, nor could God's blessing rest on them and their ill-gotten gains. Sandalwood traders murdered many of the Islanders when robbing them of their wood, and the Islanders murdered many of them and their servants in revenge. White men, engaged in the trade, also shot dead and murdered each other in vicious and drunken quarrels, and not a few put an end to their own lives. I have scarcely known one of them who did not come to ruin and poverty; the money that came even to the ship-owners was a conspicuous curse. Fools there made a mock at sin, thinking that no one cared for these poor savages, but their sin did find them out, and God made good in their experience His own irreparable law, "The wages of sin is death."

Ships, highly insured, were said to be sent into our Island trade to be deliberately wrecked. One Sabbath evening, towards dark, the notorious Captain H——, in command of a large ship, allowed her to drift ashore and be wrecked without any apparent effort to save her. Next morning, the whole company were wading about in the water and pretending to have lost everything! The Captain, put in prison when he returned to Sydney for running away with another man's wife and property, imposed himself on Mr. Copeland and myself, getting all the biscuits, flour, and blankets we could spare for his destitute and shipwrecked company. We discovered afterwards that she was lying on a beautiful bank of sand, only a few yards from the shore, and that everything contained in her could easily be rescued without danger to life or limb! What we parted with was almost necessary for our life and health; of course he gave us an order on Captain T—— for everything, but not one farthing was ever repaid. At first he made a pretence of paying the Natives for food received; but afterwards, an armed band went inland night by night and robbed and plundered whatever came to hand. The Natives, seeing the food of their children ruthlessly stolen, were shot down without mercy when they dared to interfere; and the life of every white man was marked for speedy revenge. Glad were we when a vessel called, and carried away these white heathen Savages.

The same Captain T—— also began the shocking Kanaka labour-traffic to the Colonies, after the sandalwood trade was exhausted, which has since destroyed so many thousands of the Natives in what was nothing less than Colonial slavery, and has largely depopulated the Islands either directly or indirectly. And yet he wrote and published in Sydney a pamphlet declaring that he and his sandalwooders and Kanaka-labour collectors had done more to civilize the Islanders than all our Mission efforts combined. Civilize them, indeed! By spreading disease and vice, misery and death amongst them, even at the best; at the worst, slaving many of them, till they perished at their toils, shooting down others under one or other guilty pretence, and positively sweeping thousands into an untimely grave. A common cry on their lips was—

"Let them perish and let the white men occupy these Isles."

It was such conduct as this, that made the Islanders suspect all foreigners and hate the white man and seek revenge in robbery and murder. One Trader, for instance, a sandalwooder and collector of Kanakas, living in Port Resolution, abominably ill-used a party of Natives. They determined in revenge to plunder his store. The cellar was underneath his house, and he himself slept above the trap-door by which alone it could be entered. Night and day he was guarded by armed men, Natives of adjoining islands, and all approaches to his premises were watched by savage dogs that gave timely warning. He felt himself secure. But the Tannese actually constructed a tunnel underground from the bush, through which they rolled away tobacco, ammunition, etc., and nearly emptied his cellar! My heart bled to see men so capable and clever thus brutally abused and demoralized and swept away. By the Gospel, and the civilization which it brings, they were capable of learning anything and being trained to a useful and even noble manhood. But all influence that I ever witnessed from these Traders was degrading and dead against the work of our Missions.

*

One morning, three or four vessels entered our Harbour and cast anchor off Port Resolution. The Captains called on me; and one of them, with manifest delight, exclaimed—

"We know how to bring down your proud Tannese now! We'll humble them before you!"

I answered, "Surely you don't mean to attack and destroy these poor people?"

He answered, not abashed but rejoicing, "We have sent the measles to humble them! That kills them by the score! Four young men have been landed at different ports, ill with measles, and these will soon thin their ranks!"

Shocked above measure, I protested solemnly and denounced

their conduct and spirit, but my remonstrances only called forth the shameless declaration—

"Our watchword is—Sweep these creatures away and let white men occupy the soil!"

The measles, thus introduced, became amongst our islanders the most deadly plague. It spread fearfully, and was accompanied by sore throat and diarrhoea. In some villages, man, woman, and child were stricken and none could give food or water to the rest. The misery, suffering and terror were unexampled, the living being afraid sometimes even to bury the dead. Thirteen of my own Mission party died of this disease; and, so terror-stricken were the few who survived, that when the little Mission schooner *John Knox* returned to Tanna, they all packed up and returned to their own Aneityum.

Before leaving this terrible plague of measles, I may record my belief that it swept away, with the accompanying sore throat and diarrhoea, a third of the entire population of Tanna; nay, in certain localities more than a third perished. The living declared themselves unable to bury the dead, and great want and suffering ensued. Yet, from all the accounts afterwards received, I do not think the measles were more fatal on Tanna than on the other Islands of the group. They appeared to have carried off even a larger proportion on Aniwa. I am ashamed to say that these Sandalwood and other traders were our own degraded countrymen; and that they deliberately gloried in thus destroying the poor Heathen. A more fiendish spirit could scarcely be imagined, but most of them were horrible drunkards, and their traffic of every kind amongst these Islands was, generally speaking, steeped in human blood.

This dreadful epidemic blasted all our dreams. Mr. Johnston and his wife devoted themselves, from the very first, and assisted me in every way to alleviate the dread sufferings of the Natives. We carried medicine, food and even water, to the surrounding villages, few of themselves being able to render us much assistance. Vast numbers of them would listen to no counsels, and rushed into experiments which made the attack fatal all around. When the trouble was at its height, for

instance, they would plunge into the sea and seek relief; they
found it in almost instant death. Others would dig a hole into
the earth, the length of the body and about two feet deep;
therein they laid themselves down, the cold earth feeling
agreeable to their fevered skins; and when the earth around
them grew heated, they got friends to dig a few inches deeper,
again and again, seeking a cooler couch. In this ghastly effort
many of them died, literally in their own graves, and were
buried where they lay! It would not be surprising, though we
did everything in our power to relieve and save them, that the
Natives associated us with the white men who had so dreadfully
afflicted them, and that their blind thirst for revenge did not
draw fine distinctions between the Traders and the Missionaries.
Both were whites—that was enough.

A new incentive was added to the already cruel superstitions
of the Natives. The Sandalwooders, our degraded
fellow-countrymen, in order to divert attention from themselves,
stirred the Natives with the wild faith that the Missionaries and
the Worship had brought all this sickness, and that our lives
should be taken in revenge. Some Captains, on calling with
their ships, made a pretence of refusing to trade with the Natives
as long as I was permitted to live on the island. One Trader
offered to come ashore and live amongst the Tannese, and supply
them with tobacco and powder, and caps and balls, on condition
that the Missionary and Abraham were got out of the way!

A Tannese protest

[But not every Tannese jumped whole-heartedly into the arms of
the Presbyterians. There was much opposition, much of it covert.
To show the folks back home the kind of opposition—hatred—
he has to overcome, Paton quotes several Tannese about their
feelings towards the church. (I have combined two statements
into one.) Paton's reply to this protest was that the word of the
Holy God led him to fight "bad conduct," this being a Divine
Command—"If I refuse to obey my God, He will punish me."

However, he never mentions the circumstances of the supernatural apparition that told him to tear into the Tannese.]

The Worship is killing us all and the Inland people will kill us for keeping you [the missionaries] and the Worship here; for we love the conduct of Tanna [that is, traditional Custom], but we hate the Worship. We must kill you and it, and we shall be well again.

We hate the Worship, it causes all our diseases and deaths; it goes against our customs, and it condemns the things we delight in.

Our fathers loved [Custom] and followed it, we love and follow it, and if the Worship condemns it, we will kill you and destroy the Worship.

We like many wives to attend us and to do our work. Three of my wives are dead and three are yet still alive. The Worship killed them and my children. We hate it. It will kill us all.

[Until his dying day Paton never understood why a native preferred to be himself rather than an imitation white. Beats me too, why some people prefer authenticity to sham.]

Papists as black as the natives, Paton finds

War breaks out among the Tannese. Villages are burned, men killed (roasted and eaten, too). Paton and the other missionaries, threatened daily and abandoned by their native friends (never trust a native over thirty, or under, for that matter) when the going gets rough, live in constant fear of their lives. Finally they are forced to abandon the mission on Tanna, leaving everything behind, clothing, books, sacred implements. Their work is shattered. The Tannese are rejecting civilization, retaining only their knives, guns, tobacco and a veneer of misunderstood Christianity. Paton makes a tour of England and Australia, raising money and preaching the conversion of the black world, and warning about the dangers of the French. He returns to the New Hebrides, but takes up residence on Aniwa, a much smaller island than Tanna and some twenty miles offshore. Seems safer, and his mission grows. Meanwhile he enters political life sideways, agitating for annexation of the New Hebrides by Mother England, his motivating force being as much his fear of the French and their Roman Catholicism as his desire to convert the people to Presbyterianism. Fear of Roman Catholicism runs through his life, a steady refrain in his autobiography, and he is able to equate it with the superstitions of the Melanesians.

In Glasgow, as a young man, he had had bad experiences with the Catholics. Anonymous letters were sent him, threatening his life for his staunch opposition to Popery (so he wrote). "I was publicly cursed from the altar by the priests in the Abercromby Street Chapel." As a student he worked in the Ordnance Survey of Scotland, mapping the county of Dumfries. "The men both over me and beside me, were mostly Roman Catholics, and their talk was the most profane I had ever heard." Taking ship from Aneityum after his escape from Tanna, he has the misfortune to get aboard a sandalwood trader. "The Captain proved to be a profane and brutal fellow. He professed to be a Roman Catholic, but he was typical of the coarse and godless Traders in those Seas." Etc. In the Loyalty Islands, a French colony south of the New Hebrides, where he stayed briefly, he observed that the work of the various Protestant missions was "all being cruelly undone by the tyranny and the Popery of the French." The natives "cried aloud for God for deliverance from their oppressors." And: "The French Popish Missionaries were everywhere fostered and protected, presenting to the Natives as many objects of idolatry as their own, and following, as is the custom of the Romish Church in those Seas, in the wake of the Protestant Mission, to pollute and to destroy." And so on.[11]

*

Fifty years in the missionary field, bringing the good Jesus to the darkened mind! A commendable objective. But the natives are caught in the white vice, missionaries on one side, destroying their minds, souls, beliefs, customs, and on the other, sandalwooders, planters, traders and slavers, killing, robbing, picking them up bodily to transport far away. Black man, you had it coming to you, child of the Stone Age. But not time but blackness separated you from the whites. Black skin, black mind, black heart. Black, black, black.

*

NOTICE
Dogs and Niggers are Forbidden to enter inside
the Portals of those Gates. Any Dogs or Niggers found
therein will suffer the Penalty of Death.
By order of GEORGE DE LAUTOUR
British Resident

Lautour lived on Aore about 1883 ff. He had a skull atop each gatepost with two crossed thigh bones nailed below. The notice was posted on a nearby tree. One day a dog wandered inside and Lautour shot him, as the natives watched from outside the gate. Another day, as Lautour was inside the house, a native crept up and put the muzzle of his gun through the lattice work and shot him. A group then captured Lautour's son Willie, who had been chopping wood outside. He was a popular kid. One man held Willie's arms while the killer of his father shot him. Though they liked Willie they could not allow him to live as witness to the murder. The job on Willie was finished with clubs. Poor Willie! The sins of the fathers, etc. A punitive expedition lined up the natives in a row and shot them down one by one. Sitting bucks, you might say. The village was burned to the ground. The whites (French, mostly) soon did away with the survivors, so that by 1935 there was only one native left on the island, Aore being "the most settled, all-French island" (Harrisson).

Civilization develops on Tanna

We got two kinds people here: clothed (Christian) and unclothed (heathen). Rod of iron rule. Iron hand in iron glove. The first Condominium agent, Mr. W. Wilkes, called Presbyterianism the "mailed fist type of evangelism such as I have never seen nowhere else in the Pacific."

Presbyterians got their courts and their policemen. Everybody subject, white as well as black. But white on top anyway. Drinking kava gets you put in calaboose, singing gets you put in calaboose, 'bout anything you do means the calaboose.

Fines are imposed. Prohibitions for Sabbath breaking, feasting and indulging in entertainment. Many villages have their own police force of church elders devoted to exposing and prosecuting sin. In some there are public whipping posts. Depopulation has so weakened certain villages that the missionaries must force people to regroup in new communities where they can be better supervised.

All for Jesus.

This is the famed "Tanna law" I have been talking about. Whites still mention it with a morbid interest. The native mind goes blank with rage, fear, hatred when it is recalled. In all of the New Hebrides at this time there were barely twenty (white) Presbyterians, the number being kept down by disease, death, weariness in the face of obstacles, dropping out, and abandonment by the good Lord.

But Mr. Wilkes has to admit that Presbyterian rule is better than the past (cannibalism and head-hunting, for example), though he emphasizes that it is still "defective and brutal."

In 1912 the French and British Resident Commissioners visit Tanna and order that the only court to be recognized by the Condominium is that of its Agent. But the missionaries maneuver their own people into Mr. Wilkes's court, and begin a campaign of vilification against him. Letters go out not only to the Resident Commissioners in Vila but to friends in Australia and England and to the press. In 1915 Mr. Wilkes resigns: a bigger war (in Europe) needs his aid. He is replaced by Mr. James Nicol, who originally went out as engineer on the government yacht. Sir Harry Luke (*From a South Seas Diary, 1938–1942*) describes him as a "rough and ready old Aberdonian."

Mr. Nicol's attitude to natives is demonstrated by his action when Sir Harry asks him who a certain native woman was. "He went up to her, slowly pulled up her head by her top-knot so that he could get a good look at her face, opened her mouth and inspected her teeth like a vet judging the age of a horse, and said, 'Oh that's Rosie.'"

Damn good Presbyterian, that chap Nicol.

The Church marches on, with vigor.

Jesus saves.

Depopulation

The population of the New Hebrides, in the days before the coming of the whites, has been estimated as high as one million. This would be about the year 1800. H. Roche (*Description of the New Hebrides,* London, 1846) puts the figure at forty million. Most suspect, and perhaps a misprint. However, Harrisson's estimate is three million, again a guess, though Harrisson had the weight of solid experience in the islands, first as an anthropologist, and then in an extra year living in the bush in Malekula, where he could observe native life at its closest and reflect upon the past. Alexander Don (1870) and Felix Speiser (working from a study in 1882) claim 650,000 and 600,000 respectively for those years. By 1892 the Colonial Office stated the population to be under 100,000, and by 1920 the government figure was 59,000. But the end was not in sight. Harrisson puts the 1935 figure— for all the islands—at 45,000, with the decline in population continuing.

Throughout the nineteenth century the common white view was that depopulation was caused by the sins of the natives— they died because they were black sinners—aided by a push or two from the whites, like slavers and sandalwooders. But the fault lies largely with the whites, who were introducing ways of life the blacks could not cope with. Not only did the sandalwooders and other early traders kill ruthlessly, but the arrival of the blackbirders brought even heavier losses. Natives were taken by the thousands from the New Hebrides (and from the Solomons and New Guinea) for the plantations of Queensland and Fiji and for the guano fields of Peru. At the worst period, roughly 750 out of each 1,000 laborers taken to Australia died or at least were not returned to their own islands; even the returnees were often dropped among hostile tribes, where they might be killed. Of the men sent to Peru, not a single one is believed to have been brought home. And then there was the introduction of diseases, accidental or deliberate, which brought further destruction to the islanders. Disastrous famines sometimes followed the destruction of the indigenous way of life. The places most Europeanized suffered the most disastrously. The population of Aneityum dropped from some 5,000 in 1839 to 199 in 1943. The 1967 census places it at 313. Tanna fell from 15,000 or 20,000 in 1872 to 6,000 in 1926. Pre-white figures could have been 100,000 to 200,000. Guiart's figure for the period 1952–53 is less that 6,000, but the 1967 census shows a marked increase at 10,367. Whatever the causes, it must have been a frightening experience for the New Hebridean, the Solomon islander and the New Guinean and Papuan to see his world rapidly being emptied by causes beyond the control even of his magic.[12]

NOW CARGO COME

Cargo has been studied extensively, but much of the basic material can be found in three works by outstanding observers—Burridge (1960), Lawrence (1964) and Worsley (1968), all three previously mentioned. The first two have studied specific Cargo movements in New Guinea in detail; certain aspects of what they say about New Guinea also have specific relevance to other areas, including Tanna. Worsley's work covers the broad range of Melanesian Cargo with some asides on Cargo and other millennial movements elsewhere, including Europe of the Middle Ages and the Ghost Dance of the North American Indians. I have my minor quarrels with all three writers, but the material I am going to quote, summarize or paraphrase says enough about the "natural" and mundane aspects of Cargo to give us a consensus of how it originates and develops. While it might be sociologically true that each movement is "unique," and independent of others, it is also clear that there are certain themes, hopes, trends, sources that are more or less shared in general by Cargo. One should not make blanket statements in this very sensitive field where experts quarrel at the drop of a cross-cousin relationship, but there is much to be observed in common.

Lawrence, in his study of the Cargo movement in the southern Madang district of New Guinea, makes the following points: A cargo belief (myth) described how European goods were invented by a cargo deity and indicated how men could get them from him via their ancestors by following a cargo prophet or leader. Cargo beliefs and ritual were never fixed: they could be replaced or revised after failure. The manner in which race relations developed gave the people the conviction that they could have satisfactory dealings with Europeans only if they acquired large quantities of Cargo. Native attitudes to whites passed through various alternating stages of friendship and hostility. The cargo movement eventually gave the natives a sense of unity never experienced before contact with Europeans, and developed into a form of "embryonic nationalism" or "proto-nationalism."

Other points: Very little specialization in the native way of life. Primary emphasis on subsistence economy, with no concept of profit making. No strong internalized forces of change; life tends to be stationary. Wars were common, but were rarely fought to improve a group's economic position, revenge being the primary motive, caused by disputes over love, magic, adultery, sorcery and homicide.

Religion: no clear separation between religion and magic, and no native society had any single word for it. Myths are accepted as the sole and unquestionable source of all important truth. Natives possess a sound body of secular knowledge by western standards, but except in minor matters they dismiss the principle of human intellectual discovery. "All the valued parts of their culture were stated to have been invented by the deities, who taught men both secular and ritual procedures for exploiting them. The deities lived with men or appeared in dreams, showing them how to plant crops and make artifacts. They taught men to breathe esoteric formulae and observe taboos. Even when a man composed a new melody or dance, he had to authenticate it by claiming that it came from a deity rather than out of his own head . . . Ignorance of a myth did not matter as long as it could be accepted that a myth of some sort existed and was known in the place of origin. It was enough to be sure that the relevant deity had revealed his secrets in a recognized way . . . The leaders were men who 'really knew' and who could direct the activities of others—those who did not 'really know'—to the best advantage."

The natives' reactions to Europeans were governed by two considerations: the personal behavior of the white men they had met, and an unsatisfied demand for western goods, on which they were becoming more and more dependent. The settlers regarded the natives purely as economic assets, to be exploited with a minimum of outlay and flogged into obedience. In New Guinea the Germans, the dominant white group, treated the coastal people with the greatest arrogance, stealing their land and their labor. Dispossession from the land and forced labor were the common introduction to white rule. In return the natives received little of the new wealth derived from their own lands and labor, though they were extremely attracted to the whites' standard of living. When the Australians took over the area at the beginning of World War I, the Germans were forbidden to flog, but "coon-bashing" was common, and the Australians soon adopted the Germans' racial attitudes. The natives were kept firmly in place. Eventually western goods replaced so much of the old island culture that whatever the natives might feel about Europeans, they were forced into a symbiotic relationship with them, from which they could not escape.

Cargo, in the long run, may be considered as a reaction to the preceding and as a rudimentary form of revolutionary "nationalism"—"the people's first experiment in completely renewing the world order and achieving independence from European rule." At times the hope was expressed that the whites would either be killed or expelled. However, there were traditional forces that prevented cargo followers from ever breaking seriously with their past, thus delaying the emergence of a militant "nationalism" in the fullest sense of the term until a quite late stage. Although the people may have thought that they were forming a new way of life, it was old attitudes and concepts that motivated their actions. Ideas could not be too unfamiliar; they must have some roots in the past to be accepted. "Traditional value- and epistemological-systems have so far proved extremely durable under European contact partly because of their own integration and logical consistency, and partly because the changes introduced affected only the externals of the natives' way of life without touching the vital principles underlying it."

So far we have seen how the indigenous people have been able to retain much of their own culture, still with a foot in the white man's world. But Lawrence, like most whites, sees native ways a hindrance and white ways the only solution for being a native. He says, "For the future, unless conservatism is quickly and effectively eradicated [that word should be underlined a hundred times], it may well impede the more far-reaching economic, political and intellectual revolution which we are now trying to achieve." Thus again, the native's way of life is to be annihilated so he can be an imitation white man, an attitude we meet over and over again in this polemic.

Burridge, in Mambu, made an intensive study of the Tangu people and those of the Manam island, in northern New Guinea. What he says about these people has general application, particularly his remarks about relations with whites, guilt caused by the black man's inability to handle these relations to his own satisfaction, and dreams and myth-dreams.

In the middle of the nineteenth century, says Burridge, the people of the Territory of New Guinea were living their own lives in their own way. There were no missions, no administrations. "Their cultures were rich in rituals, myths and art forms. From childhood until death their lives were ordered by a relatively narrow, but complex ambience of kin obligations. Their tools were of stone and shell. They enjoyed, for the most part, what we call subsistence economies. They produced huge surpluses of foodstuffs which were consumed in feasts to yield prestige and political influence: they were engaged in barter, trade, and food exchanges." And: "Individuals were proud, self-centered, and quick to recognize a slight; warrior values went hand in hand with hard work in the gardens, business acumen, and a fiercely independent spirit." But by the nineties these values were beginning to be affected by the influx of explorers, adventurers, traders, missionaries and administrative officers, most of them German. With the beginning of World War I, the Australians (and British) replaced the Germans.

In general, the people dislike white men but also wish to be like them. But white men cause trouble: "White men are habitual liars and hypocrites." The Kanakas have not yet found a completely satisfactory means of heading off the trouble that whites cause. The whites make their own laws, pay what wages they choose, imprison when they feel like it, according to their own arbitrary laws. Their behaviour is irrational. They are all-powerful and immune. And, "they are scarcely impressed by what Tangu have to offer. They cannot be pleased, importuned, or even corrupted directly." Whites add both new knowledge and new uncertainties to life. The Kanaka asks: "What is wrong? We are as we are—black, dirty, without learning, without Cargo, without power. Sometime in the past something went wrong. What was it? Who did it?"

The problem for the Kanaka is how to find ways of co-operating with whites, but more importantly, to persuade whites to co-operate with them; how to live in a new world which is neither European nor native; and how to transcend the divisions between Kanaka and white and make the world an intelligible unity.

Unlike the European, with his linear concept of history based on past documents, the Kanaka bases his moral, intellectual and conceptual structure on myths. "For Kanakas the present appears as an isolated time span of three generations." Most, if not all, truths and much learning and lore go into a myth or story. "There each piece of knowledge is remembered, correlated, and threaded into a meaningful pattern. The traditional myths, overtly telling of the past but also accounting for the present and linking present with past, have been undermined by missionary teachings, by conversations and experiences with administrative officers, traders, planters and other white men. Yet few Kanakas are willing to abandon the form of a myth as a means of expressing their truths. And while there is a conservative reluctance to alter the detail contained in a particular myth, over the years myths do undergo changes in content and meaning. Some parts drop out, other items are added. The chief criterion of placement is consent." Myths and dreams become interwoven.

"For Tangu dreams are not simple fantasies woven from sleep. They are a normal technique for solving a problem or finding a way out of a dilemma." Whether or not a man who claims to have dreamed a dream actually dreamt it in sleep is unimportant. What is significant is that the chosen means for expressing the desires and hopes of a man was a dream. For example, "Some men in Tangu said that they would not consider wasting their time building a pig-trap until they have dreamed of catching a pig." "A dream is useful: it predicates a future . . . It comes to the recipient from 'outside'—from the spirits, from the dead." This brings us to the "myth-dream." Burridge writes: "A myth-dream is a body of notions derived from a variety of sources such as rumours, personal experiences, desires, conflicts, and ideas about the total environment which find expression in myths, dreams, popular stories, and anecdotes. If those involved in a myth-dream were capable of fully comprehending and intellectualizing its content and meaning then 'aspiration' might have been a better word. As it is, myth-dream, because of its previous associations, better meets the case."

Worsley, who points out that cargo-type movements are by no means peculiar to Melanesia, says that the cults "serve as an expression of reaction against what is felt as oppression by another class or nationality. . . . The cults generally occur among people divided into small, separate, narrow and isolated social units: the village, the clan, the tribe, the people of a valley, etc. They occur firstly, among people living in the so-called 'stateless' societies, societies which have no overall unity, which lack centralized political institutions, and which may lack specialized political institutions altogether." They have no suitable means of organization by which they can act as a political unified force. And indeed people sharing the same culture and language or dialect—villages and clans—get into a state of intermittent hostility with their neighbors, the same people with whom they trade and intermarry. Such highly segmented societies are incapable of offering resistance to the Europeans.

"The main effect of the millenarian cult is to overcome these divisions and to weld previously hostile and separate groups together into a new unity," and they must create new political organizations to express their new-found unity. Such is the integratory function of the millenarian movements.

In his concluding chapter Worsley quotes Raymond Firth in saying that students of the movements have begun to see them in more positive and dynamic terms. "The movements are part of the process of imperfect social and economic adjustment to the conditions arising directly or indirectly from contact with the West. They are not mere passive responses, the blind stirrings of a people who feel that they are being pushed around. Absurd as they may seem [that is, to us intelligent whites] when considered as rational solutions, they are creative attempts of the people to reform their own institutions, to meet *new* demands or withstand *new* pressures. In the broadest sense their aims are to secure a fuller life."

So much for the broad outline of Cargo by leading social anthropologists. How Cargo works out in the field is something else, which is both entertaining and tragic. When you smile at the black man's naïveté, think of how you would fare if you had not been trained since infancy by toilet, teacher and the Tube.

Divine Twins, Destroying Angels, Water Babies & others

Fiji was discovered early (by the Dutchman Tasman, 1643; Cook came in 1774, and Captain Bligh in 1792). As the nineteenth century arrived, Europeans begin to come ashore in flocks, first the sandalwooders (though the supply of trees is depleted by 1813), fishermen, whalers and traders. Some of the newcomers are (almost) legitimate businessmen; most are murderous adventurers, criminals, escaped convicts, beachcombers and other (colorful) detritus. Everyone is tough (you never in your life saw such mean bastards!). The Fijian tribes are at war, and many whites sell their services as skilled military technicians and "invincible slaughterers."

Warfare increases and other cruelties grow apace. The whites continue to arrive. Native lands are sold; plantations are developed. Finally, because the warfare is so destructive, the more responsible whites (that is, those making a living out of and off Fijians), along with certain of the natives, ask Mother England to step in and rule, a move the Home Government at first resists, quite sensibly. But by 1874, when Disraeli is Prime Minister, Fiji is "ceded" to a now-willing Britain.[1] The islands are rapidly becoming civilized; the areas dominated by whites having been nominally converted to Christianity by Wesleyan missionaries.

But the natives are restless. In 1877 news of a religious cult, the Tuka movement, not "native," not Christian, filters through to the white masters. By 1885 the whites realize that they are faced with a movement that challenges their domination. In the back country, on the upper reaches of the Rewa River, groups of men with blackened faces and wearing robes of native cloth are carrying out a kind of military drill. They are armed with clubs and spears and have a few guns. This enthusiastic and committed "army" is established on a system copying the British military, though the upper ranks of leaders, thanks to the Holy Bible, are known as "destroying angels." The commander is a man named Ndugumoi who claims prophetic, miraculous and occult powers. His spirit can leave his body and move about the countryside. [It is said? No, it *can!*] Ndugumoi has once been arrested, in 1873, and exiled to Tonga, but was freed in 1882. On his return he has announced that he has escaped from the foreigners, leaving his body abroad. Attempts by the government to kill him have been unsuccessful.

Ndugumoi's message (like others to come, here and in other islands) is roughly this: he has been told mystically that the ancestors are to return to Fiji, that the ancient lands (now held by whites) will be restored along with the past glories of the Fijians; in the millennium eternal life and eternal pleasure will be the reward when the faithful enter The Glorious Paradise. For the old, youth will be renewed and sexual desire will burn with the energies of the young; the shops will be jammed with European clothes, tinned fish and other goods, and most important, the whites—government officials, missionaries and traders—will be driven into the sea. Interspersed in this vision are prominent biblical themes: Noah and the Flood, the story of Creation are primary. The Fijians, Ngudumoi affirms, have always known Jehovah, well before the whites reintroduced him to their islands. Tuka is the first "Cargo" movement in the South Pacific to attract white notice.

The Divine Twins—two legendary Fijian figures now identified with Jehovah and Jesus Christ—are about to return. Ngudumoi has seen them in a vision. The whites know this and are afraid. There are miracles (God descending in the cult temples to the sound of a low whistle is one); kava (called yaggona on Fiji) is drunk; the faithful are called upon to renounce sin, though the prophet has taken a number of young girls, promising them perpetual virginity as long as they drink holy water.

A strong anti-white theme runs throughout Ngudumoi's teachings. The fattening of a white pig—in white paranoia believed to symbolize the white man (not so paranoid, perhaps)—in preparation for sacrifice to the ancestors on the Day creates a sinking sensation among the pale faces. But now some of the Fijians themselves begin to attack the movement, particularly parents whose daughters seem to have lost the perpetual virginity the prophet has promised them. The British act decisively, the moment being propitious, and arrest Ngudumoi and a number of destroying angels. Can this be the ferocious Ngudumoi?—a native described by an anthropologist as "a sooty-skinned, hairy little man of middle age, with eyes bleary from excessive kava drinking." One year in prison for the sooty little man instead of the death sentence he has expected, because, as he later tells his followers, the government is unable to kill him. Then he is banished to another island some three hundred miles away. The government, the Tukas are able to report, has indeed tried to kill the prophet by dropping him first into the crusher of a sugar mill and then into the funnel of a ship, but the prophet has escaped both the rollers and the flames unhurt.

The Tuka movement continues under new leaders, aided by the Water Babies, an interlocking movement of younger people expressing their restlessness against the oppressive white rule. We find kava drinking, prayer, song and dance as prominent exterior expressions of the revived movement. The whites are irritated. Arrests, persecution, imprisonment follow. A. B. Brewster, an Englishman, writes (*The Hill Tribes of Fiji,* 1922): "In my opinion it was not really seditious, it led the boys to be cheeky and insubordinate, and to a certain amount of larceny. I think there is not much harm in it so long as the votaries refrain from picking and stealing, and are duly respectful to their elders, and there is certainly a fair amount of romance and poetry about it."²

Then follow similar and descendant movements—by now we have reached 1947—another Tuka cult, the Roses of Life, led by one Kelevi (the Kingdom of Christ on this earth, the return of the Twins from Europe, where they have been giving out wisdom to the whites), and so on.

That Kelevi he sleep with various Roses.

Into jail wit him.

Here come God

The Baron N. N. Miklouho-Maclay, Russian, accompanied by a Swedish sailor and a Polynesian servant, is dropped ashore at Astrolabe Bay on the northern coast of New Guinea. The date is 1871; the Baron will stay fifteen months, returning later. Objective: to establish friendly relations with the natives. They flee. The Baron strolls about, finds a native cowering under a bush, shakes hands with him. But the natives no like these invaders. In sign language they tell the whites they will be killed. The ship's company builds a bungalow for the mini-expedition, sets mines around it as protection, and fires a twenty-one-gun salute as they sail off. Honors to those who are about to die.

Showers of arrows, shot to test his divine nature rather than to kill, narrowly miss Maclay (as the historians call him), though two bounce off his head. Swede and servant terrified. Maclay, iron-nerved, ignores the arrows. The shooting stops. A new test. He is tied to a tree and spears are rammed down his throat "in an unpleasant manner." As the result of his reception he damn near die! But Maclay lives. Must be some kinda god, is native thought. The Baron got one sore throat! For a while the natives stay away from the wait-sikins. "The Polynesian died. The Swede was a perpetual nuisance," writes someone.

The Polynesian's body is pushed to sea, weighted and dropped to the bottom. It is a nighttime operation. No natives around to witness this deception. "Where brown man?" ask the natives in daylight. Maclay points vaguely at the horizon. Natives think the brown man has flown away like a bird.

Maclay shows his goodies. He has scientific equipment, firearms, a primus stove, presents. (What if no one *ever* gave a native a set of beads, a bolt of cloth, a stick of tobacco? We've spoiled the bastards!)

Maclay walks about at night with a blue lantern. Natives suspect he has some connection with the moon, though he tells them repeatedly he has come from Russia. So, Russia equals moon.

The general conclusion is that he is a deity. Something to do with the big tibut or god the Sengam, Som, Yam and Yabob call Anut. (For your information, the Seks have a different name for the big tibut. It is Dodo.)

Anut is a creator-god, some people believing he created the entire world, others (the Yabobs) that the world had already been in existence when Anut came out of a cave and straightened up the place, a sensible theory. Each tribe has numerous variations of the Anut story and his progeny, all too complicated to detail here; volumes are needed for a proper explanation. We must get on with Maclay.

The Baron begins to learn the language. He is referred to as Tibut Maclay. But the Yabobs assume he is Kilibob, a light-skinned deity who is one of Anut's two sons. At any rate, Maclay is some kind of deity, with his pale skin, numerous exotic possessions and his self-assurance under arrows and spears. Tibut Maclay has the stuff people want. He hands out steel axes, adzes, nails, mirrors, cloth, beads, paint. He also has seeds of exotic plants—pumpkin, melon, pawpaw, pineapple. The natives bring him presents in trade. The first (disastrous) step has been taken.

More: Tibut Maclay is always ready for conversation, and he displays superhuman knowledge. Advice you want? Ask Tibut Maclay.

He's got good advice, all right! Tibut Maclay knows about the brutality of the blackbirders in other parts of Melanesia, and about land-grabbing traders and planters and other white activists. He hands out warnings: watch out for the white man. He gonna getcha! Tibut Maclay tries to explain that there are two kinds whites, good (like himself) and bad. Some good ones may come, but many will be bad. His final visit ends in 1877. The Englishman Romilly and the German Finsch, both of whom have met the Baron somewhere, arrive at Astrolabe in 1881 and claim to be his brother or some such lie. But they behave fairly well. Finsch returns in 1884, a "good guy," and claims Astrolabe Bay (and more) for the bloody Kaiser. Bloody liar! Those sparkling blue waters out there are named for Bismarck. Soon the New Guinea Company (krauts) arrives to take over the land, paying two steel axes and some matches and paint for what appears to be a sweet little homesite. But out go the surveyors and their guards and stake off thousands of acres, an area beyond belief. The natives are upset. But who got the guns?

"The Bilia natives lost most of their lands and ever since have had to borrow or rent garden sites from affinal and cognatic relatives in other groups," writes Lawrence. "The inhabitants of Nob, Yabob, and other villages also lost many of their holdings." The Germans have set up a protectorate.

To protect what against whom?

Planters, traders, gov't officials, missionaries begin to come ashore.

Despair among the natives, who think the Djamans are hostile deities, not benevolent like the crazy Russky. But hope springs eternal and perhaps, perhaps, with the right magic, they will get some of the groovy things Tibut Maclay had handed out.

Cargo is off to a running start in New Guinea.

*

The century turns, off coming a page of the calendar and there is a magic new number, as if a great change can erase Rape, restore the murdered Dead. Can one revive innocence, trust, honesty, the primal naïveté?

One interesting fact develops: The Djamans not gods but people.

They die of malaria, other diseases, mysterious things. Two

native convicts escape from prison with stolen rifles and shoot down Governor von Hagen as he pursues them with a patrol.

One good Djaman!

The natives become openly hostile. Three revolting native policemen add three more Djamans and a Chinaman to the list. During the first twenty-five years of German occupation of New Guinea and the neighboring islands, fifty-five wait-sikins are killed by natives. Three wait-sikins are killed by Duke of York islanders. They are rewarded with a punitive force of 750 troops, being properly punitive. German battleships range the coasts, bombarding, shelling, sending forces ashore. After the people of Deslacs Island behave in the usual unfriendly manner, they get a sound shelling, and then natives from New Ireland, amply armed not only with spears but rifles, are put ashore with instructions to kill every child under ten. Which they do.[8]

Now Cargo come in earnest. In one small part of the Madang district on the northern coast Lawrence traces five major cargo movements in detail over a seventy-year period.

In the British part of New Guinea, in the Milne Bay area, a young native named Tokeriu is inspired by a spirit which resides in a sacred tree. Tokeriu now visits Hiyoya, which is nothing but the other world, and upon his return he prophesies a great storm which will submerge the coast with a tidal wave. But believers are to be saved from the catastrophe. Tokeriu orders the banning of the white man's goods. Discarded are tin match boxes, pocket knives and other white implements. A ship is to come with the spirits of the dead. To escape the coastal tragedy, the people are to flee inland and build new villages. Gardens are abandoned, pigs (wealth, social status!) are all to be killed and eaten. Clubbed down are some four hundred of them. In the new villages yams and taro will grow in profusion. No need of worrying about food! The coast is emptied. A missionary, one Mr. Abel, finds his Sunday service abandoned except for a catechist and his family. Abel plunges into the jungle to reason with the natives in their new homes. "Sullen silence" greets him. He attempts to bribe them into conversation. "I had in my wallet a long thin stick of trade tobacco, a delicacy very much prized by these people, and as I was sitting in the doorway of the chief's house I took it out, and threw it to some men who were sitting behind me in the dark. Almost before they had time to pick it up, it was hurled back and struck me on the ear." Tough.

Abel flees in fear of his life. But the promised riches don't come, and the people now threaten to kill Tokeriu. The government gives him two years in jail. Disillusionment brings the end of the cult.

On they go, the cargo cults. The writings use such phrases as "profuse," "rife," "reports of Cargo movements come thick and fast," and so on. Plenty Cargo coming, no doubt about that. The Vailala Madness really gets the whites up tight. It starts in 1919, when officials find that in one village after another the natives are showing themselves possessed, in trances, dancing madly, prophesying, hysterical. Some villages have magic poles, which, carried on the shoulders of several men, are able to answer questions merely by reactions. The whole area seems to be gripped in the madness, which, it seems, stems from the revelations of one Evara, who has foreseen the coming of a steamer with the dead ancestors aboard, bringing with them the Cargo. Rifles, rice, flour, tobacco and other objects are in the Cargo. Papua for the Papuans is the message that spreads about; the Whites must be driven out. Papers flutter down from heaven bearing messages for Evara. The ancestors are white! And: "Brown skins are no good. God he want all the people to have white."

The movement's members have visions of Jesus Christ. Papuans will replace the Europeans. The people dress in their formal clothes, sit at tables, as whites do. Flowers are placed in beer bottles. The air is one of formality. An Acting Resident Magistrate comes to a village to get the buggers back to work: "They sat quite motionless and never a word was spoken for the few minutes I stood looking at them. It was sufficient to raise anybody's ire to see them acting in such an idiotic manner; a number of strong, able-bodied natives, in mid-afternoon, dressed in clean, new toggery, sitting as silently as if they were in stocks and stones, instead of being at work or doing something else like rational beings. They appeared to be fit subjects for a lunacy asylum." He made his report in 1919. The Vailala Madness lasted until 1931.

*

There are more cargo cults in New Guinea and Papua than you could put in a hundred books. They say: world coming to end, throw out the whites, big ship on way with plenty stuff. God the Father turns up in Suain on the northeast coast. Four Black Kings arise at Aitape predicting the end of Europeans and the coming of new cooking pots. Wewak got its Black Kings too, seven in this case, who reveal that the ancestors had made all the Cargo, which has been stolen (as you might know) by the whites. In the Madang district there are rumors of a strange Black King who has a skin of iron and stone and many hands. At Markham, after one fella sees Jesus Christ, another gets a visit from Satan, who brings him to the bowels of the earth to talk to the dead. After a big earthquake, say the dead, they will appear with tinned meat, tobacco, loincloths, rice, lamps and rifles. On the Huon Peninsula a hermit named Upikno talks to God, takes the name of Lazarus and works miracles. Lazarus calls for moral renewal. No more stealing, fucking, no sin. Throw out the white man, destroy his goods. Cargo coming.

Those prophets, they spring up here and there faster than the government can arrest them. Plenty in gaol and in exile, but New Guinea and Papua got more than the wet-man can capture.

More Cargo bilong New Guinea side

1. Big chief Batari he promise Cargo.
Got followers long much thousand.
That day ship come long cases marked batteries.
Chief he plenty angry white traders no give him Cargo marked
his name sent by ancestor gods long sea old time.

2. Big submarine baimbai he come long America much much
   Cargo for native.

Cargo chief say all that story, chief he got some boxis long soap
   painted like radio he send out message long submarine how
   he come long shore unload plenty Cargo.

Natives he burn down house kill all pig destroy crop Cargo
   coming!

God he send much much Cargo hundred time big stuff bilong
   today.

Submarine no come cause white man he make bad magic he
   block native get Cargo.

All Right!

3. American plane he come baimbai drop plenty big eggs plenty all
   black man bilong Rabaul.

That egg he break out come American soldier

plenty tinned meat

washing machine

Mercedes automobile

much much Cargo!

4. Wewak got Cargo coming natives go Wewak town see
   refrigerators

come back bush make refrigerators long wood make wires long
   vines

sit down pray pray much much

Baimbai refrigerator door he open

give native

   ice creams

   plenty sodas

   cold

like wet-man got Wewak side

Baimbai.

5. "A serious young District Officer told me, 'The Cargo we
   had here [in the Western Highlands] was the Bank Cult. All
   through the jungle the natives make little buildings of bamboo
   in the shape of banks they had seen when they went down to
   the coast, complete even to tellers' windows. The natives
   believed they had only to wait for money to come out.'"[4]

The story of Matthias

Matthias cargo leader he read Book of Revelations
Book say Cargo hidden in that ground top Mount Turun,
    sacred mountain East Sepik district long near Wewak town
Survey markers put there by that U. S. Air Force fellas long
    1962
Markers right over that Cargo hidden long ground
Natives he look that mountain long that flash cube he see all
    that Cargo hidden from those U. S. Air Force fellas
Matthias he gonna crucify self get that Cargo bilong followers
[Fifteen thousand they are not counting woman and childs]
Concrete markers land survey there no reason but mark Cargo
    place
Matthias say small boy must die same time he crucify self,
    otherwise people no get Cargo
"You take em up those marker when we dead," Matthias he say
"And underneath that markers all that Cargo!
"Knives, forks, automobiles, trucks, refrigerators, food all that
    stuff bilong native that white man he steal
"That white man he use evil magic," is Matthias revelation
    bilong that Book
"When you got up that Cargo, Matthias he rise from dead long
    that boy. All Right?"
["The appearance of the powerful Cargo cult has presented a
    problem to the Australian authorities on New Guinea, a
    United Nations Trust territory which with the associated
    territory of Papua is scheduled to become fully self-governing
    in five years. Great delicacy on the part of the administration
    in controlling the movement is required."]
Matthias got that flash cube he got that picture too Agatha
    Christie book *Evil under the Sun* show lady doll stuck with
    pins. Native man he say, "This persecuted lady he going be
    ruler Papua New Guinea!"
Big day coming, Matthias ready kill boy, crucify self, followers

get that Cargo under markers. That Father Francis he tok tok
Matthias, plenty tok tok, Matthias he no crucify self, no kill
that boy
That Matthias he go top sacred mountain Turun, all those
people come get Cargo
Big moment now! Shovels out, crowbars, Matthias he give big
heave and pull up marker number one marker number two
Aaaaah!
NO CARGO!
White man he trick Matthias, with his western morality
Part Two Coming. Unexpected twist. Civilization he make
advance.
Matthias he run for Papua New Guinea House of Assembly, like
parliament bilong England
He cream opponent 7,200 to 435
Matthias now big bosman he got 60,000 followers know Matthias
gonna help them
He say, that independence come Papua New Guinea "me big
fella leader o'long Papua New Guinea." Matthias be Prime
Minister baimbai!
You fix em Matthias.

Marching Rule

We got one small story from Solomon Islands where Cargo pro-
liferates like elsewhere. Far back as 1908 Europeans in Tulagi
fear for white prestige when American black Jack Johnson beat
Irishman Tommy Burns in Sydney for world boxing champion-
ship. Japs come in World War II in their wonnerful Greater
East Asia Co-Prosperity Sphere. First they are welcomed with
food, flowers and so on, but soon the natives find Jap like every
other foreigner, maybe worse. (You think wet-man bad, you
outa work for Jap!) Along come Americans to fight Japs. Americans got all that Cargo, trucks, tanks, movie theatres, beer,
whiskey, food. Americans got those laundry machines where the
natives can do their wash. No more wash in stream now! But

the British, with centuries of experience various continents, know the mistake of giving natives privileges and stop access to washing machines. U.S. marines, kindly fellows, run line to native village mile away and put in washers for natives. British pretty damn mad. Americans got all that money, which they give to natives. Upset local economy, cause all kinds trouble. Plenty Americans are black, a fact which leads the people of San Cristobel to believe that these are the descendants of natives kidnapped by Mendaña centuries back. On Mailata the natives try to buy American rule, it being obviously better than the British. The war moves on, the Americans leaving piles of equipment behind. Natives build new villages along the lines of American camps. Throughout the southern islands of the Solomons the natives seemed to be organizing. The movement is called Marching Rule, a corruption of a native word masina, meaning brother or brotherhood.

The natives are openly anti-white. Villages now have stockades around them. Arrests follow because the people refuse to pull down the fences, some 2,000 men being imprisoned by June 1949. The situation becomes tense as the people become polarized between political action and a millennial, mystical surge. Gardens are abandoned for it is authoritatively rumored that the Americans are about to return with more Cargo. Now, instead of working on their gardens the people dig air-raid shelters for protection in the American bombings of the British. Hide-outs are constructed in the bush.

No Americans come, no war, no need for shelters. Plenty of arrests. R.C. missionaries first sympathetic to Marching Rule, turn on it.

Marching Rule fades away, leaving behind one big number disappointed, disillusioned, frustrated Kanakas. British rule now restored in all its power and glory, and those Lever Brothers are able to ship out that copra for making soap for pretty white ladies' faces.

*

Marching Rule has had plenty of study, it being widespread, well-organized and localized where the anthropologists and sociologists could get at it easily. Some interesting documents turned up later, which possibly could be apocryphal (but this is an apocryphal situation, or perhaps not). At any rate, there have been some native statements about the situation in the Solomons, some of poignant and pleasing literacy, the British having established a good school system. One document stating natives' grievances says a basic one is the "great distinction between them and us." Under the British the native has never enjoyed the friendship, love or sympathy of the white. And is never likely to. "We are never allowed in their houses—never to eat or drink out of their cups or plates etc., never to sit on their chairs—not even those of us who were advanced and educated and were above the standard of the majority." And: "We have been used as beasts of burden or engines for work," life on the plantation being "hard going and for the benefit of the exploiter." Also: "If it happened a [court] case was raised between Native and White it mostly fell on the native side to be the guilty party and punished with imprisonment."

Yellow shadows on the South Seas

Japs come as liberators, to free natives from the domination of wait-sikins and bring them into Greater East Asia Co-Prosperity Sphere. As natives. Kanakas welcome Jap liberators, give them flowers, food. Natives see Jap wealth, want to get paid. Japs want guides, men to work, unload ships, build airstrips. Rebel leaders arise.

On Karkar Japs promise a brilliant future for native under Imperial rule. Japs point out that Japanese work, unlike whites. Japs give tinned food, promise automobiles, horses, boats, houses and even planes if native will co-operate. Japs give loot from European homes.

Native goes into jungle to think it over.

At Rani Japs have a ship captured from the Dutch. Mansern Cargo crowd attacks, gets mowed down by machine guns. Japs capture the leader, Stephanus Simiopiaref, and behead him.

Good lesson for native. Native opposition arises in islands, ambush Jap patrols, take heads, have good kai-kai Japs. Japs forced to torture and behead to keep order. At the football grounds at Serai they call a large crowd together, then behead the prophet Mimrod. Stephanus Dawan, another prophet, talking of Americans, gets beheaded too. At Mokmer Cargo people under Jan Simiopiaref set up headquarters next to the Jap airstrip. Nervous Japs machine-gun five hundred.

Cargo groups everywhere are shot up, or down. Leaders executed. Blood-red swords, dripping with Cargo blood. Cults are a nuisance with their promises of a messiah, who likely as not is white. In the Hollandia area a man named Simson proclaims that a Papuan messiah at the moment in the Netherlands will appear and expel the strangers. Simson is taken to the Sentain airstrip and executed. At Buka, in the Solomons, the people, initially co-operative, desert the Jap labor force, begin stealing and sabotage, proclaim the coming of Cargo and a messiah. Leaders are arrested and tortured. Three executed, the others imprisoned.

Thus prosperity in Greater East Asia.

No Cargo!

Yes but are the natives friendly?, or, Mr. Clappcott founds the Naked Cult

"Mr. Clappcott sir we no like way you take woman bilong native, sir," say respectful natives southern Santo 1923. Mr. Clappcott has been described as "an inoffensive man," but somehow he bugs native neighbors over the question of immoral relations with Kanaka ladies. Some men they cut down his coconut trees a few here and there. Innocent or guilty of adulterous behaviour and other lapses, Mr. Clappcott, unknown to himself, is the subject of intense discussion. One Runovoro, Presbyterian-educated, remembers old story how when a noted native murderer was himself killed, all his victims came to life. Runovoro organizes movement to kill all the whites. Mr. Clappcott will be the first to go, followed by all other local Europeans. Native dead will rise and ancestors will return from white-caused banishment in far-off land. Movement has great promise, for Cargo will come after a Flood. Runovoro charges fee for admission to movement, up to £1. Whole of Santo is covered by organizers collecting shillings and pounds in expectation of great white ship with all that Cargo. But only for paid-up members. Large warehouse is built for expected Cargo.

Much tok-tok Runovoro raises the dead—plenty people—and one cow!

July 24, 1923. Runovoro holds great sing-sing, at which the dead (in their white skins) are to arise. Writes the Reverend Raff: "In the middle of the 'sing-sing,' Runovoro's wife died and when all attempts to raise her to life failed, he declared that Clappcott was the cause and must be killed before she would come to life. Five men were sent to shoot this planter, who was an inoffensive man, deaf and in a very lonely place. He was shot, his body mutilated, and parts of it eaten."

Inevitable reaction: *H.M.S. Sydney* shells the bush. Eighteen men are arrested, one dying before trial, net result, five acquitted, remainder convicted, three of them to death. Runovoro, already once returned from the dead, doesn't fear execution.

Movement goes underground, surfaces again in 1937 under a Santoese named Tsek. Rumors say Cargo is to be landed on spot where Clappcott died. War comes, along with Yanks and *their* Cargo. Powerful repercussions among Santoese. Americans soon pass on to Solomons, leaving natives with dreams. Yanks will come again, the standard hope. Tsek forbids families to "cohabit" at night (a missionary euphemism, that); cooking is allowed only in morning, bride price is abolished, clan laws mitigated, new order coming. Americans expected with everything people need and so Tsek orders the pigs killed, gardens dug up. Private wealth ended, no more fights among people. Purity of heart, freedom of self-expression: sex act proclaimed no longer shameful and is to be performed in public in the village clearings. Everybody looking forward to plenty good entertainment. Lovers told OK to fuck other fellas' wives, husbands advised not to be jealous. Some people beginning to get itchy over turn of events, including Presbyterian reverends. It's the Naked Cult!

Tsek has a road built from the site of Clappcott's demise to the shore and a dock is constructed for the Cargo from the great white ship that even now is on its way. Those buggers never worked this hard for us!

Natives give up church, collections off. Reverends in a panic. "Missionary warnings," resound in Condominium offices. Get the gov't off its ass.

Gov't burns down dock.

Movement changes character. Wireless sets are built of bamboo and vines to keep in touch with Americans and other spirits. People enter a new phase, with fits of shaking and prophesying. Naked Cult begins to slow down, fades away.

Baimbai Chief Jimmy Stevens Moses comes with better idea.

Cargo postscript

New Hanover, 1964. 1,000 natives vote unanimously for Mr. Lyndon B. Johnson as representative on Local Government Council. Upon being told that Mr. Johnson is not standing for election in New Hanover, the islanders raise $1,600 with which to buy him, forwarding money to Most Rev. Fred Stemper, Blackhammer, Mich. Most Rev. promptly returns money.

Natives petition Washington for annexation, presenting request to travelling United Nations mission. U.S., with more than enough (native) problems, ignores New Hanover islanders.

Meanwhile peppy young missionary, Father Bernard Miller, late of Toledo, Ohio, brimming with new ideas, has come to help get New Hanoverians on feet. Father Bernie attacks Johnson cult, and explains to New Hanoverians that they "could do things themselves without waiting for Americans," who, as likely as not (in the opinions of some people), would drop a bomb as easily as a bulldozer, considering general U.S. attitude towards natives.

Chief Walla Salo GukGuk, Johnson cult leader, as the result

of much tok-tok with dynamic young missionary, finds new direction for his people. Johnson cult now becomes United Farmers Association, "A rare example of the acceptance of modern economics by cultists as the islands prepare for nationhood," it is reported.

Natives plant 100,000 new coconut trees, buy bulldozer, motor launch, tractor and trailer, and start sawmill. Cement-block community house is built. Natives now getting wooden floors and wooden furniture. Must learn new way of sitting, uncomfortable like white man instead of easy relaxed way on ground. Surplus funds are allotted for stock in four hundred million dollar Anglo-Australian copper plant in neighboring Bougainville.

Father Bernie speaks final word: "Most importantly, everybody is doing something productive instead of waiting for Cargo."

Last word U.S. side, as committee is formed to raise money, bring Chief GukGuk America run things right. Baimbai New H. annex America.

SOME STORY LONG
NEW HEBRIDES

While the missionaries were trying to save black souls on Tanna, traders were coming ashore. In the 1870s the situation was infamous, with former sandalwooders and blackbirders ("notoriously evil," says Harrisson) settling and establishing plantations. Violence ran wild, not only against the Tannese but against other whites; there was much shooting and killing. The handful of whites kept the island in an uproar. In 1875 the settlers—largely British—petitioned France for annexation. On the island of Efate (or Vaté) the situation was hardly different: forced seizure of land, or plain swindling of the natives, whites robbing and murdering each other as well. Cases involving one white against another or a native against a white had to be heard in Australia and were invariably dismissed by the judge. In 1867 a British warship shelled Efate in reprisal for the murders of several ships' crews. A few years later, the Efate whites asked France for annexation. Other islands were also being settled, a planter or two here and there. Meanwhile, the Reverend Paton, his fear of France as all-consuming as his love for Jesus, agitated for annexation of all the New Hebridean islands by England. But before you get the idea that European intervention in the New Hebrides was merely to protect various reckless missionaries and traders, be assured the true reason was something else. Money.

The Reverend Paton played a key role in the coming formalities. He was the gray, black and white eminence behind them. To the credit of the British Government, it wanted no part of the islands, and consistently discouraged Paton's petitions as his anxiety increased daily with the arrival of more and more French settlers, supported by small detachments of French troops, under the auspices of the Compagnie Calédonienne des Nouvelles Hébrides (usually called the C.C.N.H.). Paton put the full weight of the Presbyterian Church—as far as he could control it—behind annexation, promising church support of the government. To counter the C.C.N.H. a group of prominent British businessmen in Australia ("like a miniature Who's Who of the elite of the colony," says a scholar), many of them being professed and active members of Paton's church, formed the Australasian New Hebrides Company (A.N.H.C.). Among the shareholders were James Burns and Robert Philp, who had important shipping and other interests in the South Pacific (Burns Philp is probably today the most powerful commercial interest in the area). Working with the Presbyterian Church, Burns, Philp and Company secured an annual subsidy to develop their outward shipping runs and their inter-island services, including a floating store which called at various stations with necessities for planters, traders and missionaries and bought copra and other produce. By 1890, so a Presbyterian delegation reported, A.N.H.C. was outstripping its French rival, which was going so heavily into debt that the French Government had to intervene, reconstructing C.C.N.H. as the Société Française des Nouvelles Hébrides (or S.F.N.H.), the name it still bears.

Meanwhile France and England were pursuing contradictory philosophical courses with the natives, France openly selling alcohol and firearms, which the British tried to stop, asking for an internationally agreed-upon ban. The British, under the influence of the Presbyterians, would not—in theory—sell liquor even to Europeans. But the traders went about business as usual. The A.N.H.C. bought up huge tracts of land, for example, buying over 10,000 of the choicest acres on the south coast of Santo. This land was leased to various settlers at token rentals (like a few pounds per year for some 2,400 acres). Unfortunately, many of the British settlers and traders sent in by the A.N.H.C. and some of their own agents were not capable of the kind of work in a bad climate, surrounded by hostile natives, that more adventurous, independent traders and planters could do. A.N.H.C. soon found its books in a muddle, its accounts uncollectable, its settlers losing heart, so Burns, Philp and Company took over.

Britain and France, finding themselves together locked into a colony which only the latter wanted—though Britain was not willing to relinquish the islands to its rival—came to the decision that joint rule was the only solution. Mutual agreements were reached in 1902, 1906, 1914 and 1922, which saw the establishment of the Condominium. Or Pandemonium, in the local joke, which gets run ragged, because this Anglo-French joint administration, though having the advantage of inefficiency (a blessing for the whites, because they can get away with so much before the government can catch up) has so mucked up the islands that little seems to go right, leaving them wide open for exploitation by shrewd Europeans and keeping the native on such an inferior level that he is virtually an alien in his own land. Today not only is there Condominium rule but also separate British and French departments in such areas as education, police and prisons, and health, along with some of minor importance. The lucky native gets educated, or arrested, by the British rather than the French, the latter being considered by the black man nothing more than the devil. In fact, on Tanna the native word for Frenchman is nakua, the same word as for devil.

The British are said to be anxious to leave the New Hebrides, having now only minor commercial interests there, but—that means abandoning them to the French, who would enjoy being sole proprietors, for there are suspected natural resources not yet explored in the Group, and the islands also offer a fine labor force still to be utilized with the skill the French have shown in New Caledonia and Africa. Also, the New Hebrides would be a fine addition to the impressive string of France's Pacific colonies, which include not only New Caledonia and the Loyalties but Tahiti and the Marquesas. The French have already reduced nearby New Caledonia, once a penal colony, to the level of a tropical Appalachia by strip-mining vast areas of what was formerly one of the most beautiful islands in all the Pacific, destroying jungles and mountains and polluting the surrounding sea so fiercely with industrial wastes that virtually all marine life is dead. The chief ore is nickel (New Caledonia ranks third after Canada and Russia in its production), but there is also copper, gold, silver, lead, and in lesser quantities chrome, cobalt and iron. The guess is that the New Hebrides may contain some of the same ores. The people of New Caledonia complain that life in their own land is like being in a prison (the French have retained the know-how from the past), but the pay is better than in the New Hebrides, so when there is work the Tannese and other fellow islanders go there for a period of a few years in order to earn some cash. However, they find living conditions almost more than they can stand. So on the basis of what they have seen next door and in their own islands, they ask if the Frenchies, as sole rulers, would give a damn about them.

A rhetorical question, of course.

*

Even under the formal government of the Condominium and with various settlers, traders and planters at work, the New Hebrides slid through the first half of this century with the minimum of development. Owing to the lack of a telegraph and the infrequent shipping, news of the declaration of the War of 1914 took nearly three months to reach the islands, and the war itself left them in comparative tranquility. In the 1920s an island like Tanna might be visited every five months by an inter-island ship. But the Second World War was another matter and the New Hebrides were deeply involved, being the first French overseas possession to declare for the Free French under General Charles de Gaulle. They were directly in the line of the Japanese advance; the enemy, by the end of 1942, was firmly entrenched in New Guinea and the Solomons, and it was at this time that the islands found themselves a potential battlefield: massive forces of Americans landed on two of the northern islands, Efate and Espiritu Santo, to prepare bases for the Allied push to the West. It is this Yank "invasion" that brought changes to certain of the people, and eventually resulted in two areas of Efate and Espiritu Santo, the towns of Port Vila and Santo, being incorporated into the modern world, though progress by Stateside standards has been slow. It was Tanna, more than any other area that experienced the most dramatic effects of the American arrival, this being more psychological, a searing of the Tannese soul and psyche, than physical.

Still today, Santo and Vila are the only towns to have electricity. There is no daily or weekly press, though there are some small government publications, one or two mimeographed sheets expressing some (hopeful) native points of view, and a thin monthly magazine of no great interest. There is a radio station, Radio Vila, more of a service than entertainment. ("Mr. Cooper asks Chief Bonga Bonga to meet him at the mouth of the river with the school reports," might be the kind of item one would hear on the midday news, a valuable service considering the circumstances.) There are a few movie houses, and some bars and restaurants; hotels are in short supply, and people who drop in at Vila by air, on the way to Fiji or Nouméa, are surprised continually to find that there are no rooms available.

I hope I have conveyed the idea that there is nothing of interest to the westerner in these islands, if he is looking for an extension of his own life. Before I left for the New Hebrides, knowing from experiences in other primitive lands what to expect, I talked about the lack of facilities to friends and relatives, but I was unable, failed, to convey the truth that life even in Vila is nothing like that in Merrick, Long Island.

I won't give up. More is to come, on the utter simplicity, the mind-numbing lack of sensory stimulation, in these upper islands. A minor Condominium official with a lifetime experience in southeast Asia, with whom I had several pleasant disjointed conversations, said that his first two years were "a complete dislocation." In his third year now, he adds, "I am still dislocated. I can't understand it. But still dislocated. You'll have to excuse me."

New Hebrides Biennial Report tok-tok[1]

The indigenous population of the New Hebrides is predominantly Melanesian in ethnic character, but there is some admixture of Polynesian strains and a considerable range of physical types. Indeed, in the interior of Malekula and Espiritu Santo, a few people of small stature, reminiscent of negrito, are found.

Many languages and dialects are spoken; most belong to the Melanesian family and are related to those of Fiji and New Caledonia. They have a common grammatical structure and phonetic system, but there is much variation and diversity of vocabulary. As a result, people inhabiting the same area may not be able to understand one another. In general, the languages of the Torres Islands, the Banks Islands and the northeastern section of the Group most closely resemble one another; those of the central New Hebrides are divergent; and those of Aneityum, Tanna and Erromanga in the south form another distinct section. A few languages, including those of Aniwa and Futuna in the south, and of Fila and Mele in southwest Efate, are basically Polynesian in character and closely related to one another. These languages have their nearest affinities in those of Samoa, Tonga and other islands in western Polynesia and not in other New Hebridean languages. A pidgin English (in French called Bichelamar) is the lingua franca of the New Hebrides, as of the Solomons and New Guinea (where it is now sometimes called by linguists "Neo-Melanesian"). The pidgin of this part of the Pacific has a Melanesian structure and a limited vocabulary, drawn from English (supplemented in the New Hebrides by a few French words) and stretched by circumlocution.

Native communities in the New Hebrides are usually small. The basic social unit is the elementary family of a man, his wife and their children, but forms part of a larger unit, the lineage membership which is based on unilineal descent, either through the father's or the mother's line. In some parts of the group one lineage, together with those who have married into it, occupies a whole village; in others, several lineages may live in the same village. A tribal group may consist of a number of lineages, bound together by loose ties of common languages, culture and territorial proximity. The intersection of patrilineal and matrilineal descent groups may also provide a system of marriage sections of varying complexity. There is generally an absence of strong political authority extending beyond the village. Prestige and influence rather than authority are shared among a number of "big men" in the community. Villages vary greatly in size from Mele, near Vila on Efate, with a population of almost 800, to one family occupying a single hut.

Disintegration of the pre-European society has been taking place for a hundred years and in many cases has been thorough. Much regrouping of the population in larger villages along the coast took place under Mission influence, and their inhabitants form a sharp contrast with the "bushmen" of the interior of Malekula and Espiritu Santo. The latter have had only infrequent contact with Europeans and have to a large extent maintained their traditional way of life.

On 28th May 1967 the first complete simultaneous census of the population of the New Hebrides was held. The Report on the census was completed by March 1968 and indicated a total population of 77,982, including an estimated 1,400 who refused to complete returns. Prior to the census no reliable estimate of the total population of the Group had been available. The most striking feature of the 1967 census was that the total population proved to be considerably higher than had been believed. The total enumerated in the census was 76,582 persons, of which New Hebrideans constituted more than 92%, the remainder being composed of Europeans, Polynesians and Micronesians, Part-Europeans, Other Melanesians, Vietnamese, Chinese, and Others [not defined]. The census suggests that the New Hebridean population is increasing at about 2.5 per cent per year, which means that it will double in size in less than 30 years if this estimated growth rate continues. Despite a continuing surplus of males at most ages and an overall 53:47 male–female proportion, the New Hebridean birth rate today is in the region of 44 per 1,000 population.

New Hebrides Biennial Report he tok-tok
one more time

The indigenous population of the New Hebrides is mainly engaged in peasant agriculture, producing subsistence and cash crops. The latter provide the money required to buy clothing, to supplement the local diet with imported foods, and to meet social and family obligations.

Money is also earned by employment in occupations such as stevedoring, plantation work, public or mission services, inter-island shipping, building, open cast mining, domestic services, retail distribution trade, and general laboring. [Note: these are all "native" jobs and not ones the whites do; no native ever gets a "white" job.] Wage rates are considerably higher than in any neighboring territories except New Caledonia.

[An irrelevant, ridiculous statement. Wages run as follows for certain jobs: unskilled plantation workers, $20-$30 Australian per month plus overtime (huh!) and rations, for a 45–50-hour week. Domestic servants, forty-hour week, no meals, $30-$50 per month. General laborers, no rations, $2-$3 per day, 45-hour week. Pay in New Caledonia is said to run as high as $7 per day. For back-breaking work in the mines and on the docks.]

There is still little need to take up paid employment or to remain in it for any length of time except for the few areas of the Group which are overpopulated and where there is a shortage of agricultural land [that is, the native can't use his own land because the Frenchies and the Aussies got it]. Difficulties in obtaining a ready supply of labor have led to the introduction of Wallis Islanders, Tahitians and Gilbertese to work on plantations [who get better pay than the locals]. During the period 1969–70 a significant development has been the temporary emigration to New Caledonia of relatively large numbers of New Hebrideans attracted by the high wages paid for semi-skilled and general laboring work in this nearby French territory. It was thought that the number of New Hebridean workers in New Caledonia was in excess of 2,500, although precise figures were not available.

So far no industrial trade unions have been established.

To fill out the economic scene

Big development going on in these islands. The South Pacific Fishing Company (British owned) employs some thirty vessels on contract from Taiwan, Japan and Korea, which land their catch at Palekula, near Santo, where it is frozen and shipped to America (80 per cent) and Japan (20 per cent). In 1970 over nine thousand tons were exported. Since the crews are various types of Chows, the Orientals, not the British, get the blame for this particular robbery of the islands' resources. Cattle industry is thriving and substantial areas of land have been cleared and fenced for stock. Most herds are dairy types, based on Australian Illawarra Shorthorn, Herefords, Beef Shorthorns, Murray Grays, Brahmans, Limousins, and Santo Gertrudis; also a small number of Charolais. Dr. J. P. Marty (*français*) estimated the cattle population at almost 70,000 in 1968, and Dr. H. G. Osborne (Aussie) projected it to nearly 100,000 by 1975. Quantities of frozen, chilled and tinned meat are being sent from Vila and Santo to markets in New Caledonia. The N.H.B.R. says: "At present Melanesians contribute relatively little to the beef industry, and most of the cattle killed on Efate and Santo come from European-owned plantations, but they are taking an increasing interest in cattle-raising." Interest, yes, but how are they going to buy cattle? Answer, please.

Timber on Erromanga, this being number three industry in the islands. Expansion of international airports at Vila and Santo. New deep-water wharf at Vila, to "accommodate large cruise liners." Wharf to be built at Santo. Lands everywhere being surveyed by government. Considerable building activity on Efate and Espiritu Santo. Increasing numbers of officially sponsored visitors, such as U.K. and French officers, international experts, and "persons of note anxious to see for themselves an island group receiving much new publicity." Their Royal Highnesses the Duke and Duchess of Kent arrive. "The visit, the first ever by members of the Royal Family, lasted three days, and included a children's rally, the laying of the foundation stone of the new British Base Hospital in Vila by the Duke, and a day at Santo." Pleasant confusion all around as work stops for this grave but smiling fambly.

"Both the import and the export business are dominated by branches of four large firms, two British (Burns Philp and South

Pacific Fishing Company) and two French (Comptoirs Français des Nouvelles Hébrides and Maison Barrau)." There are some smaller firms, including Chinese, and some stores run by Vietnamese.

Prices are high.

Mining jointly controlled by British and French gov'ts, but only mining lease now in effect is held by Nouméa-based consortium (sounds nasty, that) now styled Le Manganese de Vaté (L.M.V.), in which Southland Mining Limited of Australia has a 50 per cent interest. Export figures (1970) are 28,545 tons, all of which go to Japan, gaining in peace what she lost in war.

The number one crop of all the islands & elsewhere

Copra is what they sell, when they can sell. It accounts for roughly 50 per cent of the New Hebridean exports, with fish second. The price of copra drops periodically, and planters go broke; natives, being already broke, have little to lose, except a chance to fall out of a tree or some wearying hours in the copra sheds. Copra is made from the nut of the coconut palm, which is dried; from the dried nut an oil is taken by an elaborate process discovered by a canny Djaman sometime in the nineteenth century, and this oil is turned into soap of the kind that makes complexions lovely and invites admiration from gentlemen and envy from other ladies. Coconut trees grow best at low levels, and so plantations are concentrated on the coastal plains. The temperature, rainfall and soil are most favorable for coconut palms in the New Hebrides. Coconut growing "gives a high return for work, since it is simple and unexacting if high yields are not sought," says N.H.B.R. European-owned plantations cover about 50,000 acres but are now being let go because of the "high cost of labour [!] and the difficulty of obtaining and keeping it, reluctance to invest in a very long-term crop when the political future is uncertain, the low and fluctuating world price of copra, and the rival attraction of beef cattle rearing."

"New Hebrides copra is smoke-dried and generally of inferior quality." France is the major market (27,754 tons in 1970), Japan a poor second (3,443 tons same year), and no one else interested. There are some attempts at raising the quality, but meanwhile the trees are under attack by certain insects (Axiagastus Campbelli and Aspidiotus Destructor), rats, and weeds, and in general the yields are low (palms produce too small nuts, natives won't work, and then there's that fluctuating market). When I was in the islands, the market seemed to have hit a standstill, variously ascribed to the soap manufacturers' shifting to other (synthetic) oils, a dock strike on America's West Coast, which led the Filipinos, a major exporter to the States of highquality copra, to send it to France and Japan, thus taking the New Hebridean markets, or a general worldwide depression. Anyway, a fat herd of cattle pleases a planter more than a bunch of aged palms. Needs fewer natives to do the dirty work, too.

However . . .

"Copra is still the principal export from the Group but . . ." You sonofabitch, that copra he drop from $132 Australian per ton to $30 and down down down. Copra even higher after World War II and down he come and up and down, a trick the white man play to keep native poor. Now native no longer make living outa copra. White man he go into cattle, fish, timber, airlines, tourist business, minerals. Native he eat (yams, taro, pottaters) but white man he make money, buy all that good stuff tinned from Australia.

You think native start airline? You betcha, but white man take over, run it, make money. "Thirteen hundred natives put money into Air Melanesia," reports R. U. Paul, one of the founders and directors of the line. "We give Mr. Paul money for Air Melanesia," says native, "but when we ask for it back, he give two or three people money. Rest he says, 'Kiss my ass.'" Native pissed off at Bobpaul keeping money. Bobpaul rich man, say native. Bobpaul got long story how 1951 he come ashore on Tanna to pick up copra for sell in Port Vila (price copra P.V.

$90 ton Australian to sell, $30 to buy in Tanna) and missionary, that Dr. Nicholson, meet him with rifle. Missionary no want white fella come ashore upset natives fuck up missionary work already rather shaky. Bobpaul tell how he get pistol from ship, show down missionary like in some bush opera from Outback. Turns around, says, "Shoot me in the back you bastard I dare you." Reverend no shoot Bobpaul. From that day on Bobpaul he big power in New Hebrides. Got finger, hand, foot in everything. "I was the first man to hire a native driver," says big, affable, blond Bobpaul. "The whites hated me for that. Tried to drive me off the island. I was also the first trader to have native help in a store. The whites couldn't stand me. Some of them wouldn't say hello." "That sonafabitch Bobpaul he most hated man in islands," says Tom, Henry, John, Jimmy, Sam, Joe, Ben, etc. long every goddam islands Banks to Aneityum & everyone in between. "That Bobpaul he take native lands all along coast. He got best lands. Four copra plantations. Bobpaul cattle graze on our lands. We like to shoot his cattle on our lands, but that fella put us in jail. No shoot."

Tom, Henry, John, Jimmy, Sam, Joe, Ben, etc. just black fella. No leverage.

Bobpaul is a big handsome chap, sort of like Errol Flynn in the days when Errol was all there, not boozing too much. Bob's an all-around chap, flies, hunts, fishes, fixes the refrigerator in the store, loves the natives, speaks pidgin, gets his photo in *Pacific Island Monthly,* travels all over the world. Some chap, Bob is!

Our excellent state of health

We got diseases here to enchant and enthrall the tourist. We got
   hookworm, roundworm, malaria ("the most important
   disease in the New Hebrides"), leprosy, tuberculosis ("the
   cause of much morbidity"), filariasis, intestinal parasites,
   diarrhoeal diseases, tetanus and scabies. ("Other causes of
   morbidity and mortality are complications of pregnancy and

childbirth, accidents, fish poisoning and untreated surgical emergencies.")

That not all, not by a long shot. We too got whooping cough, measles, chicken pox. You want yaws? We got yaws, back after WHO done its best. Yep, yaws come back.

Venereal infections? Yep, that we got.

Tourist, you better get your shots afore you come see untouched native in untouched primitive charming surroundings.

Otherwise we give you dose of somethings!

Our capital city

Port Vila is a dusty little town, miserable in its heat and rain. Facing the West, it overlooks a magnificent bay. In the afternoon the sun drops quickly like a great red orange that suddenly goes plop into the ocean amid swirls of pink and purple clouds. Plop, and all is dark.

The day begins early, for the heat is frightful. The two in-town hotels, the Rossi and the Vaté, offer breakfast at six and lunch at eleven when the offices close. At high noon people huddle around their air conditioners like Alaskans around a stove in mid-winter. A useless effort, because there is barely enough power and there are more and more demands on it each day, the humidity is frightful, and the slightest movement brings torrents of sweat. The banks reopen at 1:30 and other offices later, up to 4:00, some of them being likely to remain open until 6:00 or so. Vila has an unenviable history, which we will disregard, echoes of it have preceded us and will return on later pages. The Chamber of Commerce through its Tourist Information Bureau, reported 960 whites in and around Vila (with the figure increasing daily), 5,640 New Hebrideans, and 360 Asians (primarily Chinese and Indo-Chinese, a few Indians) and 1,040 other Pacific races and mixed.

The Rue Higginson runs the length of Vila. On it, right in the center of the town, are the Rossi, constructed 1958, thirty-two rooms (seventeen of which are *"climatisées"*), and the Vaté, constructed 1964 with twenty-four rooms (*toutes climatisées*). The Rossi, older (it seems like a century but it isn't), is said to have more charm—atmosphere anyway. In its bar one can find the usual group of French planters and officials and their eighteen-year-old Indo-Chinese mistresses—sloe-eyed, round-cheeked and reeking with the promise of orgiastic sex. O those devilish Frogs! But the French love a good meal first, and through their transparent shirts (open to the navel) one sees rapidly growing bulges of flesh, even on the young men. They wear shorts also, and ankle-length socks and sandals, and their hair is thinning. Dashing? You betcha.

The ambience is French (*Bar des Sportifs, Alimentation Générale, Centre Culturel, Le Snack Bar, La Boutique,* and so on), though the town is supposedly half French, half English, the English being not only English but more likely members of inferior races like Australians, New Zealanders and Canadians. But after the French the true ambience is southeast Asian and Chinese, the yellow peril, clustered along the Rue Higginson and in the center of town (we find Kwong Yuen and Fung Kuei and their fellows running shops, while Mr. Lam Lo boasts of his fine new *immeuble commercial* being constructed near the Condominium offices; Vietnamese and Chinese restaurants are the chic dining places). All over town there is new building, high rises for the banks and tax refuges and for Herz and Avis and other patrons of civilization. The most imposing structure of all, with its façade of perforated cement block *à la* Edward Stone's American embassy in New Delhi, is the Bank d'Indochine, though the interior is a sardine can of French, Indo-Chinese, Fijian and other foreigners, plus the usual lone, trained New Hebridean sambo, at desks that would shame a nineteenth-century American sweat shop. Is there *climatisée?* The sweat rolls in streams.

Flies stick to everything, flies like raisins with gluey feet. Toyotas and Citroëns are cars of choice.

There is a third hotel, Le Lagon at Erakor (once a nice "native" village) done in Polynesian style. Polynesian, in the heart of Melanesia! The mysterious white mind! It is owned by Belgians who have already constructed 48 *climatisée chambres* with *piscine, boutique,* bar and *salle de conférence,* and plan on a total of 130 C.C.'s. Here the tourist can enjoy the ambience of the native village with none of the discomforts. The exterior is of pandanus and palm leaves and palm thatch. The natives are said to have come from miles around with the materials, which were used to make a womb of the Hilton interiors, and were paid in New Hebridean francs and Australian dollars, which in turn were exchanged at Burns Philp for corrugated tin for their own homes. Progress it is, going sideways. All over the world natives are trying to move out of their bamboo houses and get rid of their charcoal stoves in favor of kerosene, electricity and gas, and meanwhile, back on the patio, friend husband is demanding, Where the hell is the charcoal lighter? How the hell can he cook without the lighter?

Chinese on bicycles, their women in black trousers, teeth red with betel. Inscrutable.

The movies have the latest. *Typhoon sur Hambourg, Tarzan chez les Coupeurs de Tetes, Les Léopards de Churchill* (WIN-STON CHURCHILL—*un homme! Un mythe! Symbole d'une poignée de courage, voués à la mort*), *Les Derniérs Aventuriers.*

The Aussies are a great sight, if amusement is what you are looking for. The accent drives you up the wall and around the bend, but they're good-natured, which is more than you can say for the Frenchies and the Chinese. The Aussies wear knee-length white socks, shorts, carry folders of papers or briefcases. Some of them drink beer all day, perspire freely and, and. One carries a canoe paddle from the Solomons. We may have a flood.

The New Hebrides are progressing. There is a great future coming. Land prices are skyrocketing. The land your grandfather sold for a bag of rice, a rifle, a stick of tobacco is now offered at $250,000 Australian. No kidding. Right next to the Hotel Vaté on Rue Higginson is a plot that, after pacing off, I estimate to be forty by one hundred (feet, not yards) at the asking price of a quarter of a million dollars. "They'll take less," says a Condominium official. But not much.

Native, you one goddam fool. Why don't you offer a bag of rice for it? Two bags, because it's appreciated in value.

Other bargains abound. The South Pacific Real Estate Agency offers a nice parcel on Rue Higginson by the waterfront: 3,500 square meters with water and electricity for $400,000. Between the Condominium and the old Post Office is a block of three thousand square meters at $200 per meter, two thirds down. Residential sites follow the same kind of pricing, and a nice little ranch of two hundred acres, twenty miles from town, with "native housing quarters" (no charge for dirt floors) and forty head of cattle, just went for $50,000.

The reason for these prices, for land that a few years ago was virtually without a potential and which had been bought (or promoted) from a native for a few cents' worth of some western goods, is that the New Hebrides (a) are believed to have great tourist potential, and (b) are now a fantastically successful tax haven. There are no income taxes in the island, and the Condominium expects the imposition of none. Stateside, European, Asian and Common Market companies set up dummy offices in Vila, which are used to siphon off or bury funds traveling from one branch or subsidiary or partner company to another. Goods flowing from one industrial nation to another are double-invoiced. For example, a raw material from Australia gets billed at a loss to a dummy corporation in Vila which then "sells" it to an affiliate in the States at an excessive cost, thus reducing taxes at both ends. Or money may be "lent" by the dummy corporation in Vila at excessive interest to a foreign client, which may likely be the true lender. The variations on these themes, and the multitude of other possibilities, depend only on the skill of the businessmen and their lawyers.

The number of foreign corporations with offices in the New Hebrides stood at some five hundred by the end of 1972 and was growing steadily. Consequently, high rises were going up all over the tiny town of Vila and its outskirts, to provide office space and apartments for the foreign staff members; private housing has been in short supply, and residential land commands proportionate prices.

And the banks. Native, do you need a friend at a bank? Here are seven for you, where you can put your $2.50 per day in complete confidence. When you have a job. You have a friend in all of them! Don't be shy. That trick of looking right through you to the opposite wall is just the white man's way of showing his great liking for you. But try them: Banque de L'Indochine, the A.N.Z. Bank, Commercial Banking Company of Sydney, National Bank of Australia, Ltd., Bank of New South Wales, Commercial Bank of Australia, and The Hong Kong and Shanghai Banking Corporation, Ltd.

Things seem casual, though the money machines are counting at top speed. Too goddam hot to worry about certain details. On a hill overlooking the bay (and right around the corner from the Paton Memorial Church) is the British prison. The guards carry sticks, but the prisoners each have a bush knife. Just to hack down the shrubbery around the Governor's house. In ten years in the four prisons in the islands (Vila, Santo, Lakatoro, Tanna) only one prisoner escapes. "He has not been re-captured," remarks the Biennial Report, adding, "Escapes are rare." Why escape? Prison is a home away from home. "The main external problems faced by the [Police] Force were excessive consumption of alcohol, which often leads to the commission of offences against the person, neglect of the family, etc., and the deplorable standard of driving in urban areas."

*

A French woman, Lillianne, is sitting at a table outside Le Snack Bar, writing letters. "I am going out of my mind, going crazy," she says aloud into the air in English. "Going crazy." She has been waiting for a boat to take her to the northern islands. Days lengthen, become a week, ten days, two weeks. "Always it is tomorrow. So boring here! I am going crazy. Nothing to do, no place to go, no one to talk to." The food is terrible, the cinema hopeless, no culture, no conversation, nothing but bureaucrats and businessmen. "But if you really want to go crazy, go to the Gilberts and Marshalls. Yap, you will kill yourself on Yap. But I go crazy here too."

The sun burns overhead, the bougainvilleas, in their brilliant reds and purples and oranges, begin to wilt; other flowers don't open until the cool of the evening. A sudden slight rain squall comes spattering a few drops, the dust rises in swirls and part of the sky darkens. The natives on the street stand against the wall of the S.C.N.H. warehouse looking suspicious. Black bastards!

The whites are now concerned that native morality is breaking down. Bad stories all over the town. Lots of petty thievery is claimed. Lillianne says that her borrowed car, sitting before the house of the homosexual painter at Erakor, has been stolen. She had left some valuable papers in it. A missionary says that Le Lagon was pilfered steadily, but—happy ending, all the loot was found in the homes of native maids and bellhops. "They got the idea that what is yours is theirs and what is theirs is yours. Not real stealing of course," says liberal understanding missionary. Transistors, watches, cameras, tape recorders, clothing recovered. Meanwhile tourists have flown on. Question: who now gets the loot?[2]

Please, sir, our cry come to you

Santo, that island got big future coming. One Eugene Peacock, Hawaiian real estate entrepreneur he bought ten thousand acres choice jungle land, divided up (in his head) into ten thousand one-acre plots to sell to ten thousand choice American families. Vacation homes, retirement sites. Escape to your own paradise. Go native! Buy now! Live in the sun on sunny Santo. Yours to enjoy! Can you imagine ten thousand Yanks and their famblies on one small corner of one small island? Marinas, motor launches, ranch houses, skin diving, gas stations, shopping centers, wheaties, no-phosphate detergents, charcoal grills, TV, twenty thousand automobiles, air conditioners, movies houses (incl. porn hard & soft), Sears, Two Guys, Ramada Inn, *The New York Sunday Times* (seven pounds if an ounce, delivered on Tuesday), Safeway, Grand National, Colonel Saunders, Doggie Dinner, Howard Johnson's, King Kullen, McDonald's. Complaints about the servant problem.

One fucking big Cargo cult!

Mr. Peacock he get damned rich!

But the Condominium stopped it, thank God. Ten thousand Yanks, perhaps forty thousand Yanks even with ZPG, boggle the mind. The imagination goes limp. Condominium make new post-factum laws including fifty per cent added-value tax on profits from the sale of lots by subdividers, right to refuse subdivision of more than two lots, and other headaches for Mr. P. But he got a hotel anyway, the Lokali at Hog Harbour on Santo, and other white folks see big future for you, native, like that same place bilong Mr. Peacock. Presbyterian Board of Missions (Australian branch) still feel deep feelings about native, worried about his future, writes in pamphlet: "Just around the bay is a new luxury hotel [the Lokali]—first of a possible thirty[!] hotels. With an airfield, golf courses, marinas and other tourist amenities planned this area could become a thriving center." Next sentence reads: "But for whom?" Why the native of course, because "There will be work for the New Hebrideans—taxi drivers, doorkeepers, bellboys, cooks." The reverend writer neglects maids, washwomen and prostitutes. An afterthought arises: "Could there be work for New Hebridean gardeners supplying vegetables and tropical fruit for the overseas visitors, or will these be imported too?" . . . Native, your white mission friends and their friends—those bankers, businessmen, hoteliers and gov't officials, Limies, Aussies, Frogs, Yanks—they all got BIG plans for you! Bow down and kiss their asses. No, someday you wish you back in Queensland cotton plantations. No, you wish you back in jungle with kava, custom dancing, magic stones, ten wives, long and short pigs, circumcision, head-hunting and a good feast—old-fashioned, *honest,* things.

Here come Chief Moses

The white people tell you bad stories about Jimmy Stephens which are probably true

Jimmy got seven wives

some young enough to be his daughters
    but three run away
    and then there were
                four.
Jimmy uses other people's money
for having fun
    traveling (Australia, New Caledonia, Fiji)
    women, whiskey
    (sins white man never commit).
What bugs whites though is that Jimmy leads
a movement to get back
    native lands.
Native stand up to whites
whites try to destroy native
bad stories in P.I.M.
uppity native
no morals.
Jimmy bad guy
arrest him!
stop him taking whites to court
over land they stolen
jail for Jimmy
"Jimmy's pretty much discredited"
"All talk"

Jimmy get petition to U.N. drawn up by uppity Indian lawyer
    in Fiji. ("Ramrakha likes to fish in troubled waters.")
"To the Honourable the Secretary General of the United
    Nations, New York—
"The Humble Petition of Chief James Tupou Patuntun Steven
    Moses sheweth THAT:—
"New Hebrides is one of the most backward, most neglected
    areas of the Pacific, and your Petitioner is most disappointed
    that no United Nations team has come to visit New Hebrides,
    in the same way as teams and missions have been sent to
    Papua-New Guinea or to West Irian.

"Although New Hebrides is backward in many ways, and many of its people lack formal education, and know-how in the modern sense of the word, the indigenous peoples are nonetheless entitled to their rights as human beings.

"We New Hebrideans are quite ready to rule ourselves, and if there is a transfer of power to the people we will be able to rule the country better than either the joint government or either of the two governments.

"New Hebrides are passing through a slow process of genocide, and the administering powers are directly responsible for this.

"No action is being taken except to drive the indigenous peoples out of their traditional hereditary grounds even when they are living in the 'long dark bush' and not harming anyone and minding their business, and living by substence agriculture.

"The indigenous people's only source of survival is their land, but the land laws favour those who acquired land for a mere song. Now, substantial tracts of land are being cleared, and natives being driven out.

"The protests by the indigenous peoples have been ignored. The Administration says it must honour the land laws. Natives are being imprisoned and in many cases they have been terrorized off the land.

"The Administrations have proved extremely callous and indifferent to the cries of the indigenous people and new and sophisticated methods of clearing us off our land have been devised, and the methods of using police dogs have struck a new terror in the hearts of the indigenous peoples.

"The dispossessed indigenous people have not been able to find other land, and many are bewildered and stunned that land, which is theirs, is being taken away from them.

"There is no effort to preserve the social, ethnic, and economic patterns of the indigenous peoples with the consequent breakdown of the living patterns of the indigenous peoples without any satisfactory substitutes being given.

"The non-recognition of the [native] marriage laws is an

attempt to break down the social and the moral order which prevails in the New Hebrides, and which is accepted by the majority of the peoples.

"Protests at the free sale of alcohol have been ignored by the authorities. There is no real control, and indeed, many indigenous people drink freely and pay the consequences dearly in broken homes, broken lives and broken jobs.

"We plant many crops such as yams, taro, banana, tapioca, corn, peanuts, ginger, rice, garlic, kava, curry roots, chili, sunflower etc. etc. but we do not have any market for our crops.

"No real attempt has been made to educate the indigenous people. The burden of education is borne by the Missions. There is a grave shortage of teachers and the division into French-speaking, and English-speaking indigenous people is dividing the country into two fragments.

"Your Petitioner urgently requests U.N. Mission to visit territory and examine unjust and iniquitous land laws designed to deprive illiterate indigenes of their land. Such deprivation amounts to genocide as indigenes have no other resource. We PETITION that land laws be changed immediately and no occupancy by indigenes or any land be disturbed further, that country be given independence and one man one vote constitution based on single government and single citizenship."

Etc. U.N. listen, yawn, take year to answer. "Matter under consideration." Fuck you, native. We got tourist industry to worry about, tax shelters to develop, high rises coming, minerals to explore, ranches to fence in, factories on the drawing board, Chamber of Commerce luncheons. Don't bug us. It's all in the past. Byegones.

"The law says a native has twenty years in which to present his case against the alienation of land. After that it incontrovertibly belongs to the expatriate who registered it." Mr. Ramrakha has complained to the U.N. that "The present laws which provide for notice in the gazette place the onus on the indigenous people to prove that the land was acquired through fraud etc., and in such cases, since the cases are heard after so many years, the indigenous people are unable to offer any proof even if the original alleged transferor of the land is alive." Native has no books of registry, no deeds, no title searches, no mortgages, no tax receipts, no redtape. Ask some questions: Who made the laws? Do the laws protect the natives or the thieves? Who controls the courts? Who got the lawyers? What language is law in? Who can read and who cannot? Who got the leverage?

*

[You project same situation to Australia, America North & South, Africa, even Asia, and you got one bad situation.]

Anyway, some of these natives sold the land two or three times to people. Cost us a lot of tobacco. (A quarter of a million dollars worth?)

"Jeemee eez veree bad mann," says French planter in Rossi's, feeling rounded rump of his Tonkinese mistress, like patting young heifer of his new herd. "Eee cause much troubles for us."

"We had a lot of respect for Jimmy in the beginning," reports a Pommie, "but then he filled up his house with those so-called secretaries. Completely destroyed our faith in him. For a while he looked like the first real native leader."

Jimmy Stephens his story

One English sailor named Thomas Garfield Stephens (Jimmy also spells it Stevens, or even Steven) comes ashore at Tanna in the 1890s. A restless man, Stephens gets bored with Tanna and moves on to Aoba and then Espiritu Santo. Still itchy, he goes off to Tonga, where he marries one Sela Tupou, a member of the royal family. In 1904, now the father of three children, Stephens runs into some kind of nasty financial trouble and decides to leave. He loads his family and a boatload of watermelons (their only food) into a twenty-five-foot whale boat; there are also two men who want to leave Tonga too. The seas off Fiji damn near swamp the boat, but the escapees sail on, living off the thirst-quenching watermelons. They safely reach Erromanga. Soon the Stephens family moves to Ambryn, then Malekula and finally Santo. Old man Stephens, a crusty, sexy old goat, has ten children before he dies in 1951. Meanwhile one of his first-born, Tupou-Luther, has married a girl from the Banks islands, one of their children being a boy named James, now approaching fifty.

Jimmy works for the Americans at Santo during World War II. When the Yanks go away, young Jimmy, as later gossip says, does "very well for himself." He digs up caches of equipment left behind by the onward-moving Americans. Good sales from the Yank stuff. Then Jimmy works a while driving a bulldozer, injuring his leg in an accident with one of the machines, is caretaker of an R.C. church and then skipper of a B.P. inter-island steamer. But the leg injury begins to bother him and he finally quits work, though he has a large family to support.

He is a big, patriarchal man, with an air of authority. Old friends say he has not changed over the years, with his heavy-set mien, graying beard, stomach hanging over his belt, imposing air of prophet and leader. A man to respect, if he wasn't a native.

He drifts, anxious, talkative, restless. Then circumstances bring a focus for his energies. In 1962 some fifty bush people move down from the jungle toward the open plain near the town of Santo. They are led by a chief named Buluk. Jimmy encourages Buluk and the bush people to squat at a place known as Vanafo, on some land owned by S.F.N.H., some fifteen miles from Santo town. The squatters feed the Stephens family with produce from their gardens and "wild" cattle shot on the S.F.N.H. lands. Much talk between Jimmy and Buluk about the injustice of the alienation of land. Early in 1966 Jimmy and Buluk hold a meeting in a bar in Santo to discuss the problem with other New Hebrideans. Over eight hundred people, including twenty chiefs, attend, hear Stephens and Buluk announce the "Act of Dark Bush Land," claiming all land beyond

Man Tanna: suspicious, reserved, independent.

A Tannese child dressed for a custom ceremony at Leminuh, the sacred festival grounds.

New Hebridean effigies, carved from gigantic ferns.

A custom dance at Leminuh revives practices banned by missionaries for over a century.

In the cool of the late afternoon, Tannese men gather to prepare kava.

(Above) The rocky beach at Green Point, where John and Nakua fought their heroic, bloody war.

(Left) The liver of the giant, Sem Sem, is still preserved at Leminuh, Tanna. It is now hard as stone.

(Above) Lauchman Tani, one of the first to be imprisoned for support-
ing John, is now a village elder.

(Left) Joe Nalpin, whose letter to Sydney village was intercepted by
the British District agent, thereby setting off the John Frum "affair."

John Kalate, mystic and poet, leader of the inner circle of John Frum followers.

Sam Tacuma, former church elder, who serves as an interpreter of the movement.

(Above) Sulphur Bay, one of the central villages in the recent resurgence of John Frum.

(Left) Mellis, John Frum leader at Sulphur Bay. Mellis sees John regularly, spends long periods with him in the bush.

(Above) Tom Hiwa, John Frum leader at Bethel village.

(Right) Tom Navy (otherwise known as Thomas D. Beatty), the Sea-Bee who became a symbol of American generosity to the Tannese forty years ago.

A John Frum cross stands silhouetted against the sun near Yasur, the sacred volcano, "bank" of Tannese hopes.

the known European plantations for the indigenous people and demanding its return. Jimmy and Buluk state that they do not challenge plantations already under cultivation but they regard lands the whites are turning over to cattle as Dark Bush Land.

The movement gets a name, NaGriemel, after two plants used in Custom ceremonies.[3] The chiefs want rifles, and Stephens agrees to get some. He collects the money but does not deliver. The chiefs complain to the Condominium. Jimmy is jailed. Then Buluk intercedes, persuading the bush chiefs that Jimmy's intentions have been "honorable." The chiefs petition for his release, and he is freed. Jimmy gains a new ally in one Pastor Abel Bani on Aoba, the leader of the Church of Christ. The pastor is long known for his opposition to the Condominium and his attitude of nonco-operation.

More land is occupied, this belonging to a French planter, and trouble begins to develop. Meanwhile Vanafo, an "attractive" settlement, with neat houses, gardens, a flagpole where the Na-Griemel flag is run up and down daily in impressive ceremonies, bathing rules strictly observed (at three o'clock in the river for the men, at five for the women), grows from twenty-seven in 1967 to over two hundred in 1969. Jimmy is baptized by Pastor Abel, against his will, and is given the name Moses because he is leading the people in the wilderness. The French planter has Jimmy and Buluk arrested and tried; they get stiff terms for leading the trespassers on his land.

The Condominium, which has so far publicly ignored Na-Griemel, is now getting firm overtly. Not a word in the official British and French newsletters, not a word on Radio Vila in its news broadcasts of local interest. Quietly, though, the French have offered a school at Vanafo and the British a medical clinic, in order to help NaGriemel develop "along reasonable lines." Same old question: reasonable for whom? Obviously the natives are becoming too powerful. Jimmy, in prison, now claims ten thousand members for NaGriemel, even twelve and fifteen, figures most suspect to this writer. But he does have a lot of indigenous support.

Mr. Ramrakha gets the sentences reduced to a few months each, but the fat-headed Condominium has made martyrs out of Jimmy and Buluk. The power structure is so naïve! The NaGriemel message goes out to all the islands via tape recorder.

A joint statement by the Condominium's two Residents belatedly pays a back-handed tribute to NaGriemel—"Forward looking in land development for cattle and agriculture," yet "they seem preoccupied with the past, inasmuch as they talk a great deal about custom law." Tough! "Although it was necessary earlier this year to punish some of the people involved in the NaGriemel movement for illegal entry on land, we are watching its activities with interest [I should say so!] and shall not oppose any desirable project which will not disturb good relations between the various communities."

Cut the horseshit, whitey, and give us back our lands!

*

Footnote: One estimate by A. G. Kalkoa[4] is that seventy-five per cent of the land in the New Hebrides is now in the hands of (mostly white) foreigners. The whites number less than three per cent of the population, and of these most today are paid contract employees of the foreign business interests. The Condominium itself puts the amount of alienated land at 36.1 per cent, but again, they control the statistics. Of the alienated land, about eleven per cent belongs to British nationals or optants; the remaining eighty-nine per cent is held by French interests, the biggest of which is S.F.N.H. with some 170,000 hectares already registered or under claim. On southeast Santo the S.F.N.H. holdings run to 13,000 hectares. The French Government, which is a major stockholder of S.F.N.H., also holds 95,000 hectares.

Native, you got one big court battle ahead of you. Meanwhile whitey gets dug in deeper and better, with his buildings and barbed wire.

*

A sign is posted at Vanafo, by the neat cottages and the well-arranged gardens:

Nagriemel committee claim
Please, sir, our cry come to you

Help us natives to get our land back under Nagriemel
Please the European or New Hebridean who wants to work
in the natives' reserve after coconut, cocoa, coffee plantations
please they should pay rant
go to Nagriemel

THE WELL-WATERED, QUAINT ISLAND OF TANNA

A brief history of Tanna under Mr. Nicol

To catch up: Mr. Nicol, ex-chief mechanic on the British resident's yacht, the *Euphrosyne,* is appointed District Agent on Tanna at the end of 1915, replacing the unlamented Mr. Wilkes. Nicol's rule—there is no other word—is to last twenty-five years, twenty-five frustrating years from his point of view, because the natives will just not get in line. The first general regulation found in the files is dated 18 November 1918, ordering all magic stones to be either destroyed or thrown into the sea. It took twenty years to get rid of them, but he succeeded. One had to begin again after his death. Guiart writes that the measure was "objectively justified" because of the tremendous fear the people had of magical powers. What happened, though, was that the sorcerers went underground. In the twenties and thirties, with their own magic in abeyance, some of them learned another kind of magic, more deadly, it is said, from the people at Ambryn. Cost them a pretty penny for the knowledge too, but worth it, in the long run.

Nicol's other big campaign was getting rid of "vice," that is, sex. Now, that is an uphill battle anywhere. Tannese—native—marriages are not like western marriages. One is hard put to make generalizations for the practice, since marriage differs so widely throughout the world. The Presbyterians, of whom Nicol was a fervent one, saw marriage only in their own terms. So Tannese practices—polygamy, controlled sexual initiation of the young men, a little bit of "adultery" here and there—infuriated the Europeans. The general rubric "adultery" was a catch-all phrase for dealing with the unruly native, no matter what his crime, and it was freely used during the John Frum period. Sex seemed to have been suppressed, but when the island was loosened up after World War II, "adultery"—that is, polygamy and sexual initiation—surfaced, as strong as ever in the past.

To control the natives, Nicol and the missionaries moved them into new villages, large clusters of people from here and there, of different clans and tribes and languages. That some were ancient enemies made no difference to the rulers: they were all natives. Nice new names were given the villages: Jerusalem, Sydney, Melbourne, Samaria, Athens, Macedonia, and so on. Made the natives easier to handle. This was a common policy in the Pacific. After World War II the natives drifted back to their own villages and hamlets, but some damage was done to traditional structures.

In 1925 the French, seeing the southern islands of the Group firmly British, slip in their own delegate. Trouble comes, because the French District Agent is a doctor (as is his successor), gives medical care and medicines free, while the Presbyterians charge what the native could bear and more. Nasty frogs! Can't trust a Frenchie when it comes to subverting the natives.

More headaches come, but they are spaced out over the years. However, in a place like Tanna, a headache every five years is more than a man wants. Natives complain (1926) and again (1932) about the presence of land surveyors marking off their lands for Burns Philp and other unwanted whites. In 1933 the natives try forcibly to prevent the surveyors from working.

This must have been a bad decade, because a Roman Catholic mission (under the Marist fathers) and the Seventh-Day Adventists both arrive to set up counter-claims to the Christian truth preached by the Presbyterians. The latter are quite vexed. In 1936 Nicol punishes a native, member of S.D.A., who says that the Adventists should be tried only by Adventist courts and not by government or Presbyterian courts. The Adventists have a good selling point: they teach *English,* which the Presbyterians have refused to do, preferring pidgin as a medium of communication. In 1932, as the Adventists were getting settled, Nicol commented sourly: "When a school native was vexed with his fellow villagers, he usually left the school and retired in a non-school village and drank kava. Now it seems fashionable to join the Seventh-Day Adventist Mission instead. A certain amount of irritation is caused, but it will probably die down when the newness wears off and the S.D.A. missionaries get to know the bad eggs. Most of the troublemakers and agitators in Tanna [he means the men the Presbyterians cannot easily control] have been sent to Aore," where there is a training school for S.D.A. Two years later Nicol writes: "People whose grandfathers have been driven off their land, are trying to use the influence of the S.D.A. mission to press their claim, and the Presbyterians consider that they have the right to hold the land of any convert to the S.D.A. whose land is included in the survey of Trust lands." What this means is that when a native had been converted in the past, the Presbyterian mission automatically took title to his land, holding it for him, so generously, in a mission-controlled "trust." And when he left the church, he then lost title to his land, not that he still had it. A practical system for the whites. Later Nicol wrote that there was plenty of land for the natives, except for the area around the volcano, this meaning that the best land had been taken by the whites, but if the native wanted to clear the jungle or sweep off the volcanic plain, the land was his. Until the whites wanted it.

Meanwhile, with all these administrative problems, the Presbyterian mission was running into its own difficulties. The mission was now in its third generation of missionaries, and, frankly, they lacked the fervor—one might say, the killer-instinct—that old man Paton had, for preaching the truth of Christianity and making the world safe for Jesus. The natives had their fill of Scotch Calvinism, and church attendance, much as the reverends tried to enforce it, was slipshod. Among the islanders there was much discussion about whether or not they should put themselves under the protection of the French District Agent. But they saw that it was the choice of two evils—they did not rush into the so-called "French" church, the Roman Catholics, preferring, if anything, the Adventists. In January 1939, Nicol's head count of religious persuasions showed 3,381 Presbyterians, 656 Adventists and 72 Roman Catholics, with 1,659 people still listed as pagans. Conditions were worse than Nicol and the reverends suspected that year. For now we are at the time of the great Parousia, John Frum.

Tanna, when John Frum first appeared in the 1930s, was an isolated island, barely known to the outside world, despite the steady intrusions of Presbyterian missionaries and traders, planters, sandalwooders, blackbirders and other foreign offal. White presence at any one time ran from, perhaps, half a dozen to twelve or fifteen, rarely more. Unlike the northern islands, which were and are heavily French, Tanna (and the neighboring islands) fell under British influence. In 1892 a head count showed eleven British subjects (traders and planters), a German and a Portuguese, both also in business, and five missionaries, again British. It wasn't until after World War II that the foreign population increased markedly. Roads were and are quite primitive, merely a number of ancient, well-traveled native trails which were expanded under Mr. Nicol by the use of labor produced by the Presbyterian courts. For a long time he was the only person on the island to have a car (at times he had two), most travel being done either by foot or on horse, the animals being brought in by the missionaries and planters. Some of the horses escaped and their descendants now run loose and wild on the plain at the northern end of Tanna. Until R. U. Paul founded New Hebrides Airways Limited in 1961 (it is now called Air Melanesia and is controlled by Qantas and B.O.A.C. and uses their equipment), traffic to and from Tanna was slow and infrequent. A boat came about once a month or so, staying two or three days. Supplies were landed, island produce taken off, and people caught up with their mail and answered it. Daily plane service began in 1961 between Vila (which is serviced from abroad by Fiji Airways and UTA) and Tanna, the island being favored because it is Mr. Paul's home. Later Air Melanesia extended its routes to eight other islands. Tanna is in the world, but not of it. Conditions are still primitive, wherever you look. There are now some sixty to seventy motor vehicles, most of the Land Rover type, a Japanese version being favored (the general term for a vehicle is "truck"); the majority of the trucks are white-owned. Three or four Tannese have gone to New Caledonia to sweat out the mines, saved their money and bought old Land Rovers, which now serve as taxis, running them around the island on a community basis. There is still no electricity save for a few generators owned by Paul, some of the whites and the institutions like the government and the missions. Fuel must be brought in by ship. And of course there is no movie house (though the Presbyterians will sometimes show a 16mm film), and no bar or café, no restaurant, no hotel, no accommodations for strangers outside of the native-type bungalows that Paul rents out from time to time. Visitors who stay overnight must buy food at his trading post and cook their own meals.

The island is very beautiful, with lush vegetation, some high mountains, deep valleys, picturesque coral and black-sand shores. It is often described as "well-watered." Its fertility is staggering: tree trunks and branches cut and planted as fence posts quickly root and branch. It is heavily wooded, with great banyans and other trees, vines, wild flowers, bougainvilleas, wild Swatow oranges, limes and papayas.

Tanna's shape is that of a fat crescent moon, or, perhaps more accurately, like a Stone Age handscraper roughly chipped to shape, with the bulge along the west coast. From North to South it is some twenty-four miles deep, and from Lenakel to White Sands, the widest point horizontally, it is about eighteen. There is a great mountainous range which begins in the South and runs halfway up the center, where it fades away into low hills and a plain. The highest peak is Tukosmeru, 1,084 meters high; this is John Frum's mountain (or Kalbapen's); a few miles to the South is Mount Meulen, where Karaparamum resides. Sometimes the abodes are switched; it depends on the speaker. On the eastern coast is the volcano, Yasur (also called Iasur and Yauouey), 361 meters high, dominating Sulphur Bay and the White Sands area with its irregular booms every few minutes, which send up puffs of black smoke and showers of rocks onto the ashy plain at its base. At Yasur's eastern foot is Lake Siwi, the scene of certain miraculous events. The terrain around Yasur is lunar, like any we have seen on TV; the recognition is instantaneous. Yasur is promoted by the Vila Chamber of Commerce as a great tourist attraction. People come down by Air Melanesia for the day to see it. Hibiscus Tours: "A thirty-minute hike up the edge of the volcano will bring you to the crater, where the bubbling red hot lava and constant rumbling will hold you in awe." But it's actually a devilish climb, ankle-deep in volcanic ash; however, little old ladies and little old men, most of them tourists from Australia, take the tour and make the climb as part of their pre-mortem excursion through the conquered primitive peoples of the South Pacific. Climb the sacred volcano and get a heart attack. Yasur is all smoke and flames, hurtling rocks and periodic bangs, big and little, and showers of sparks at night. Its fine ashes float across the island, leaving a gray-white powder on everything—food, utensils, clothing, bedding, the people. Yasur will play a role later on.

There are two separate racial groups on Tanna, as different as white and black, which is what they are, the whites there to exploit the island and the natives, the blacks there because it is their birthplace, their home far back into the mists of time, because Tanna is sacred and is the navel, the umbilicus, of the earth and the universe. The white population is roughly half French and half "English," that is, one or two English and the remainder Australian and New Zealand. The whites number about sixty to seventy, and these figures include some two dozen women and children, the men being missionaries, government officials, teachers, doctors, planters and traders. European influence seems strong, almost overwhelming, and it is in the coastal areas, around Lenakel, White Sands and Port Resolution, yet a few hundred yards inland life goes on virtually as if Europeans didn't exist, except that almost everything that motivated Tannese life in the pre-missionary days has been destroyed. The Tannese population is again growing. The census of 1967 put the native population at 10,367; whites estimate it at 12,000 in 1972, and the Tannese at 17,000. You can take your choice, though any figure is a sad reflection of the estimated 100,000 to 200,000 of the pre-white golden age. The people are spread out in hundreds of tiny villages. The latest and only map I have seen, an excellent work by French cartographers (dated 1962), shows some 130 "major" settlements; there are many unnamed hamlets not included on the map, some being groups of two or three houses. The Tannese speak three different languages, with varying dialects, of immense complexity. The only white I knew of who could speak any Tannese language was a Catholic missionary, a nice gentleman, who had spent over twenty years on Tanna, and would be there the rest of his life, waiting for, and hoping for, the eventual conversion of the Tannese to his church. That was his Cargo, I thought. But the other whites, as far as I could learn, went no further than pidgin, a degrading language for the native.

Native culture is something of the past, lacking the great art still practiced on Ambryn, Malekula, the Banks Islands and elsewhere in the north. The only cultural forms I saw were the Custom dances at Sulphur Bay in honor of John Frum. A (guilty) Presbyterian minister has been trying to introduce some types of native carvings—copied from forms used on other islands. It hadn't occurred to him to see if the Tannese could develop their own art again.

There is adequate food, in the shape of vegetables and starchy roots. Plenty of calories but not much real nutrition in the form of protein. Anthropologists who like to measure such things (keeps them from causing troubles in other areas) have estimated that four hours' work a week in the garden will produce enough food for the average native family.

Tanna gets a big play in the tourist literature, but frankly, tourists are rare. A few come down from time to time for the day, see the volcano and the wild horses. The bungalows are rarely used, and Paul has not bothered to replace one which blew down in the hurricane of 1972 (he had six originally), the same hurricane in which three people were killed, one of them a Tannese child in his mother's arms, who was hit by a falling coconut (damn things weigh four or five pounds; never sit under a coconut tree). Not much to do on the island, aside from seeing the volcano blow up, watching the wild horses at White Grass run away, or driving past the quaint natives and their quaint John Frum symbols, the crosses. There are John Frum crosses in various places, painted red and surrounded by neat little fences. The English-language folder prepared by the New Hebrides Chamber of Commerce, Industry and Agriculture says, "the red cross is a tribute to the volcano [not so] by the followers of John Frum, the quaint and primitive religion of Tanna." (The French version says, somewhat less inaccurately, *"la petite croix rouge est placée près du volcan par les adhérents du culte John Frum, religion étrange et primitive de cette île."* But there are crosses over much of the island, though the Lenakel side has none and the people pretend not to know why the other side (Sulphur Bay, in particular) has them. Far to the North the people there put up signs with the figures 2 and 4 superimposed over each other, and smaller ones with the word PARISEN (prisoner); these symbols are in black rather than red.

The Chambre de Commerce D'Industrie et D'Agriculture has issued a pretty good bulletin which makes the trip to Tanna sound like something you would want to make, though it is heavily sprinkled with the usual misinformation and absurdities. "We asked them to check it down there for us," says the director ("them" meaning the whites), "but they never answered, so we put it out anyway." The bulletin reads in part, after describing the exciting plane flight and jeep trip across Tanna:

"The road begins winding down to 'King's Cross,' gently sloping towards the volcano and turning gradually into pure volcanic ash, until suddenly you will emerge from the bush into the Sewe desert. This 'moonscape' area, brick-red in colour with old lava flows and the sulphur-coloured lake, surrounds Yasur Volcano.

"The village of Sulphur Bay, home of the famous John Frum Cargo Cult, is nearby and from here permission will be granted for your visit to Yasur. These people own the volcano and have certain religious beliefs pertaining to the stones, which you will be requested not to remove.

"This religion, based on old customs, using some Christian ideas; and with the arrival of American G.I.'s vast quantities of equipment during World War II making a great impression on the people is so strong that the leaders keep in touch by 'radio' (a crude resemblance of a radio and aerial) with John Frum who will one day return bringing everything that is desired by 'Man-Tanna.' Regular meetings with large attendances are held on Friday nights close to Yasur Volcano, which is also part of their religion and where thousands of 'devils' are forging weapons for John Frum. It is interesting to note that the stones of wisdom were supposed to have been taken from Yasur by Captain Cook during his landing at Port Resolution in 1774, and 'Man-Tanna' therefore claims that the White people have taken his wisdom.

"Customs have been retained by the people and are referred to continuously. These include dances, circumcision ceremonies, witch doctor practices, land tenure, etc. The crude symbols of the John Frum cult such as gates, birds, crosses, all of which are usually painted red, may be photographed, but please do not touch them. When visiting Tannese villages never enter a native hut or man's house unless asked. Your guide may arrange it for you . . .

"There is no restaurant on the island."

The climate is rather pleasant, at least along the coasts, where constant breezes blow, and easily far superior to that of the northern islands with their furnace heats. The humidity is high, and inland in the dense jungles heat and humidity become unbearable, and in the constant rains suffocating. January, February and March are the worst months, hot, humid, rainy. A planter's wife says that "Everyone becomes short-tempered, we wonder what we're doing here, we want to leave, and then it becomes pleasant." Earthquakes are frequent, sometimes coming in waves for two or three days, and as high as seven on the Richter scale.

And what about the people? Gentle, subdued, intelligent, existing under the white occupation. Polite to whites, they stand aside on the road when a white passes. At the trading post they defer to a white if he enters after them. The whites ride their jeeps and Land Rovers, the natives walk, and such is the Tannese way that a woman will turn her face away completely when whites pass. Around whites Tannese dress in the manner their parents and grandparents learned was acceptable, the men in trousers and shirts, or shorts or sarong (here called lava lavas), the women in knee-length flowing mother hubbards or in blouses and skirts, the latter either cloth or pandanus leaves dyed in bright colors. Inland men are said to wear the penis wrapper if they think no Europeans will spy on them. In the mountains and valleys life continues rather close to the Stone Age level, with the modifications of steel knives, nails, some tinned foods from the trading posts or the co-operative stores, cigarettes, and printed cottons from Taiwan.

I hope the reader gets the picture of the simplicity of Tannese life. The people live in small houses—huts would be the best equivalent in American—of bamboo, thatch and pandanus leaf, sleeping on mats on the earth. Some houses are raised and have wooden floors. Cooking is done on outdoor fires. The diet is simple, as I have said elsewhere: taro root (tasteless), potatoes, yams, some fruit, occasionally a chicken or fish. And bread: it is both a staple and a luxury. A Tannese with ten cents will buy a loaf of bread at the trading post and sit on the ground outside, his legs stretched out before him and slowly, with relish and delight, devour the entire loaf. Protein foods are scarce. Pigs run all over, but are not eaten regularly. The pig is a measure of wealth, saved for a feast; then forty or fifty will be killed and presented to another village, which in turn must do the same. There are chickens running about, but their meat is something of a luxury and eggs are not a regular staple (the Lenakel trading post imports eggs from Australia, along with oranges and other items which could be grown locally, if anyone thought about it). Though the surrounding seas are full of fish, fishing is not a regular occupation. In general, the Tannese get enough to fill their stomachs from their gardens, and know nothing about calories, fats or proteins or carbohydrates.

There are some large herds on the island—cattle, sheep, goats —but ninety per cent (at least) belong to the whites, primarily to R. U. Paul; there is fresh meat every Monday at the Lenakel trading post, but few Tannese can afford it. Paul is careless about boundaries, apparently assuming the island is his, and he lets his cattle run over the natives' land, to their great frustration and anger, and it is only recently that a Tannese has dared take him to court over the intrusion.

To the whites, in the Condominium and elsewhere, the Tannese—Man-Tanna, as he is known—is an ornery bastard. He is soundly criticized for wanting to protect his rights, to be independent. A government official at Vila remarked to me, "Man-Tanna is very strong-headed. They're all like that. 'This bit of land—you can't take it.' There is a basic distrust of all the island people for the government, especially on Tanna. They've got their reasons, mind you. It's worst on Tanna, mostly due to the change of District Agents every two or three years, who don't know the language and the way of life and will say something, make some promise, which their successor doesn't deliver. Old beliefs are very strong. Even when you educate them they will go back to Custom, witch doctors and so on. You think that they are following a rational way of doing something that is rational to the white, and then they'll do something else which to you or me is incredible." I thought he should have left me out of the equation, but whites assume all whites stick together in the colonies.

He adds that the Tannese wanted an airline. They built the first airstrip themselves, way ahead of the administration in their thinking. They bought shares in it, "thanks to John Frum."

Magic plays a central role in Tannese life, in a way that I think whites don't understand. The whites I talked to, on Tanna and in Vila, seemed to dismiss magic as inconsequential, a native pastime that they really didn't take seriously. It is this inability to accept the indigenous mind, the native way of thinking, as valid in its own way that has caused so much dissension throughout the world. Once I had made contact with the John Frum people and we had developed some mutual trust, people began to tell me about the use of stones. Tom says, "We can control the weather with stones. We don't tell this to the Australians because they don't believe us." I say I believe it. Lauhman Teni asks me about the Americans: Can they control the weather? I have to think for a moment, and then I remember the Red Indian rain dances. Tom adds that when papaya, banana or some other tree is not growing well, they make a hole in the trunk of a tree and put certain stones in it with some leaves, and this makes very good fruit. Stones are also put in gardens. Both Tannese and whites tell me about the use of stones to make good weather for the Queen's birthday, the whites finally admitting to a fact that baffles them. For a number of years the chiefs had approached the District Agent to say they could get good weather for the celebration of the holiday; the D.A.'s always rejected the offer as so much native nonsense. Finally, after steady rain each time, climaxed by a nine-inch rainfall that completely wiped out the festivities, the chiefs were allowed to make good weather for the Day, and it has been celebrated under sunny skies ever after.

Shortly after I arrived on Tanna a severe hurricane struck Fiji, which is some six hundred miles due East of the New Hebrides. The next morning, as I was shopping at the trading post at Lenakel, the trader's son, Russell, remarked that he had just heard a radio report of the hurricane: sixteen dead, more feared dead, a tidal wave, severe devastation, and the storm heading right for Tanna. I mentioned this to Joe Johnson Hiopel, a teacher at the local school, who assured me that it was all right, they knew about the hurricane and the chiefs were working on it with their stones. That day the storm veered off at right angles and hit the Gilbert and Ellice islands. We had only heavy seas. Six dead in Gilbert and Ellice.

One rainy day Henry Weiwai and I are walking along the beach at Green Point, the same beach where John Frum and the evil spirit Nakua had an epic battle years before. The beach is full of heavy boulders and smaller stones. I ask Henry if he can tell which stones are sacred; he says "No," though I suspected he didn't want to tell me, and he adds that one has to be specially trained. We are trying to go further inland to visit the Green Point villages where John has first appeared but there is some problem. I had been extended an invitation, through John Kalate. Now John Kalate has disappeared, but he returns. Something is wrong. John and Henry explain to me that Nakua won't let me inland; he is afraid that I will find out too much about John Frum. There are now two factions in the Green Point villages, those following John Frum and those following Nakua. Henry adds that Nakua is a very bad spirit; he has given babies to many ladies. A heavy rain breaks over us and we go into an abandoned house near the beach and John Kalate builds a fire so we can dry out. Henry returns to the subject of stones. He is annoyed at Tom, who has been trained in their use (Tom never told me about this), and now he is not only using them for legitimate things, like the weather and the gardens, but he is also using their powers against people.

Another disaster had also happened recently, one which intrigued the Tannese, since it had not affected them. On the day of the great island festival, celebrated, for the first time since the Presbyterians came, at Leminuh, the most sacred spot on Tanna, the Air Melanesian plane returning to Vila had crashed over the plain where the wild horses ran. This was the second crash of the year for Air Melanesia, which was now down to three planes. The whites claimed that the pilot had been flying too low; some of the passengers had wanted to photograph the horses; the plane, a bushplane about the size of a VW bus and even less comfortable, hit a sudden rise in the ground. Wipeout. And earlier in the year Bob Paul's son had been killed in another—third—plane crash in Australia. There were two Tannese explanations for the crashes—one (from Green Point) that the most recent crash was the result of the white's tampering with the Sem Sem stone at Leminuh (I will come to this later), and the other that John Frum was punishing Bob Paul for his treatment of the Tannese.

Whatever happened, the Tannese felt that they were constantly being victimized by whites. An anthropologist named Kal had come through recently. "Who this man Kal?" several people ask me. I say I didn't know him but had heard about him. He had a bad reputation among both the whites and the New Hebrideans. Finally an older man tells me that Kal had asked the people to take off their clothes so he could photograph them as they had looked in the past. A lot of discussion about what to do, and finally the Tannese, eager to be accommodating (for Kal claimed to be an American), agreed and Kal photographed them as "primitives." "Now we are angry," several people say, having heard the conversation. "Kal made fun of us." I hear later from another source that Kal had persuaded a number of the women to be photographed nearly nude, too, and now the women had been put out by their husbands. Kal was a hated man at Sulphur Bay, where he had appeared in the company of a New Hebridean woman, fondling her in public and making a display of her. The Tannese are a bit on the conservative side in matters like this and don't like whites taking advantage of their women. Even among themselves moral codes are strict; an unmarried boy or man who seduces a girl may be tied to a tree and whipped; in the distant past he might even have been killed. But sexual practices for the unmarried were carried on in certain controlled ways, the most common being the employment of a woman who would live in the bachelor's houses and initiate the young men into the rites of intercourse, taking them one by one into the jungle, where the boy would lie down on his back, and the woman would lower herself over him, covering her pelvic area with her grass skirt so the boy could not see her genitals. The Tannese have a great feeling of personal propriety. Nevertheless, what the natives do along these lines seems to the reverends and to the British District Agent (at least in the past, if not even now) very much like prostitution. The Custom house woman went through what appears a rather rough sexual initiation herself at the hands of the chiefs. Nicol fought an endless battle trying to stop this Custom. Now such practices are somewhat more open. A certain H. rents out his wife for the night, sending a formal bill the next day typed on an old machine he bought from a trader for a quid; and there are girls who hang around the police station at Isangel who will do "it" for a few bob. Later on they take the boat to Vila, where more than a few bob can be had. The whites, among them the Belgians, are looking into the business for the tourists. Tanna

JOHN FRUM HE COME

girls are prized now for their talents, as Tanna men were once prized on the cotton, sugar and guano fields a century back.

Thus, well-watered, quaint Tanna, with its picturesque natives and its charming John Frum crosses. But there's more exploding than windy Yasur . . .

TANNA STORIES

A Tanna story

[*Told by Sam Tacuma. Mr. Tacuma used "he" and "she" indiscriminately in referring to the woman. Pigeon is the generic term for bird.*]

A giant he's ate all the people while he ate them he missed that
    little baby a girl and when he went away this baby cry and
    kick and break the root of a tree that root nanuman and he
    suck the root it has a juice and he broken it and suck it
From that tree then he becoming big and while he is strong and
    able to walk he went down to the beach and he used the vine
    to make love to himself to fuck himself and when he broke
    the top of it he used it to fuck himself and by that he became
    conceived and he bear these two children twins two boys
She look after them until they grow up she circumcized them
    in the fashion we do now with a bamboo knife they five or six
    years old when they grow to manhood she began to show
    with them how to shoot bows and arrows and spears
She learned them all these things until they could spear anything
    then she asked them if they could do anything
They said, What thing?
She told them this story about this giant one of the giants has
    eaten all the people and I carry you too and I'm asking if you
    could spear him
Kill him!
But the older one said we can't kill him we are not able (and
    that is why his name is Kasasau he shakes he is afraid)
But the younger one said I can kill him (and his name is
    Kaniapnin willing to kill him he's brave)
When it showed the younger one is brave to kill him she
    prepared a spear to kill him when she prepared spear she
    put it on the road to the south to Lenakel one on one side
    one on another

After she make ready the spear she went up the hill from Sydney
　　on Mr. Paul side she kindled the fire there
This giant up at Nagyum [Aneityum] eating the people he see
　　the smoke from the fire he told her I ate everybody but who
　　is making the fire? I go see somebody I missed it
He come across swim across we don't know how he come
They begin to spear the children are hiding to spear him the
　　mother is dancing on the road
He said I must eat her
When he come near these hiding children they began to spear
　　him all along the road while the mother is dancing one goes
　　to one side of the road to spear him the other goes to the other
　　side and spear him
That spears made from all the different trees she put the names
　　all along the road the names are kept by people now
He see the names for all the spears he was speared with the tree
　　nene (and that is why we call the place Lomannebe the place
　　of nebe)
But he not dead yet they still running after him to go to the
　　place where they mother made the fire they chase him to the
　　place of the wild cane where the wild cane was cutting his ass
He swear at them and said you are doing nothing the wild cane
　　is cutting my ass I'll eat you
Then they put the last spear in his forehead that last spear we
　　call nesiko the name of a tree and we call that people there
　　after that name nesikomin
Afterward they put that spear on his forehead and he fell down
　　dead
When he falls down they not know if he dead because they call
　　all the different pigeons to see if he is dead because they are
　　afraid of him
Pigeon with a red head [the honey-eater] they sent and he put
　　his head on the giant head and he come back and said he not
　　dead yet
And they sent another one like a sparrow with a red head and
　　wings and tail [a kind of parrot] this pigeon he went right

through the mouth right through to the ass and they know he
   really dead
He got it!
When they cut it they cut it to pieces and they call all the names
   of the people he ate them and they call all the pieces after
   the people
All the tribes now called after the pieces of this giant
When they cut it from every place they could hear the sounds of
   the cock crowing and they people talking and laughing he ate
The people are alive again
The belt and feathers for the chief man they found in the giant
   so they send them to all the chief man
At that place where they cut it when they share all the pieces of
   the body but there they cut the liver
That liver today hard like a stone you can see at Leminuh

                  *

[We have been sitting in a raised bamboo house owned by Mr.
Tacuma's son. It has been raining outside and the heat and
humidity in the house are unbearable. Some of the men present
begin to laugh when they think of eating the giant and of the
pieces of the body they are named after. Leminuh, where the
giant's liver lies half buried in the earth, is the most sacred spot
on Tanna, and was barred to the Tannese by the Presbyterians
during the mission's most oppressive period. It is now held in expectation as the place where John Frum will again appear someday, to lead the people out of bondage.]

The Ark of Tanna

Noah built the Ark here—the place is on the way to Sulphur
   Bay, at King's Cross. Hammer, saw, tools—some of them
   were found there. People take them away. Now it's a rule not
   to allow visitors. So the Ark was built by Noah so all the
   families got in with all those animals like lions seen in other
   countries but not here.

A big rain came and took it through Port Resolution. If you go
there you will see there is a track showing how the Ark floated
away. So the flood was all over the place—no sea—but Noah
was told to put the Ark facing East, going along, until he was
told when the New World would come, on Ararat. The flood
rose fifteen fathoms high.

We have Ararat on the other side of Tanna but what people
see is Mount Ararat in America. Ararat is name of mountain
and has a meaning, "The land is here." So what the New
World formed is the separation of islands. Before the flood
there was one land, afterwards, many, many islands. The
Second Creation, separating the islands. In the first place
there was only one land, that is, here, Tanna.

Now what we got in mind is that everything was left with the
Americans on mountain of Ararat in America—everything—
education, tools, all the things we need.

Why? Because we can prove it. Because the education is starting
from American instead of from Tanna. It must be true
because the people who are closer to that place, that mountain,
have more information than people far away like Tanna. If
you visit that place, you will see it is still true. The tools are
there.

There is a place on Tanna called Sumeria. Babel is here. That is
proof Tanna was the beginning. These things happened and
spread all over the world.[1]

On top of Old Smokey

Before the war an American was hauled very high in the sky in
a net. He came to Vila and talked to the Tannese men in the
calaboose. He talked in the door or in the wall, as John did
later. He was hauled in the sky in something like handcuffs.
He had irons on his legs, a kind of chain. Had his legs bound
by a chain. They put him in a special calaboose. Like John he
came out, eating something. They made him a warm tea, they
gave it to him, he just drink. They gave him a pencil and he

wrote something even with handcuffs. He spoke American wisdom. We didn't understand what he means, true or untrue. In handcuffs two or three months.

He stood on something white, like a plate. In a minute, two minutes, he went to America.

We didn't know his name, but we called him Nabnab, Mr. Nabnab, which means Fire. Because always, he's just playing with volcano smoke at Tanna. When the wind blows that cloud somewhere, he's just sitting up on that cloud. Well before the war, it was, somewhere between first war and second.

The American we understand, but only when he comes by himself, like John.[2]

WHITE MAN HE MUCK UP JOHN FRUM

[*A white planter*] The John Frum business would have died in the beginning if the government had let it alone. A kick in the ass would have stopped it. Just look angry and they back down. They don't have much courage except when they're drunk. They're not warriors, they're assassins. Their own warfare was assassination. There's still a lot of feuding today but the government keeps it from breaking into violence.

I was up in Vila a few weeks ago when I saw a crowd of them standing on the street, looking ugly, probably thinking of getting into trouble. "PISS OFF!" I said. You should have seen them scatter.

*

[*A Condominium official*] Your Melanesian is inclined to become aggressive and fight when he is on alcohol. I much prefer them to stick to kava. I don't care what they do or think if they don't cause trouble. But when my doctor wanted to inoculate them on the other side of the island, they refused. I can't have that sort of opposition.

Don't feel sorry for them—they're always feeling sorry for themselves. Western rule has been for the better, not only here but everywhere [and he lists a long string of present and former British colonies].

*

[*A white*] If they don't want you to know they shut up like a clam. You don't know if they are putting you on or not when they talk. A lot of fantastic stories.

There's a lot of misinformation in John Frum. South America and the American South are all the same. Then there are terms like New California which apparently is tied in with New Caledonia.

John Frum is pretty free from violence. The only violence you see is against the women. They have no say. They're vassals. Get beaten.

*

[*R.C. missionary on another island*] They left the Presbyterian church forty years ago because of the ban on dancing, kava, and because of too many collections. For a while they thought of coming under our umbrella. But then they stayed as they were. A curious thing, it is. In the beginning there was a person—not John Frum himself—but some kind of emanation. Since then their education has resulted in a good deal of progress. Many realize that John Frum is just foolishness.

When they left Presbyterianism we maintained two priests on Tanna because the day may come when they have to go somewhere. We may be able to pick them up.

The Presbyterian system of tabu may have been the best thing at the time for people in the Stone Age, because the early traders would sell them anything. The missionaries were right to stop their drinking. However, now, psychologically speaking, such prohibitions as were in effect are not good. Today it is against the law for natives to drink hard liquor—but not outsiders. The people from Wallis and Ellice, for example, can go into a pub and get a drink.

*

[*A white resident of Tanna*][1] John Frum was started by Jack Kohu and Manehevi. Kohu gave out a story how he had seen a man on the shore, hanging about like a man waiting for women. The man ran away and jumped over a pandanus tree. The man was not human. Kohu was told by a sorcerer how to cook a chicken in a certain manner in order to catch the fellow. Next thing we hear, the villages near Green Point are being cleaned up. This person Kohu has been talking about is to be there. No one saw him during the day, only in the evening. No one was ever sure who it was, whether the same man or someone else. But it was Kohu, I'm certain of that. He was doling out medicine, giving injections. You never saw the doctor at all—you stuck your arm through the door and felt a prick. Not a western-type injection but a scratch. There was a woman in her thirties who was doubled up in pain. Couldn't straighten out. She got an injection and was cured. People used to come from all over for treatment.

The movement originated with Kohu and he was the dominant figure, at least on the West side of Tanna, until his death in 1971. He got polio and was crippled from the waist down. The man rotted. He was still alive but the flesh was falling off him in chunks. Full of maggots, the flesh just dropping. But he was carried from one village to another and talked about John Frum. He said that John Frum was "feeding" the people, was feeding the villages. When he died he was delirious but still mouthing John Frum sayings.

I think Kohu might have started the Frum business as a bit of a hoax. Then it was taken up by Nambas at Sulphur Bay on a more practical basis, as a way of getting out of Presbyterianism. The local chiefs met and talked things over. Nambas had been a teacher in the church schools. Frum was not anti-white originally, and there was no Cargo at the beginning. Cargo came from the White Sands side. Nambas saw a tremendous opportunity, his own glory. He had a far superior following than Kohu ever got. He was able to use Kohu's image and then Kohu picked up things the White Sands people had invented and talked about Cargo.

The movement has been going downhill since Nambas died. Mellis, the fellow who took over at Sulphur Bay, is not a good leader. Nambas had vision. He would run up a flag and call people together and tell them what it meant. Anything. The original focus was Green Point. I don't know why it shifted to Sulphur Bay. There are some great gaps no one can fill in. The movement has changed character—it's not the same as originally. Some change in dynamism that no one can account for.

Joe Nalpin was one of the ones who imitated John Frum and said he was John Frum. Nalpin pretended to be Frum in a house near Sydney. There was a partition in it, with the men on one side and the women on the other. Nalpin said, "You must do exactly as I tell you. This same night the world will turn over and all the whites will go. You must do exactly as I say. Give me a girl. The girl I want is Tom Kaliwok's daughter." There were a lot of protests, particularly from Kaliwok. Nalpin said, "If you don't give me your daughter, the world won't turn over and the whites won't leave." So Joe got the girl. The next morning the sun rose, the earth was as it always was, the whites were still there. The day passed. They waited all day. Nothing happened. Kava time came. The next night passed. Still nothing. Then someone recognized Joe Nalpin's voice and he was reported to the District Agent and deported.

When they imitate John Frum they dress to the eyeballs— white talcum powder on their faces, big sunglasses, fancy hat with a ribbon. They disguise their accent—talk in pidgin or the accent of another village.

Everybody who imitated John Frum got something out of it. Nambas used to get presents all the time. The same with Jack Kohu, right up to his death.

The movement progressed into one to get out of Presbyterianism, which was virtually the only religion (there were no Roman Catholics to speak of, perhaps two or three). At a given signal everyone quit Presbyterianism. Normally a Tannese who wanted to leave the Church would not have gone to the minister and said he was quitting—there would be too much pressure on him.

Kava was brought up the road from South to North. Everyone had to take a sip as a sign of accepting John Frum. This was the symbol that meant a return to Custom, the violating of a Presbyterian taboo. Two young men, Roman Catholics I believe, refused and were threatened with death. Later the British agent was menaced with guns. Among the Presbyterians everyone accepted kava. Then they were having drills, like an army.

Things came to a head when the leaders were deported after threatening the District Agent—thievery in the stores, their getting rid of their money, abandoning their gardens [no thievery, says another westerner, who has heard this]. But tickets were torn off in the store. We never understood the reason for it.

What undoubtedly influenced the Cargo theme was when

they were working in Vila for the Americans. When the Yanks got new supplies they would throw away, or give away, the old stuff. There was a tremendous superfluity, a lot of excess there. All they learned about the Americans came during the war. No Americans had been here before the war.

I think the name John Frum is possibly a corruption of John Brown, the American general who liberated the blacks in the States. Possibly some American Negro spoke to them at Vila, and they picked up the name. However, the movement had already started by that time, before the war.

Eleven years after the arrests they returned. That started the second phase of John Frum.

Irving Johnson came off the *Yankee* when the movement was going strong, in its second phase. Johnson turned up with his white boat and crew. People gave him baskets of fruit and vegetables and kava and took him up to the volcano. There was a big meeting there on the volcano plateau and Johnson addressed the people. He was advised by the local whites to tell them to work, that nothing would ever come except by work. It was translated by Nambas into Tannese. I'm damn sure that Nambas didn't tell them there was no hope of getting Cargo except by work.

They had been waiting for a white boat. The *Yankee* was not big but it was white. The people would paddle out to sea at three in the morning to see if anyone was coming off the boat to give out secrets they wouldn't give in the presence of the local whites.

Nambas apparently was the key man in getting the second phase of John Frum underway. It started something like this: One day a fellow named Nakuma came to me and said, "I want to tell you something, it's hard to believe. I was with Nambas at the foot of the volcano. He said, 'Do you know, if I were to scratch the sand with my foot the whole place would open up. You would see everything there—American troops, guns, Land Rovers, refrigerators, everything. But if it opened up you would tell everybody.' So I said to him, 'But you must tell me. I won't tell anyone else. But I want to see it.' 'OK,' says Nambas. And he scrapes the ground with his foot, and the volcano opens.

Everything was there—American troops, guns, iceboxes, all the things he said. Then he covered it up. Nambas said not to tell anyone, but how could I not tell you?" This gave Nambas tremendous prestige because everyone knew what he had done. You couldn't stop the story.

There is a relation between the volcano and Cargo. They talk about Cargo coming in a boat, but they also believe in the volcano. About 1959 or so a Russian volcanologist, Haroun Tarzieff, came to study Yasur but they wouldn't let him down because they claimed the whites know what there is in it and want to take it. There have been a lot of stories, like those of people marching on the plateau on top of the volcano. Both black and white, they are. I asked some of the natives how anyone could live there. They say that there are several vents, some for fire, some for water, that's how. Seems easy to live there, they think. That's how they think about it—no problems of gases and heat. On the other side of Siwi they say there are underground tunnels. Two women fell into them and are still there. The story is that they will rape any man who wanders in, so the men are afraid of that side of Siwi.

A fellow told me he had seen the ground open up at Lokatai. Saw bodies of people. A snake [a lizard in another telling by the same white] addressed him and told him the symbolism. There are six corpses there. The snake [lizard] held up its hand and said John Frum is going to bring Cargo. I said to this fellow, "How can you tell me a bloody lie like that?" He said, "Sir, how could I lie to you?" He knew bloody well he was lying, but ten years later he would believe it, every word of it. The same fellow would go around with a piece of copper wire about his waist and swear he was getting news from America on it. Now he's sort of sheepish about the wire.

This fellow Hyawak claimed to be the spirit of John Frum. He wore a wire around his waist; it was supposed to be electrical. He had a series of women, Queen One, Queen Two and so on. Said he was the voice of John Frum just to get women. Hyawak would climb a tree—people were not supposed to look up—and this disembodied voice would make profound statements. People knew Hyawak was the voice of John Frum. One day somebody snuck up with a torch and said, "What are you doing up that tree, Hyawak?"

Tell a deliberate lie first and then come to believe it. Like Kohu, who began to believe what he was saying. It's very common here. When John Frum was in the early stages, someone would dig a hole and get in it and put his ear to the ground. He have an accomplice up in a tree and he'd shout out the news from America. This fellow in the tree would pass it on. That was the way things would be told.

Someone said a submarine had landed in the South. Americans were coming ashore at night. If the whites went to look, they would see only dogs, but actually the soldiers were there. They turned themselves into dogs to fool the whites.

Then there was an invisible bridge between the volcano and Port Resolution.

There was too much noise about John Frum at one time, less now though there still are stories. A fellow came to me and said in a casual conversation, "Friday I was coming to the church but the others want me to come to the John Frum dance at Sulphur Bay. When Mellis went to Vila [Mellis is the Frum leader at Sulphur Bay] he then went to America on a mysterious thing and when he got to America he met some soldiers who said everything is ready and they showed him an eagle crouched and said when the eagle goes, Cargo will come."

A local woman went completely nuts. She wanted to become a Roman Catholic but her husband said No. He was a sorcerer. She defied him and went to Benediction. The husband brought her up before the chiefs. She told them she had seen an enormous big hole with trucks coming out. Plenty of Cargo. The chiefs were impressed and didn't punish her.

*

[*The same white, more philosophical*] They've come bang with a flash to what has taken us two thousand years. Obviously these things they want—Cargo—don't come with a bang but they want to do it with a bang.

In New Guinea they've seen Cargo coming ashore and are convinced that it doesn't belong to the whites, but here they're more sophisticated—they've bought things themselves.

One should *not* look too deep. If one looks too deep, one looks far too deep. The movement reflects the image of the man who is in power at the time, who exhibits the signs and portents.

Up to very recently they had no idea where material goods came from.

They do everything by magic—make yams grow, potatoes. They feel the whites have something similar.

Reasons for the John Frum movement in my view are, one, getting out of Presbyterianism, and two, the profound effect that western culture has had on them. They want to produce something comparable of their own. In a lifetime. By magic they want it now. The reason Frum continues is that the movement is theirs.

The basic structure is simply the form Kohu and Nambas gave it—why go through all the trouble of the whites when we can have the same with a minimum of effort? Many of them were teachers, as was Nambas. They know about the Second Coming of Christ. Perhaps John Frum is John the Baptist come back. It isn't one thought by any means, but a range of thoughts, memories, Custom, Christianity and whatever other influences may have come in through the impact of Europeans and Americans.

How does John Frum fit in with the aspirations of the Tannese people? One reason it continues is that the Tannese have produced "our thing." The original John Frum members in 1941 are now over thirty years older, in their mid and late fifties. They could never admit they made a mistake.

Put yourself in the skin of the Tannese at the time, the late nineteen thirties and early forties. How they got their information, how they lived. As the sun goes down man-Tanna picks up his news at kava time. "You hear what so-and-so said?" The John Frum story comes out. "So-and-so was in Vila—met this bloke who saw John Frum." They want to believe. In the beginning it was just a rumor. Next time they get some more news from a different source and Frum becomes a reality.

Communications were limited. The Europeans were a closed community. They were there, we were here. Cargoes come direct from Australia. Two days to unload. The natives don't see money change hands, as when they buy something from the trader himself. No idea of geography. Australia could be the same size as Tanna. The original transport was by horse. Not until the Americans came did they see motorized vehicles.

Another point. Anyone who was five then has had no education since. Now forty and ripe for believing anything. Born into John Frum. Second nature. They believe implicitly. I've never heard anyone who will say no about John Frum. Even men like Iolu Abbil, who is pretty well educated and traveled and doesn't believe in Frum, complained to the District Agent that some other man had caused a hurricane.

*

[*Another white*] The Presbyterian mission was completely despotic in the nineteenth century. The Presbyterians claimed that the time before their arrival was "a time of darkness." They had the island bombarded by British warships. People are still finding the cannonballs and bringing them into Bob Paul's store. Presbyterian bigotry was responsible for John Frum. The name John Frum was in use in the late nineteen thirties.

It was Bannisters at White Sands where they took off the price tags. I still can't get to the bottom of this. John Frum broke up into fragments because of jealousy. The people at Sulphur Bay are showmen and exhibitionists. They had to go Green Point one better. At Sulphur Bay Nambas used to hoist the flag and call the people together and then give them some new angle, some new story. First the flag was red calico. Quite an insignificant flag. Then he got something fancier. God knows what the red crosses mean. Up north they got a different John Frum movement, with black crosses and signs.

*

[*A planter*] I was up at Vila looking for a boat ride home—this was before the airline was started—when I met this American, Irving Johnson. I told him about John Frum. He was interested.

He was writing some articles for the *National Geographic*. He has a white ship, the *Yankee*. So we got on the radio telephone to Tanna. The operator down here flipped when he heard the American accent. We arrived in a storm. All Tanna knew the boat was coming, and they were waiting for us. Must have been a magnificent sight—Johnson put the sails up even though he was running on his motors and we came through the fog, the white ship from America. Johnson came ashore with twenty-two men. Off to Sulphur Bay they go. Presents along the way. Up the volcano. Two hundred people come too. They all stand on the plateau below the crater. Crew full of American gadgets, tape recorders, cameras, field glasses.

Johnson was getting concerned that the thing was going too far. He decided to stay in the background and got a fellow named Chris Sheldon, one of his mates, to address the people. Sheldon told them that if they want everything, they have to work. Bob Paul translated it into pidgin. Sheldon said he himself had worked for seven years and so on. But they heard what they wanted. All along the road back to Lenakel people offered fowls, fruit, kava root. Johnson went on board. There were canoes all around the *Yankee* with people throwing letters aboard for what they wanted. Johnson was quite concerned and wouldn't go ashore again. But the Tannese thought that he just wouldn't speak when the other Europeans were around. The people waited all morning hoping he would deliver. But at no point did he take the people for a ride.

*

[*A trader*] The Tanna Army started about 1956. There were rumors of people drilling at Sulphur Bay. They had very well-made wooden rifles. Lethal looking bayonets of wood or bamboo (bamboo is very sharp, and the word for it is the same as that for knife). The rifles were exactly like U.S. carbines, excellent copies.

One of them knew the drill, a chap named Kauya. He'd spent some time in jail. He was the sergeant. The officer in charge was Nakrumah. They drilled like mad. Everyone got very excited, particularly weak-kneed Europeans. The government, that is the D.A., went over to Sulphur Bay. Found the barricade. They wouldn't let him in. Sulphur Bay is screaming defiance over the gate. So the government people went back. Took them six weeks to get reinforcements, guns, tear gas from Vila.

Meanwhile the Army broke out and went on a march across the mountains. People were terrified, having seen the government retire. Villages had to feed them. Army headed towards Lenakel. Lauhman Teni suddenly became John Frum and the Army went to rendezvous with him. The idea was the Army would march through the Presbyterian church grounds.

The Army came right up to the gate of the mission at Lenakel. They said, "Open the gates." "You're not going through here," say the missionaries. The Army got more demanding. I was standing behind the gate with the reverends, listening. They got more and more insistent, rather ugly, so I jumped over the gate and said, "PISS OFF!" and they scattered.

Up to that point they looked pretty good. They had American-type uniforms. A lot of Yank stuff was still around even then. But they had to retreat. A lot of confusion.

Even so, the administration decided to bring in three boatloads of native troops from other islands with British officers. They had machine guns, Bren guns, and command trucks and cars and tear gas. They wanted to attack the Tanna Army! So they all get together, this crazy invasion force, and they went over to Sulphur Bay and up to the barrier. Nambas was on the other side. "Where's the Tanna Army?" says the British commandant, because by this time everyone had scattered and all he could see was a bunch of natives in different kinds of clothes. Nambas wouldn't say. The commandant is getting madder and madder and Nambas more and more silent. They couldn't get a word out of him.

Meanwhile I was sitting in back of the administration forces. A lot of the Army boys were straggling in from the jungle. We're all outside watching, the Army and me, while the British argue with Nambas. The Administration stood there for three hours trying to find out where the Army was. Finally everyone got bored and went home and the whole thing faded away.

One of the boys gave me a gun as a souvenir. Well-made job, it was.

*

After the Army had gone home, I went into the village to look at their radio. It was a cast-iron boiler with the side missing and on the overhead handles there was a piece of rope which went out of the house and up to a tree. It was the same old thing—they were always putting up rope and vines as aerials and tuning in to America.

*

Somebody once asked me about the snake at White Sands. "They've got a snake in a box," he says. There are no snakes on Tanna, though there are on some of the other islands. The Tannese are terrified of snakes. If you throw a gecko at them they run a mile. Anyway, it was Yatik again, up to a trick. People would come from all over the island to see this snake. Yatik said it was the snake from the Garden of Eden. But whenever you went to see it, it was sleeping and you couldn't look at it. . . . I picked up a rubber snake in Sydney. Had it hidden in my shirt when I went over to White Sands one day. I pulled it out and Yatik took off like a shot.

Besides John Frum they had these other characters, like Jacob and Isac. It was Nambas trying to get on the bandwagon. Then Man World appeared, rather like Jacob and Isac. It was Yatik who had a vision of Man World. A big flap, like John Frum. The government agent had to send a circular to the Europeans to keep calm. The whites were getting worked up. Weak-kneed crowd. But Man World never developed. It was an effort on the White Sands side to start another movement. Happened when John Frum leaders were in exile and the movement was dormant.

I think the movement is going down [a white planter who is sitting with us agrees]. Mellis is weak. Frum needs a colorful character to keep it moving, someone like Nambas. Once he had a bit with a partition. There was an old woman in it who muttered garbled talk. Nambas would interpret it as John Frum talk. Boat coming, you must go to Sulphur Bay on Fridays, whatever he wanted the people to do.

*

[*Allan, a native Presbyterian Teacher from Erromanga*] John Frum was an American, a white man, but he spoke our language perfectly. He has not been seen since the early days, but the people are still waiting for him. He was real, not a dream, not imagination. Some people say that John is John the Baptist. When the church showed *The King of Kings* a few months ago, people said, "See, John the Baptist is John Frum." The movement is confined to Tanna, though a few people on Aniwa believe in John. They come over to Sulphur Bay and get the latest news and add their own lies.

Custom is much more than they tell you: it includes a life-for-life vindictiveness, the poisoning of enemies, black magic. The people at first seem nice but later another side shows: callousness, vindictiveness, jealousy. There are many problems here and on the other islands. We have to learn four languages, English, French, pidgin and our own. There is not enough work. Only two or three men in a village will have a job, mainly working for the Condominium on some kind of menial labor.

The Church's work here is frustrating. They have been given the Light but they will not accept it.

AN ASIDE ON THE
STONED AGE

A relic of the Stoned Age

You may have noticed the continued references to kava, and wonder why it was forbidden. The reason is simple: kava is a pleasant narcotic, a heavenly Trip. Pleasure being sinful in the eyes of the Presbyterians, kava was banned. But such a Trip one gets from kava! I would drink it every day if possible.

*

Kava forms the climax of the day for the Tannese, as for many other peoples in the South Pacific. About three-thirty in the afternoon the men begin to get restless, and those who have watches continually glance at them. The others estimate the time from the sun. At four they begin to drift toward the kava grounds, a clearing outside each village where women are barred. Often the clearing has a small house which is used in bad weather.

Kava must be prepared fresh each day. It does not keep, and is drunk immediately after preparation. Kava is the root of the plant *Piper methysticum* and is a cousin of *Piper betle,* the betle nut chewed by many people in Asia and the Pacific. Betle, in certain forms, is a narcotic. Kava, as prepared in the New Hebrides, is also a narcotic, a very pleasant and enjoyable one.

The method of preparation is this. Various men in the village go into the nearby jungle, uproot good-sized kava plants (the bush grows to five or six feet) and lop off the trunk and branches, retaining the root, a thick, twisted mass. Each man who is to drink kava then cuts off a piece of the root (as many roots are brought in as will be needed, but no more, as one does not waste kava). Then the piece of the root is chewed at great length until it is completely pulverized. The masticated pulp is then spit out gently on one or two large leaves. The regurgitation is frankly quite unappetizing in appearance. Meanwhile there is a steady flow of conversation as men come and go, bringing in more kava or going off on errands and returning. This is the hour when gossip and information are exchanged. If a visitor is present a root with a branch attached is brought into the clearing and laid on the ground. The visitor is invited to break off the branch as a sign of friendship and chew that particular root. When enough kava has been chewed, a few men will begin to strain it into coconut shells or a bucket, using as a strainer a fiber from a coconut palm.

Then the kava juice is mixed with water in a pail or in coconut shells. In the past (and today in some other islands) kava was mixed in handsomely carved wooden bowls. Now, in most villages on Tanna, a plastic bucket is used. Finally the kava is poured into coconut shells and drunk. Some men will pour the last few drops on the group as an offering. As the drinking begins, food is brought to the kava grounds and placed on long benches.

The effect of kava is immediate. At first the tongue and lips become numb, and then it strikes the brain. Ordinarily the drinker becomes silent. "It's not you who decide not to speak, it is the kava who tells you to be quiet," say the Tannese. The drinker immediately eats his supper, the usual taro, yams and potatoes, with perhaps some bread, and a pudding made of taro and coconut milk, and in a matter of a few moments, it seems, the kava has him sitting on his haunches, deep in thought. "We talk to John," says Joe Johnson, a regular drinker of kava. "We drink kava and talk to John." Occasionally a man will go to the edge of the clearing and give a long yodel or a falsetto call. No one pays attention to him.

Silence. Peace. The quiet of the jungle. John instills our souls with his message of love.

*

Austin Coates has written: "Many attempts have been made to explain what kava tastes like. It has been compared with all kinds of things in the chemical and medical world. It was not thus that it struck me. As I drank it I was conscious of earth after a shower of rain at dawn in a wood, and of the green young shoots in a primeval spring. Never in my life have I been so conscious of man's descent from his own antiquity. If anyone had told me that I had by magic been transported back in time a million years I would not have been surprised. As far as man today is capable of conceiving what it was like to be the first human beings in the world, living in forests, this was what the liquid conveyed. It is, I feel sure, the most ancient drink on earth."[1]

Coates, however, drank kava prepared by mashing the roots in a bowl, not chewed. So if this improper method can bring such a feeling of delight, think of the effects of kava prepared in the correct, time immemorial manner.

In Fiji, once one of the great centers of Pacific culture, kava is now ground to a powder and sold commercially in baggies in grocery stores. Merely add water and drink. The Fijian Tourist Office makes a big event out of its kava known locally as *yaggona,* and issues a kava certificate to the tourist. The Tannese say that Fijian kava is "like lemonade," and laugh, lemonade being the generic term for any kind of soda drink. Fijian kava no send you on a trip.

There are some untoward effects from kava. It weakens the motor facilities: legs are first to go, and hardened drinkers, who will toss off five or six coconut shells of it, drop to the ground as if felled by a pig club. Harrisson, who was a confirmed kava drinker during his time on Malekula, says, "Kava negates the legs. You cannot walk any more when you get enough of it on board. Your arms later get almost unliftable. But you can usually crawl over the soothing earth floor to get another suck at the dope. Your head is affected most pleasantly."

Kava was and is believed to prevent gonorrhea. It was formerly used as a medication for the disease. Harrisson states that on those islands where kava is not drunk, gonorrhea is prevalent. He also adds that he drank it for a year, but "From the day I left I never craved it any more. So it is not habit-forming. It never did me any harm. Every white who had lived on that coast before me had soon died of blackwater fever. I didn't." Continued excessive use is said to bring the phenomenon of "double skin," a layer of whitish skin that resembles the common ailment of leukodermia that affects so many black and brown people in the tropics. Harrisson ascribes this problem to the use of green kava (as on Tanna); on Malekula the root was first smoked.

The missionaries faced up to kava head-on. Wipe it out! was the order, and they damned near did. It was almost totally uprooted on Aneityum in 1856, and it took nearly twenty-five years before a respectable crop could be grown again. But when kava was banned by missionaries, the natives turned to alcohol, a much worse affliction. Liquor was freely sold by traders and ship captains, who could easily outwit the missionaries. Where kava produced peaceful intentions ("You cannot hate with kava in you," wrote Harrisson. "And so it is used in the making up of quarrels, and in peacemaking."), alcohol brought violence. The old fire water business, as witness that famous victim, the American Indian. Today natives may buy beer in the New Hebrides but not hard liquor. A funny situation, that—a Melanesian from outside the islands can have all the liquor he can buy and more than he can hold. But not a New Hebridean.

The old Presbyterian laws against kava are no longer observed, and throughout most of the New Hebrides it is drunk every day. Nowadays on Tanna the ritual is considerably simplified. Any man, from twelve or so on, may help prepare it. On certain islands in Melanesia teenage men prepare it; on others virgin girls, the chewing itself not being intoxicating but only the drinking of the prepared liquid.

*

My own experience, as a convert to kava, brings a different reaction to that of the kava-ordered silence. My mind goes off in a hundred directions, soaring and swooping like a graceful flock of birds; ideas rush and tumble, arise and fill the treetops, and I am extremely vocal. Tom the magician, the one man in the village who did not drink kava during my first trip, has been talking quietly to me about stones. I am suddenly aware that everyone else in the clearing is quite silent. The fire flickers gently in its own quiet. I look about. The veneer of the West has gone; we are again in the Stone Age, where we belong. Tom steers me out of the clearing—I am making too much noise, and kava drinkers cannot stand sound (nor light either)—and into a jungle trail. It is still soft daylight as we plunge into the brush, but my next memory is of pitch darkness, with a pair of auto headlights approaching me. It is the British District Agent in a jeep. "I'm stoned out of my skull on kava," I say by way of introduction, this being our first encounter. "That's all right," he replies, "I'm stoned on martinis." At my bungalow I give him a beer. He says, "I don't know how you feel about Vietnam, but it's been the wrong war for you Yanks. You don't know how to fight a guerrilla war." "We did once," I reply, "and we won." "When was that?" "1776," I say, and add that I'd like to look at the government files on John Frum. He refuses, saying that they're classified. I offer to steal some great secret American document (bad joke, that, considering Watergate et cetera) in return, but the District Agent says that even if he had the authority he will not give me the John Frum file.[2]

JOHN FRUM HE COME

[*Sam Tacuma*] When the earth was formed the first man was
Kalpaben. When John came he said he was the Son of
Kalpaben.[1] He's brought up with the earth.

John must be someone sent by God, because when I think of
the Bible, the Lord's story, no other being can come but by
God. While John came here, I thought nobody would come
besides God, and when he brought back Custom, I thought
it must be someone God knows.

They first found a man on the other side before John came.
Isac came first. After, when the people heard someone has
come, they came and repeat to John that someone has come,
he said: "That is Isac."

Some say Isac was a Red Indian. Sometimes when you walk in
the jungle you find there a man who is red, not white like a
European or black like the usual people.

After that they don't call for Isac but they call for John.

Joe Nalpin's letter

Joe Nalpin he work as police boy in Vila. He wrote letter to some
big man here saying put up a small house for John Frum. To
have house ready for John to come and live on it and speak
to the people. So the letter came. It was very strict at that
time for letters. So Mr. Nicol took the letter and broke it
with a scissor and then closed letter and send it across here to
Somo. Soon as letter come here, police come and arrested
him with others. This was the first punishment. When they
arrived in Vila from here, the police uniform was taken off
from Joe Nalpin and put him in jail.

[The letter was written in one of the Tannese languages. Nicol
and the Presbyterian missionaries had it translated by someone

loyal to them. It was written to Robert Somo, Nalpin's father, and to Sam Nako, a chief, both living at the time at Lenakel.]

DEAR FATHER SOMO,

I am Joe. I forgot something I had to tell you I say to you Somo and Sam Nako that I come here to Vila. The Government at Tanna tied you up but that is nothing. Do not forget the tobacco which came to me from John Frum and Nauka. John Frum wanted Nauka to show him the road to come out. Nauka did not know the road so he sent the tobacco to me, to you Somo and to Sam Nako. I made the road so that all the chiefs could go and shake hands with John Frum because I was not there but Karaua softened his heart and showed the chiefs John Frum. John Frum only spoke to them because he did not see me with them. He asked Karaua where I was and Karaua told them I was in Vila.

John Frum and I were together and we arranged that all the others should come to Vila. We talked together about them [the chiefs] and we arranged that the chiefs should follow us when we came out of jail.

John Frum and I came to Sidini [otherwise known as Sydney] to look for a place for a house. John Frum pointed where his house was to stand just alongside mine but he did not describe what kind of house. So listen well you Somo and Sam Nako: Nako will provide three men, Natoga will provide three men: Bangor will send three men to build the house and Sidni will provide the food for the workers.

You are not to say that the house is for John Frum or for me, but just say it is a company or a communal house.

We two are only waiting for the chiefs to go back to Tanna and when the house is ready you will send word to us and John Frum and I will come to the house you will have prepared at Sidni. Then John Frum will gather the white men and talk to them. He will send his son to America to bring the king. You must not be afraid. He showed me aeroplanes at Lonopina [also known as Tukosmeru] as thick as the bush.

You must conceal the contents of this letter. This is not my
letter, John Frum is sitting by me as I write. This is the end
of my letter, but John Frum's is underneath.

john the great
my brother here is joe : my name is karapanaman
every thing is near to us
see us two joe captain cockle shell

I am Joe. I am saying to you brothers and father that this spirit
writing speaks to you these four lines only wich you see. See
how his writing has no capital letters. He says cockle shell.
The meaning of this is that we two fit like the two halves of
a cockle shell. Everything will come from Sidni John frum
wants you to answer this letter by the Morinda.

Lauhman Teni speaks

The first man that John appeared to was Jack Kohu. This man
[John] appeared near Green Point; the villagers were afraid
that he was coming to take their women, that he was a thief.
They took a shilling to divine the future and gave it to a clever
man whose name was Noga. When Noga found out about
John through his magic, he knew that this man was something
special. Noga told Jack Kohu that John was a man of wisdom.
So Jack Kohu took a ripe banana—a banana, not a plaintain,
which is cooked—and gave it to John outside the village.
John ate it. Noga said to give this man fruit, bit by bit, cold
fruit at first and then cooked fruit. So for several days John
is waiting outside the village being given fruit. Finally Jack
and his people went to the beach with a fowl and roasted it.
Jack took the leg and ate it himself while walking up the beach
and met this man. Face to face, direct with John, and gave
him the rest of the fowl. John ate it. The people began to talk
together with John.
John ate as a human being. We never knew if he could have
been a human being or was on the other side, but he showed

us that he was a human being. Next John told Jack Kohu to
go to the beach and catch a fish. Jack did so, and brought the
fish back to his wife who roasted it in leaves in the fire, and
when the fish was cooked Jack took the fish down to the beach
and met John and gave him the fish and John ate it. After he
finish eating, John gave the bones to Jack Kohu. Jack gave
the bones and the leaf to the village and told them to burn the
bones at the time when the morning star rose, right before the
dawn. So they did this—burned the bones when the morning
star rose. After burning the bones Jack met John again.
John said: You have done according to what I said.
Then John said to go shoot a bird (a certain bird we call iouin
atvan, a large bird with white chest, the biggest bird on Tanna
island, a sort of king pigeon, edible) and then Jack shot one
and gave it to his wife who roasted it in leaves. The next day
Jack gave the bird to John and did the same with the bones.
He burned the bones again according to John's instructions.
"By doing all of these things you have grasped all of me," John
said. The people have done all John said and grasped all of
him.
John said: "There is somebody else coming after me. He will
dress in the same way but you must be careful of this man,
because he isn't John but Nakua. He is John's enemy."
John is really man, but Nakua is satan, an evil spirit. John says:
"If I come, I will come direct, close, but when Nakua comes
he will stay faraway. That is how you will know."
Nakua has been near the village for several days but he has not
come close. John is the man who comes directly to them.
John has told Nakua that by standing far away it is not good.
"Let's both of us go close and sit with them as they are
ignorant. They'll have to prepare two plates." The people
have prepared a plate each for Nakua and John. The meal is
ready. John told Nakua to go first and that he mustn't hide
in a spiritual way but must go to the people clearly, but when
Nakua approached he did not enter directly into the village
but sent only his spirit. The people didn't see him. He ate in
a spiritual manner, that is, his spirit ate the essence of the food.

John was the only person to notice this. He was waiting
outside the village. When Nakua returned, John was angry.
"I asked you to go in your human body, but you went as a
spirit. So now I'll go myself in my human body so they will
see me." John went into the village and sat down and ate
together with the people. After eating John went outside
the village again where Nakua was waiting. Now Nakua
was angry. He said to John: "You went with a human body
and the people talked together with you." But you know that
Nakua is a powerful man too: he put John in prison.

Nakua thought that John was still in prison and afraid to leave.
But John saw the people again. Now they started a war, just
John and Nakua. It began at Ielaik and raged around all of
Green Point.

When the war was beginning John announced to the people
that there would be a war, but he gave them a warning:
"When you hear the whistle, you must escape from
Eriapagkakil to Ienamihia, going around the point. You must
escape, otherwise you will die!"

When the war was being fought, the people could hear the noise
of the guns but they couldn't see the battle. They had to stay
at Ienamihia and keep listening to the whistle. When the
whistle was blown they had to escape back to Eriapagkakil.

When it's only John and Nakua, then John's brother-in-law
Karapanimum—he comes and he's helping John in the fight
against Nakua. From Green Point they chase him up to the
Lenakel side of Tanna and then the war was ended. They had
won the battle against Nakua. When the war was ended, the
people saw Nakua's blood in the sea, all over the sea at
Lenakel. John and his brother-in-law appeared again to the
people. This is the first time they saw John and
Karapanimum. As they appeared to the people, the people
liked to see Karapanimum, to be more conversant with him.
Karapanimum said: "I'm just like you, like Jack and the
others. Don't come to me. I'll live and die just like you. But
John is living forever. He's the only person people should
follow."

By "forever" Karapanimum means that you can change into a
young person again. A kind of rebirth, regeneration. John will
always be young.

Karapanimum speaks again: "My father is Atumi and my
mother is Ivi. That is, in English, Adam and Eve, from the
beginning. These are the words that appeared in the Bible.
And when the world was made, John lived. John IS."

They disappeared and Karapanimum did not come again, but
only John.

This is the main part of John and it is all you need to know, but
there is more if you are interested.

*

So far John has appeared only to his village. Now he appears to
important people around Tanna. He called all the big men
from this place. I myself did not see John then but my father
did.

In the beginning, in the 1930s and early 1940s the people kept
the news of John to themselves—the Gospel among the
"heathens"—but not given to the Christians. John made
himself known where the missionaries were trying to end
Custom, though the people believed in the Communion he
could be put in prison, the church prison at Aneityum. This
was before the British and the French came. Dr. Nicholson
punished the people with the help of the Christian converts.
They were killing our Custom. They called us "heathen."
Heathens! for what God had given us and they were trying
to take away. That is why we can no longer trust the whites.
We were afraid. The people didn't know how to get help.

Only a few people were able to retain Custom, most of them
being people who had been taken to Queensland and had
returned. Some of them asked the captain of a ship about
government and they then requested a government from
Australia to save them from the missionaries. This was before
the time of the Condominium.

The first governor lived at White Sands. But we realized
that he did not help the people but sided with the missionaries

and the converts. Again we did not know what to do, so we asked for the French. That was another mistake.

We made an agreement for the French to come. Now the Condominium is formed, but Custom is not allowed to return. Everything seems lost. Custom dance is not allowed for Christians. There are only a few "heathens" left.

Then about 1912 an American named Mr. Hambris, a tourist, appeared. He had heard about Custom and told the people they must practice it. A custom dance was held at Isangel with Mr. Hambris. He wrote it down in his book and took it back to America.

All this time the Church is moving slowly, trying to cover the whole island, trying to take away the Custom. Custom is almost finished. And now it's the time when John came. If John hadn't come Custom would have been lost. John came to put everything in order again. John said: "The Ten Commandments—that God gave." But the Christian commissioner blocked drinks, dancing, circumcision, polygamy and food prepared by "heathen" people as unclean—this is what the missionaries say. John said: "The Ten Commandments are real but so is Custom real."

John came and asked for Sam Nakou because he was a member of the Church and understood the Bible. Sam brought all the men from around Tanna together, the Christian elders and heathen chiefs, at Green Point to meet John and talk to them. That was sometime about 1930. When the people met John he started talking to them, telling them to go back to Custom. John said: "There is nothing wrong with the Bible. The Bible is true—(he told Nakou)—what God has made is clean. Jesus came to fulfill the Law, the Son of God came to fulfill the Law, not to destroy. Everything in Custom is right. There's nothing wrong with it. What people eat won't destroy the life of man."

After Nakou met with John he was afraid to let the government know what has been going on. But John said not to hide it, to tell everyone including the missionaries.

Finally Nakou told the government indirectly that someone has come and spoken to the people. John had told Nakou that he wanted the British District Agent, Mr. Nicol, to come and shake hands with him. Nicol was afraid and sent Nakou to see if John is really human or if he is an evil spirit. Nakou himself met John and returned to Mr. Nicol. Nicol asked what John looked like. Nakou said, "He's a human being." Nichol got angry that Nakou believed John was a human being. (Nakou was an officer in the government.)

So John went to all the big men on Tanna in one big meeting. It was held at night at White Sands, in east Tanna. Among the men present were Nambas, Boida, Chief Koukare and various others. They met John, and Koukare and the other people talked with him. Koukare whispered to some of the others that John was not a man but an evil spirit. However, Nakou and his people said, "He is not an evil spirit but a man."

Koukare and his people then whispered to each other and talked about one of their own men who had just come to White Sands just like John and knew what they were talking about and what John said to Koukare and Nambas and Boida. They said to John, "We have just been talking about one of our own men just the same as John." John said to them: "What is the name of the man who has just come out?" They said, "His name is Isac." John said: "Do you know the meaning of Isac?" They said, "No, we don't know." "The name Isac means 'everyone is crying.' The whole village cannot escape death."

Now the people are divided, White Sands against Lenakel. The people at White Sands [on the eastern coast] began to take Nakou and his people and put them into jail. The missionary from White Sands, Dr. Reverend Bell, and Koukare and his people made up their minds with the government to put the people on this side [Lenakel] into jail. Mr. Nicol send everyone from here to Vila. From the Lenakel side sixteen people were arrested and sent to the calaboose at Vila, and from White Sands side Nambas, Nakou, Boita and Mellis and some others. Twenty-five or twenty-six in all.

We were arrested by the police. In handcuffs. Some of us were taken from our homes. Just brought before the "court" and then sent to prison. No charges against us, no opportunity to defend ourselves. We are in jail. Mr. Nicol, Chief Koukare and the Reverend Bell were the judges. We were given fifteen years each and put to work on the roads at Efate breaking stones.

There were ten prisoners to a room. We worked on the roads until four, and then we had our showers. At half past four John would come. The door was locked, but when he came it would open by itself. Or he would come through the wall. Every afternoon John met us at four or five and talked to us. He told us what to do and what would happen. "The war is coming soon," he said. John was calling for the Americans to come to Vila and help the prisoners. The Americans will free them and they will work in Vila. It was very secretive: only the prisoners knew that the Americans were coming. On Friday John told us that the next day an American plane was coming. John knew but not the government. The plane landed at sea and the man came ashore and talked to the Resident. The prisoners already knew what would happen. The plane landed and the man talked to the Resident. This was the only place where they knew the plane was coming, and the man would talk to the Resident. Saturday afternoon about four o'clock John came and told them: "You'll have to watch the horizon and exactly at eight you'll see something there." So what happened?—by half past seven we had seen nothing, but exactly at eight the American boats were all over the Vila harbor. These were the open boats [LSTs] and the troops went in straight away. They went all over the island.

Our case was going to be appealed to the court. The American officers appeared before the British and French Residents and asked for men to build the road. The prisoners were willing to do it. The Americans were on our side.

Then we worked on the roads with the help of the Americans. When we worked before they came, it was with our hands, but with the Americans we put the stones in a machine which ground them up. After work we went back to jail at four o'clock. After our bath we met with John in the prison.

John told us that the next day the Americans would come to take us out to work. We worked alongside the Americans, which displeased the Resident. We received $6 per month plus food. The Americans wanted to pay more but the Resident blocked us. Then the government took us out of the prison because we were too close to the Americans and moved us to another camp. We still worked on the road. John appeared at the new camp.

Now he had another message for us. "If one of the prisoners should die, Tanna will change and the people will see what John is saying is true." Then on Saturday evening John came and promised them that one of the prisoners must go to the American camp. It was a camp only for the top officers. John himself was staying there—the Americans don't recognize him because he has changed his appearance. Now he is white.

The next evening John came again and asked: "Who is willing to die?—who is willing to die for the good of Tanna?" It was a hard question; we were all afraid. I was having my bath when some of the other prisoners came to me and asked me to volunteer.

John said: "I asked the big men, 'Who is willing to die for the sake of Tanna?'—but none of them is willing. . . ." I then said directly to John, "If what you have been telling us is true, then I'll die for the sake of Tanna so someday it will have a better life."

As soon as I was asked, John gave me two tiny sticks, two of them, and told me to take the sticks to the American camp. He said that I was going to talk with a big man in the camp; but: "Before you talk, put both sticks in your right jaw and chew them." In front of the camp there were three soldiers guarding it. As soon as one soldier saw me coming up, the first one, he fired at me—he didn't bother to ask what I was doing—just fired. I jumped. The bullet went through a truck and made a hole in it. The other soldiers grabbed me and brought me inside. The rest of the soldiers were at mess. When they saw me they were all afraid and ran outside. So I was left inside the house with the top officer. Mr. Honest was the leader, the captain. Captain Honest. I stood there for about an hour when one of the soldiers came up to me and began to talk. We sat at a table (I was chewing the sticks as John had instructed me); the officer said, "Why have you come here?" I said, "I have come to meet the leader." The officer said, "No, the leader isn't here." I said, "As soon as I entered the room I saw the leader right in front of you." The officer was trying to discourage me. So I asked him for a Bible. He had a small one in his pocket. I said, "The Bible tells the truth. I've been taken prisoner, so my Bible has been left behind. I left my Bible behind but my Bible tells the truth. I don't know about your Bible—"

So the officer admits, "Yes, the leader is here." Then three times I asked to meet the leader and three times the officer says, "No, that is impossible." He says, "Just tell me what you want to say and I will bring your message to him." Then I said, "I didn't do any killing, why did I get fifteen years? What is the reason?" I wanted the leader to promise to tell me the day of my release from prison. John has already told me that I will be released on Wednesday. This is why I have been sent to the American camp, to find out if what John tells us is true. The officer (his name is Mr. de Fauncey) brought the message to the leader, to Captain Honest. He confirmed the message— the following week we will be released and sent back to Tanna.

"As soon as you are sent back to Tanna the American troops will go home to America as well." On Wednesday at six P.M. the Burns Philp boat *Marinda* arrived at Vila and loaded cargo via dinghy and went to Santo and back all in the same day [a physically impossible task]. This was the boat that was to take us home to Tanna. John came that night for the last time in the British jail. Our final conversation was this: he told me "that the work you have done must not be a story for the Europeans, but what I say must be done in the future.

Tomorrow you'll be leaving Vila for Tanna. As soon as you leave Vila the Americans will go. The road you built will have to be damaged so the British do not have it for their use. The dozer and the truck will have to break up the whole thing." So we broke up the road. "As soon as you return to Tanna," said John, "you must send your children to school. Hang on to your jobs as teachers and government workers, attend church worship." John's final words that night were: "Now I'm going."

Now he's going and the prisoners are released from jail. This is what he had promised them. He's going away and they are coming back to their home. Someday we'll meet each other at Laminuh [the sacred spot of Tanna] by Lenakel. Then the people will be as many as ants.

John came to do something, to help us. But the two governments are so strong against him, blocking him from helping us, the Tannese people. John is putting pressure on the British Resident to make him do what the Tannese want. But often the Resident doesn't do what John wants, the way John wants. All the pressure is on the British. The French block us completely, the British only part of the time. That is why we were taken to prison. We were the leaders. Though we were prisoners, John appeared to us.

*

The Americans came directly to Tanna to get men, not to Malekula or Santo. John is trying to connect Tanna and America. At first the Americans asked for some men from Malekula to unload a ship but they took a month, so then they asked the prisoners at Vila if they could get men from Tanna. John told us while we were in prison that men from Tanna were being brought to Vila by the Americans. The first boat took five hundred men to work for the Americans, and then the second boat took five hundred more to work for the American Navy. They worked for four months for the Americans, mainly in Vila and Santo, and some in Malekula, because there the people do not know how to work hard. The wage was then $6 per month U.S.; the same work would now pay $60 or $70.

*

Nicol went to Vila about 1943 and died in a truck accident. His own truck. Nobody knows who did it. It might have been John. Mr. Nicol got this expert from Vila with strong equipment to catch John but he could not. Next Mr. Nicol got this Frenchman, some name like Mr. Enna. Mr. Nicol got this launch from Condominium and told Mr. Enna where place is where John is. They took launch and go South. As soon as they got outside on the sea by the beach at Lenami that Frenchman says, "There he is sitting, watching us from the mountain." Mr. Nicol thought Mr. Enna going to do something. Going to Green Point, almost at Green Point, Mr. Enna says, "There he is, but I'm afraid I cannot do anything, our equipment is not enough." So without doing anything they went around and came back. Mr. Nicol was very annoyed with Mr. Enna and sent him back to Vila. And very soon Mr. Nicol had an accident.

So you see!

*

[*Sam Tacuma*] I said to that man[2] that John came to us to lead us out of bondage. When the missionaries came they stopped our Custom—kava, dancing, circumcision. They put us out of church if we disobey. The people hear of other islands, but Custom is not stopped there. We wonder why the missionaries stopped us. Then John came to lead us from the bondage of the mission. That is what I think.

John is a white man like you [Sam Tacuma says to me]. He wears shorts and a shirt.

John Frum, when he came, he came like a thief, like a robber. They thought, "Somebody coming to rob the girls." While they watch with a bow and arrow and the spears to kill him if he come to steal. Why, they watch every night to block him. He run to this side and to that side and they got hold of him.

Jack Kohu was the man who blocked John. Jack forced him, he jumped over the stone, one big rock. He wanted to escape out of Jack's hands.

By and by he talk to Jack. He said: "You kill a fowl for me and roast it. I'll come back and eat it." Next day Jack he kill fowl and roast it and that man came back in evening about six o'clock when they give him the piece of fowl. "Take this bone and put it in the fire," this man says. Jack promised when seeing morning star, put bone in fire.

They did that. Again he ate with them. On the next day he began to talk to them, to one man, Jack Kohu, to make a small house, to make a partition in that house. John stand on other side and talk. He's living with them about three years, I think. He told them many things. Sometimes he make like a commander. He tried to train them like a police. He did many things. Many stories. But because they are a heathen people they did not understand well. He called my father because he was a chief and a chief from the other side, they both went up to meet John. When they went, some other men they are waiting. They formed two lines for John. He walked in the middle and shake hands with all of them. He came up to the place where they put a seat. He sat with the two chiefs one on either side of him. When he opened his communication with them he told them that story like Moses that he had come to lead them out of bondage.

He came like that, in that manner. It should be the end of our story, but he told them in the old days, when you went to Queensland, you came back and put your money in a basket instead of spending it. Now you must spend it on your bodies. Everything is finished. The people took out all their money, thousands, and traded it. The white people don't understand. Everything is finished in Burns Philp and Hollandia in Vila. They might hide it because the war is coming. Makes me think, the war is coming, the shops are empty. That is why John said it is finished. When we went to Vila we can see nothing in the shops. They are empty.

Johnson told my father, Johnson in America, that man will
raise the price of copra. The people will get back their money.

*

When John talk to them, he asked about their braveness. When
the white people punish them, they will be brave. Put them in
the calaboose and keep them in prison and make them work on
the road. The people say, "We are ready for punishment."
John: "If they should shoot you, will you be brave?" They
said, "Yes!"
That was the Condominium government he was talking about.
After, when he saw their braveness, John asked them what they
needed, what they wanted him to do for them.
When John asked them, one said, "I want to be in the white
house, live like white people." And one said, "I want to be
rich." And another said, "I want to know the English
language." That is, he wants to be educated.
When John turned to my father and asked what he wanted, he
said he wanted to be changed, change his form of body like a
crop, because we had in our history someone changed his
body. My father wanted to be young again.
But when John asked them if they drink kava while in church,
they said, "No, missionaries stopped us." But John said:
"The dancing is all right, kava is all right. The missionaries
and the converts put on extra load commandments. What
God has given is all right."
When the people hear that anything is not hallowed, they said,
"We must go back to your drinking and dancing and let the
white people take their church because they have told us a
lie. That is why we left the school. So they are going to punish
us for it. Expulsion from the Church. They tell us lies to make
us church people, but then they expel us for not believing lies.
In our Custom, before the missionaries, the devil spoke to us.
But the missionaries told us about God. When they punish us
they keep us from the Lord's Supper. We come to church but
they keep us from the Lord's Supper for six months.
The man through whom John was speaking on this side of the

island died last year. The people at Sulphur Bay, they have
another way of speaking to John. John came to Jack Kohu
all the time.

This is our side of the story, but at Sulphur Bay there is a man
John is talking to. That man is Mellis. John told Sulphur
Bay about the crosses. Now John talks through Mellis.

Mellis

Mellis is a John Frum leader at Sulphur Bay, one of the first
villages to accept John and today one of the central points in
the movement. He is a tall, thin man, reserved, almost angry in
his features. At kava time he mingles with the others and greets
newcomers from other parts of Tanna, but still everyone seems
a bit distant from him. Less laughter than with anyone else. A
dangerous man, perhaps.

Mellis has taken over after the death of Nambas and wants to
be regarded as the key spokesman for John, a role not willingly
granted by certain other men, since there is much jealousy between Sulphur Bay, Lenakel and Green Point, and the smaller
villages.

We are sitting in an open house in the center of the village;
the house is made of wood and thatch and has no walls. The
floor is composed of black volcanic sand and small volcanic peb-
bles. Yasur hangs over the village and every few minutes sends
out a loud boom, a deep rumbling belch and a cloud of smoke.
Mellis is very silent for a long time. He demands my credentials,
and I speak for several minutes. More silence. He sits crouched,
his arms across his abdomen, his face surly. Then he draws a
circle in the sand with his forefinger and puts his finger in the
center. "What does this mean?" he asks. I have to admit that I
don't know, though it may be that he has drawn the world with
Tanna in the center. But that is not what Mellis has in mind.

I say nothing. There is a long silence. Some scattered comments by a few of the men sitting around us, speaking in low
rustling whispers.

Finally Mellis speaks. "This is where we are. We are trying to break out. But we are blocked," he says.

Any comment would sound fatuous so I say nothing.

Silence.

I am restless but contain myself.

Silence.

Mellis gets up casually, disappears, returns in ten or fifteen minutes with a nice little Rhode Island Red hen, her feet trussed. Mellis places the hen between us on the black sand. She sits docilely. The other men had seemed relaxed when Mellis left; now they are tense again.

I realize that some two hours have gone by.

Then Mellis begins to talk.

*

You already know about John's earlier appearances. When John comes again before all the people John will appear from the "branches," Tanna being the root.

John first appeared in 1937. All the people around Tanna went to Green Point to see John. I was arrested in 1938 along with many of the others and was taken to Vila. I was in jail until 1941. At first we were held at Isangel. The government asked for $200, saying that the money would release the prisoners. The money was collected and given the government, but Mr. Nicol broke his word and sent us to Vila anyway as prisoners. We were in Vila until 1941 and then one of the Americans— a major, as I recall, the chief, anyway—told us that we must go back to Tanna. But we were arrested again by the Condominium and returned to Vila.

Then a second group of us was arrested and jailed in 1950. These were men from Sulphur Bay only. We were sent in exile to Malekula for seven years. Then we were released again and sent back to Sulphur Bay. We were at home for a year, and then came more arrests. Five of us were imprisoned at Vila for a year. All these arrests, the terms in jail and the exile, were because we believed in John and followed him. We stood by John even though it displeased the government and meant imprisonment for us.

When the first group returned here in 1957, John ordered us to make a bamboo fence and to raise the flag. John said to tell the people that this sign means the last punishment. The flag had been given us by the American commandant. John was seen by people at that time, and I myself am still seeing him today. John left me a few days ago, saying he is going to America and will come back. How long he will be gone I don't know, but he left on Saturday and sent me to the South. He went away and promised to come back today, Friday, but he may come back tomorrow.

After the last punishment we were still going to the church. But we had a bad preaching: whoever is a John Frum member is evil-smelling and not near God. That is what the Presbyterians told us. So John said to us: "Right, let's have our crosses in the village and be there with them instead of going to the church." So we built crosses around Sulphur Bay and other places. The red paint is only a sign showing the red from the flag that was given us by the American leader.

We raised that flag on fifteenth February, 1957.

    *

John is a Tannese, but because of friendly, spiritual emanations he's going on visitations from America. He often visits America. He does not change. He looks the same today as he did in the first place.

Who is John? As I have said, I am tired after all these years of answering questions, but I will explain once more.

Kalbapen represents the European word for God. In other words, John is the son of Kalbapen. But I myself think that John *is* Kalbapen. John *is* God.

John has been with me all these years and will come again. How, I am not sure, whether here or someplace else, whether friendly or not. We cannot be sure how we will see John again.

    *

[After this there is more silence. Then a slight, bearded man in a green turtleneck shirt and a lava-lava begins to talk angrily at me. Other voices join in, and Mellis takes part in the argument.

Everyone is becoming enraged, really furious. Finally there is a silence and Mellis speaks again.]

How long are we to wait? We have waited so long and we are tired. What should we do? Should we continue to wait or should we do something else? Mr. Johnson came here with his people in 1957, the same year that we raised the flag, and made us promises. This person Johnson came and spoke to us but his words are unfulfilled.

That man has cheated us. We cannot recall exactly what he promised but nothing has come. We took him to the top of the volcano and did a custom dance for him. We gave him presents. He had his brother with him. He came by boat to Lenakel, and then from there to here by truck. Then he went back to America and became President and forgot about us. That man Johnson has cheated us.

How long should we wait?

Tom Hiwa, S.D.A.

[Tom Hiwa is a member of the Seventh-Day Adventist Church. He was once a Presbyterian, and is said to have been an R.C. for two years. He lives in a small house with his family on the side of a mountain, near Bethel, the S.D.A. village at Ebul Bay.]

Was one American man. He started long time one ship he named *Mortau*. Raise sail, run engine. Ship run copra New Hebrides bout 1920's. Sam Nakou worked on *Mortau*. In Vila one big man BP come pick up copra. Finish work long nine o'clock, go shopping. All right. All fellow go ashore. That man American look Sam Nakou. He speak: Sam you long Tanna. You want, I give you something. He gave five pounds gold money, he tell Sam you takem that money, you takem long Tanna that ship, you go village you hid that money long box, you take long store, you pay something but you hid it that box.

Sam, he pass, 1930. You watch him, 1940, something happen.

He no tell anybody. All right! Something started in South, 1938. We hear smallsmall news. We talk about small story gold bout 1939 story got more big. All right, 1939 we call close to end 1939, November, Sam, my brother Natomah. This man Natomah, Sam Nakou, he told him, he prisoner Vila. Sam now he tell me something, he walk long that ship *Mortau* he give him five pounds gold, he watch him years 1940. Sam told me: listen, the name John Frum come.

Mr. Nicol go down South, sits around. Mr. Nicol he start asking questions. Long that young man Samson Kurau, you look, man, he says yes. Kaikai, he eatem? He got name? Yes, he got name? Who? JOHN FRUM.

Mr. Nicol he write letter long Vila same day. He go back. We talk about small story we hear name JOHN BROOM.

Nother day. We heard name John Frum about one month more. He send this Samson Kurau. He come village where we live, village called Loana Bilis, he got one old man, Green Point he deported here. His name Peter Koiniimana. This young Kurou say you find him someone he know English. He told Mr. Nicol, me John Frum you want Sam Nakou he come shake hands.

Everything start trouble now. He just go. By six o'clock he got inside, hear voice. No look, only listen. Now he ask Nakou some question. You speak, Sam—Sam he listen.

Mr. Nicol he not go Green Point. Send policeman, made people come here. Police burn down John Frum house later. Police report. Mr. Nicol send them back burn house. Now trouble is beginning.

John Frum speak, Custom good, church good. When people come home he speak. Leave school, all young people leave school.

In beginning long time ago line big men John Frum come up and shake hands long Green Point. Looked like Samson, Jack Kohu, but John Frum different. He stand over there.

John Frum no American soldier [as Trumbull reported]. He speak Tannese like Kalpaben, Karaparamum. He come through window in Vila, smoke cigarettes but he look

something different. He spirit. Some people think John Frum
he spirit, some think he man.

When you go long Green Point, house where he talk, you sit here,
John there. In other room. No body but voice.

We wait there, he come there through this door by us, go in
room, we hear his voice. He speak Green Point Tanna. He
talk bout Bible, Old Testament long Israel people in Egypt.
Bad king he drag him long work. He talk bout that question.
He say native here like people long Israel. We hear story might
help us. Long time, 1940.

He just go. "You watch him something will happen."

In war time Vila all big men in prison but we watch him people
long America we work with we look, savvy. We work, look
shadow belong John Frum.

Native say, when John Frum come through, you get money like
white man. Build road get money.

But, yes, long war time Vila people come North, South go Vila.
Tom [the American in charge of construction] he one good
fella man. Money, more food. Plenty food. Money, small kai
kai meats. Now Tom ask where we been working come Tanna,
two three trips. Say he come back.

"Some time we meet again," Tom say.

That what Tom he say. Thin man sweating away. In between
young and old. Plenty good man for native.

"Some time we meet again."

*

John Frum he went away. He not come here but there.
Everywhere you look he somewhere else.

We help one another but whiteman no want. John only mouth,
he speak only story. No help.

All prisoner he come home every one. Three men Samson Munhil
Nalpin all big men he stay here five years.

Now this Tom Navy he bring company home small ship. He
ask, you want anything, you want go home quick Tanna? Tom
bring boys back Tanna.

People wait for Tom Navy he come back.

Now people wait for John. Years and years people wait.

John coming soon? I don't know. All people wait and wait. Some people say, Aaah . . .

Perhaps he never come.

Only like that, like spirit.

Some story John has a son? . . . All right!

*

Two years belong S.D.A. Big talk talk American very weak, England strong long time ago. Now England sink, America rise up. Ten kings rule that earth. Now last king. That spirit come, powerful king he come, come through here, through Tanna. Not Jesus Christ but some other spirit. You steal something, put in pocket, spirit see.

S.D.A. no believe John Frum. No allow Custom, no kava, no pork, no drink wine.

Red Cross long Sulphur Bay something like Roman Catholic. Same as R.C. I look at R.C. church but not go in.

Long talk Roman Catholic might make big trouble big persecution people. Bible say that. One strong power, R.C. Me think, read Bible. Roman Catholic very powerful, got South America.

Me think John Frum save people from Roman Catholic.

Some story John Frum come Tanna, save Tanna from R.C. Me think long Bible prophecy Roman Catholic got South America, more power got much power. Roman Catholic make big trouble.

Prophecy third three world wars coming. All nations destroyed, world finished. Only God can save. It is the end. No man can stop war. God alone. That is prophecy. One war, two war. Third war is end.

Everything be okay along island Tanna plenty people he die long end of this year but we pass along to next. Now we can't look what happened long this year good or bad we try we see, we ready for Second Coming is very near.

Who have kept the truth will enter in and receive their reward this is my last word.

Man-Tanna he speak

[*Various voices*[3]] Up hill man give small rice for land, top hill, government compound now, for small small bag rice. Worth plenty money but native get only small rice.
Mr. Paul he steal but now we get wise.
White man fill pocket sell you rubbish.
Once I go Mr. Paul store now I get angry his store.
No copra, no penny. Man work Condominium get money.

*

White man give two rifles my grandfather for small piece land for building house. Two or three acres says white man. When white man register land he claim three hundred acres, running down to sea. How can we trust whites? They come to say they our friends and then they take everything. I think, find out price two rifles, offer same money to white man grandson. But I think, he tell me go to hell.

*

We were terrified when the whites appeared. We thought they were evil spirits. When they landed here, the missionaries, they used only the Bible. Bible only. We're not speaking English as well as you because we're facing only the Bible, nothing on the side. Thinking like this it is our lights to leave the place where we go when we leave this earth to our God in heaven. That's why we know that Jesus he come in the world, he died for all mankind. That's why we understand Jesus is Son of God. When John Frum come out, we all left the church. John said: "You understand the Bible already. The government doesn't do his duty."
John said again: "You go, just go everyone of you, to the church, put your children in the school." But no school at that time. Nobody go inside the church. My father and I and Joe Johnson [the elder] we went to Mrs. Armstrong [wife of the missionary] and asked her to teach our children. Now they

speaking English well, not like the old days. We are starting schools in all the New Hebrides now. In the past they learned the Bible only, now they learned everything. They learn quickly.

When we come back to Tanna after the calaboose, things are still bad. A man says the name of John he go to jail again. The British D.A. and the French D.A. they both say they no fight against natives, go ahead with movement. As you please. But if a John Frum man, Catholic, Presbyterian, S.D.A., Custom, he goes to jail. Otherwise no punishment. Just for being John Frum man.

The Americans promised to take care of us someday. They will give us what the British blocked us from having during the war. Some of the Americans at Vila spoke Tannese among themselves but not when the officers were present. They were whites. No one knew how they learned our language.

We don't see John now because he just gone away from us. We don't know where.

John just come by that way. The Church blocks Custom, that's why John come. He doesn't say any bad words, just what's in the Bible. One great man! He has a power. You stop our Custom we are like white people. Custom is our life, our past, our future. Without Custom we are but whites.

John says: "Go ahead just like the Bible." Custom. John is like Jesus. Regeneration. We are afraid to say that, then they are against us, the Churches. They don't like to hear about John and Jesus.

When it is John's will we will meet him again someday. We don't know when.

No one has written down what John has said. We keep it in our minds.

John says he is not against the Church, only he wants all the people to live a good living and be happy in their own island. All the people from this island they must face the place where the Gospel come, the Good News come. That beach where the Word was brought ashore. We must watch the same way on the beach. First the missionaries come ashore, then someday

John will come by that beach at Lenakel. On that beach is a
coconut tree planted from a coconut John sent. That is the
spot where John will come.
By and by it will come that way where the missionaries brought
the Gospel to this island. "You and your garden face that
way!" That's where John will come.

*

Tanna is bank—the treasury—of the world. Custom people and
Christians they all believe this. In the highest mountain
Tuposmeru is treasure. Mountain is treasury. It is very true
that at night if you go there something is shining like a bright
light, something like a diamond is there. It is the treasury.
Someday John Frum will come and unlock it.
John says we are like all the peoples in the world. We are men,
not "boys."
Men.

*

We fear the Frenchmen. In New Caledonia there is no land for
the natives. The Frenchmen they have taken it all. Frenchman
he have full control. That is why we are afraid here, that the
English will go and the Frenchmen he take everthing from
us. English say, someday New Hebrides will be free but the
Frenchmen say he will never go. So the English must stay
to protect us, otherwise Tanna will be like Nouméa, a prison
for the native.

*

Now it is almost four. Time to prepare kava. At five o'clock we
drink kava and talk to John.
We are waiting for John to come.

A dissident point of view

[Ioulu Abbil, a well-educated Tannese who is Assistant Coopera-
tive Officer for the Southern District of the New Hebrides and

the Tannese Representative for the National Advisory Council. The John Frum people dislike him, a fact he knows. He has been abroad—to France, America and the other islands—and is well aware of the European world.]

I think my views are quite correct. Sulphur Bay is saying too much about America, using it as an excuse for not doing anything. They don't want their children to go to school because they might lose Custom. However, one of the aims of the National Party is to include Custom in the school syllabus.

There are signs now that the situation is changing. Even the missionaries now say that Custom is all right. Both the government and the church no longer object to Custom.

The John Frum movement is essentially anti-western. Its purpose is to save the people from destruction. The Tannese make a comparison of civilizations. They believe that if they lose traditions, they will not be quite sure of the future. They don't know where to go.

Our civilization is different—communal living, gardening, subsistence economy. For example, in my own village, people make gardens on my land and don't pay rent. I don't ask them. We build each other's houses. We carry on all social activities together. One may speak of poverty but we support each other—all on the same class, not like Europeans or Americans. Everybody participates in things like feasts. There is no really rich man. One man may have more land but he is not selfish. Anyone can garden on it without paying rent. The Europeans say that education is good, but what is the end of an educated man and an illiterate man, a rich man and a poor man?

The Tannese look at it this way: if we go full into a capitalist society, a capitalist economy, some people are going to be poor immediately.

That is how I look at the John Frum movement. It is only a strike against western civilization. This is what they're afraid of, the differences that will come with Europeanization. A couple of men will be rich, more and more will be poor.

It is a strike.

If capitalism comes it will destroy their way. That's why we have
cooperatives on Tanna. Ten now, all but one of them working
very well, and the tenth coming along.

I've always been thinking that the old men are frightened of
Europeanization. I don't want Europeanization. How can
we maintain our culture?

Western civilization is very selfish when you take ours in
comparison. When you look at the world today only a few
men are getting rich. I speak against capitalism coming to the
New Hebrides today. We've been looking at the Europeans
settling on our island. If this is what Europeans are, obviously
we are going to lose our Custom and people will suffer.

The Presbyterian Church collapsed just like that when the John
Frum movement began. All the villages had little churches, all
run by missionaries, mainly from Scotland, Australia and
New Zealand. There were a few native elders but they were
not trusted by the whites. Now the churches are gone from
the villages and there are only a few in central places, like
Lenakel and White Sands.

I do not agree with the John Frum people. I tell them that. I do
not accept John Frum. But the movement is a strike, a way of
protest. I speak out against tourism. If we share, perhaps, but
not when the money goes abroad. The tourist pays in Paris,
London, New York, Sydney—that's where the money
remains. We get a few poor jobs as bus boys or maids or sell
some handicrafts for a few dollars. The same is happening all
over the Pacific, all over the world, when the whites move in.

And that's why the Tannese turned to John Frum, to regain
their dignity. They tried to do away with the white man's
civilization. They stopped going to his churches, took their
children out of his schools, even threw away his money.

It is a strike for their own way of life.

JOHN KALATE

During my early talks on Tanna, John Kalate stayed in the background, letting others tell me about John Frum. When I went to Sulphur Bay to see Mellis, John Kalate was one of the men who accompanied me, and it was he who interceded when Mellis was reluctant to talk to me. Mellis was quite suspicious of my intentions, and was nervous about my coming to Sulphur Bay. Mellis, who has tried to establish himself as *the* spokesman for John Frum, claims to have been mystically transported to the States, and he lets it be known that he sees John even now.

After hearing what other men were telling me about John Frum, John Kalate sent me a message that there were other things I should know. We began to talk, and I realized that I was in the presence of a truly remarkable man, a kind of natural mystic who has arisen untaught but knowledgeable and in touch with other worlds. John Kalate has given John Frum considerable thought, has had (apparently) mystical experiences involving John, and is able to discuss him in concepts and terms well beyond those of other men like Lauhmen Teni and Mellis.

John Kalate is a slight man, with black skin, a quiet manner, a gentle voice. He worked briefly in Nouméa when World War II began, and then for the Americans in Vila. He told me that he is the grandson of a forest spirit. The spirit was playing with some fruits, tossing them back and forth. One of them rolled into a garden where a young woman was working. She and the spirit were married, and so John Kalate is the couple's grandson.

There seems to be a John Frum within John Frum, this inner circle being represented by John Kalate and certain other men, who, however are most reticent about making a display of their beliefs. What most Tannese talk about and what the Europeans pick up is the surface of the cult, the flash and the sparks that cause gossip and attract the flighty and those incapable of deeper thought. The inner core is almost secret, private, esoteric, and John Kalate and his close associates are deep within it. This inner core, closely tied to and dependent upon Custom, encompasses much that the average believer is unaware of.

Several times John Kalate and his people said that on the day before I was to leave, he would talk to me and "tie things together." In my head I wondered why this tying together could not be done sooner, but John Kalate was insistent on waiting until the time of my departure before speaking of certain things. My leaving was delayed several times, and moved ahead and back again, but John Kalate remained calm. The day before I left he appeared at my bungalow, as he had promised, along with Henry Weiwai, and we sat on the tiny verandah and had some lunch (the usual tinned Australian food), and then he began to talk, illustrating his words with a huge diagram he had drawn on the back of a poster.

At first glance much of what John Kalate (and others) said may seem to be influenced by Presbyterianism—and Cargo in general has been criticized for its borrowings from Christianity —but Christianity itself is influenced by many other sources, drawing primarily from Judaism (which itself draws not only from Revelation but various middle-eastern and eastern religions). This is not the place to discuss the non-Christian and non-Jewish sources of these faiths, but the point I want to make is that religions do not spring full-blown from anyone's head or soul or psyche and that even Revelation is enclosed within a full body of nontranscendent teachings and many mundane events. Thus it is unrealistic, and unfair, to expect John Frum or any other cargo movement to be completely original. John Frum is a fusion of both Christianity and Tanna Custom, with a touch of western materialism, and this does not denigrate or weaken it or make it any less valid for its believers.

What follows falls into several sections, the first being an account of Tanna's involvement with America and particularly with the figure the Tannese call Tom (or Tom Navy), who has grown to be a significant member of the Tannese pantheon. I was able to track down Tom Navy, and later on you will find his account of the happenings involving the Tannese workers and the American Seabees during World War II. John Kalate's final sections become more reflective, more mystical, and here you will see some of what motivates Tanna in its involvement with John Frum.

John Kalate speaks

I was living with some friends in Erakor village [now the site of the chic Le Lagon hotel]—this was in 1939 and 1940—and was there until war broke out in Europe. The French began recruiting people to go to New Caledonia to work. While I was there the war with Japan started. The Australians and the Americans they came to Vila and they began to recruit people. They built stations there, one at Vila, one at the radio station and a third near Eluk, burying the mines and so on. The Australians found the pay scale was getting too high so they asked for help. As soon as the Japanese reached the Solomons the government spread the news around Efate to send people back to their islands. So I came back to Tanna and didn't leave again until Christmas [1942] when the American forces arrived in Vila. Mr. Nicol got a message from Vila to send workers, laborers, to go to work there. As the message went around Tanna asking people to come—they were frightened and didn't come—I was asked by Mr. Nicol if I would join the work force. My uncle Isac told him I would be one of those to join. So I went to Mr. Nicol, who explained about the war and said, "Would you be happy to go to Vila and die for your own people?" When he asked me I felt frightened, but my Uncle Isac he touched my shoulder to reassure me, and some friends joined at the same time. Other people signed up afterwards from Sidni and Isangel, people from all around Tanna came to sign.

As Mr. Nicol got answered from people coming to join, he said, "Right, you have come, now get ready at Lenakel. The *Marinda* will come to get you."

In the morning, looking out at the horizon, we saw a black thing coming. The boat went facing Green Point and turned facing

Lenakel beach. So it was not the *Marinda* but a United States Air Force boat. It arrived early to collect people. Two doctors came ashore to check us for our health. People with sores, sickness, were left behind for medical reasons. One of our people got into the boat without being examined. There was a second check at night and he was found. We were very surprised that the doctors found this man and sent him back to shore, out of five hundred people. As soon as everything was fixed one of the American doctors asked us to sing. We thought he meant church hymns or European songs. We had left our song books at home, but that man said, "No." He wanted our own music. So we knew he meant Custom songs and dance, nalena and nimaviang, just like on land.

When we were finished singing and dancing they brought out a case of apples for us. But there were too many people—the case was too small. Each man took an apple from the box and there were still apples remaining in that little box. Every man, and there were five hundred, got an apple. In that small case there were still apples remaining. That man, the American, said to us, "You must finish it," but we said, "We are satisfied," and he brought back the case with half the apples remaining. We didn't know what manner of man could feed five hundred people from that small case.

That man he divided us between ⚓1, 2 and 3 decks. He told us to go below but said if you want to go to the latrine you must go quickly now [on land]. None of you can come up. He divided all the boys into three groups.

The ship is going out now. It is about ten o'clock at night, going to Vila. We arrived at Vila about eight A.M. That man took us and divided us into different camps, those from west Tanna at Vila town, and from White Sands at eastern Efate.

The Americans wanted to feed us but the Condominium he himself insisted on feeding. The Americans said, "OK, you can feed them." The Condominium feed us for only two weeks and then he getting poor because he have no food, no more meats, flour, biscuits. One of our boys saw this and he get angry and start making a row. That American say, "What's the matter?"

"We have no food now," we say. We tell him that we go to a Belgian store and he have no rice, no flour, no meats, no sugar but nothing. We go straight ahead to B.P., same thing. So we return back to see that boss fella Tom at HQ. We talked together. Then going up to Joint Court of Condominium. They meet two Resident Commissioners, British and French, and talk about boys' food, who can feed them. No food enough for the boys. So French and British say "All right, you Americans can feed them. We have not enough to feed those people." At HQ they asking Americans, "You willing to pay and I'm going to feed them." British and French agree four shilling per day and no pay for overtime, four pounds per month. No house to live in only a copra set shed. But Tom he move those people to another place and those people start to make their own huts, grass house. He divided them, some unload cargo, some carry drums of bread, rice, flour and other stuffs. They were eating rice and meats. All around the camp leftovers they burned. Some of them made a new road around Efate. Promised three months work, three months passed and keep going.

We been talking about Tom. He divided them into works for Army and Navy. Tom took five hundred men from Tanna to work for Navy at Vila.

We walk around and find those cups and plates the Americans throw away in their rubbish and we nail them in a small case because we want to bring them back to Tanna. Tom he find the pile of cases and he asked, "What's inside?" All the boys say all the rubbish belong Americans they want to take back home, their own home. Tom he said, "What's inside? I want take out and see. Open cases," and Tom spread out meat, fish, OK. but cups and dish into the drum. All the boys very sorry for all the boys they moved out.

Tom take off these things they sad. Tom he got them together, he say, "You must listen what I say." Tom he says to them, "Your grandfather, your father they work. Went Australia,

New Zealand, Nouméa, Fiji. You know, Americans one impatient man, he rich man, but if you take these things back to your children, if you take rubbish back to your home by and by all the people say Americans rich man throwing out all that rubbish."

Ship take us back, same ship. Tom said, "I must load that ship right up with the cargo and bring them back to Tanna." Tom said, "OK?" They said, "Yes, we are happy."

Tom says, "I must ask permission British and French." He goes see them, waiting in their camp. When Tom go meet Resident Commissioner they say, "No, if you give those things to those people to take back to their homes they will not return. Work stop on Tanna because you have given them a lot of things." Tom going back to camp says, "Sorry." The boys sad again. British and French, they block Tom.

Resident Commissioner he tell Tom, "We get half money from the trader in tax when they buy from him."

Tom said to the boys, "That's all right. You will not go on that ship I've been promised but on British or French ship. I myself, Tom, must go with you back to Tanna and I will return to Vila." Tom giving the promise, "When I return back to the United States, U.S., then if God's will and still alive, we will meet again at Lenakel."

Tom wants a club.

They give Tom that club. (I carve that club, myself.) Tom says to those big men, "You see that club you give me, I will bring back this club and you will see it again." I myself designed it with an owl. I tell Tom, "We use feathers of owl only for chief." Tom says, "In America, the same. We use eagles." Here in coronation of Tanna chiefs owl feathers are bestowed.

That fella Tom he leave us all in north Tanna. Tom want to come back to Lenakel but too many waves. Mr. Nicol pick us up in his launch.

That fella Tom he like a general. Carried a walking stick with picture of man head on it.

We still waiting for Tom.

Come back Tom! With your club!

TOM NAVY

Tom Navy

The older men remember Tom clearly and he is a legend among the younger ones. On an island where virtually everyone knows everybody else it was difficult for people to accept the fact that I did not know my fellow American, Tom.

Tom was remembered as a tall, thin man, perspiring freely, wearing a dark jacket and light trousers, unpressed, unshaven, smoking a pipe, left-handed. He was generally known as Tom but a few people referred to him as Tom Navy. Tom Hiwa, I think it was, thought his name might be Tom Patti or Party. With the physical description of Tom and the knowledge of his job and the clue to his name, I was able to locate him through the U. S. Navy Public Relations office. Tom is Thomas Duncan Beatty (pronounced Bay-ty) of Corinth, Mississippi. He was born on 10 December 1905, grew up in Mississippi, went to Syracuse College in New York State, graduating in 1928. He worked for a while in New York and then returned to the South. "I had a million different jobs," he says. When the Japanese bombed Pearl Harbor, Beatty tried to enlist in the Army but was rejected as being over age. However, on his thirty-seventh birthday the Navy accepted him and he became a member of one of their Construction Battalions—a Seabee—though he says he didn't have the slightest knowledge of construction work.

With the rank of First Class Bo'sun, at $75 per month, he arrived at Efate island, in the New Hebrides. The date was the fifth of April 1942; he was to spend twenty-three months in the New Hebrides, and another fourteen in other parts of the Pacific. After the War ended, Beatty returned to Mississippi and took up residence in Corinth, a small, active town in the northeastern corner of the state, about twenty miles south of the battlefields of Shiloh. He married a local girl introduced to him by his sister and now has two daughters, both in their early twenties and married. From his home Beatty runs a small promotion organization, Allied Advertising Agency. He had three salesmen in the field, selling pens, pen and pencil sets, datebooks, calendars, cigarette lighters—"anything to give away"—that might be used by businesses, banks and other organizations for publicity. Beatty had no knowledge of the respect that the Tannese still had for him, nor did he know that he had become a figure in the John Frum movement. When I visted Tom Beatty, I asked him to talk at length first before I told him what had happened on Tanna after his departure.

*

I landed on Efate on April fifth, 1942. The Navy had put in a base at Port Havannah on the west coast of Efate, but the entrance was too small and they thought the Japanese might bottle them up there. But they overestimated the strength of the Jap military. I think the Japs had written off the New Hebrides and New Caledonia when they went back into the Solomons. The Coral Sea battle had started at the time we arrived.

The Navy found they had made the wrong decision about Havannah. By this time they had most of their forces up on Santo and a lot on Efate around Vila. The Army had a young sergeant in charge of native labor at the airfield, but he was an alcoholic and I was asked to take over. We had maybe two hundred natives out there on the airfield. One or two months later I was in charge of all the natives the Army was using. We needed about eleven hundred natives at Vila but couldn't get them locally, so we got a few from Malekula but most of them from Tanna.

A Belgian had been recruiting down there for the U. S. Army—a rough character. The men would run away when he appeared so he'd threaten to take the women and children. So then I took over recruiting too. There were about sixty-five hundred people on the island. I'd take two hundred and return them and get another two hundred. I'd send word I was on a recruiting mission and the people would turn up. From time to time, in order to get the rest of the village, I'd take some old men who should have been in the hospital, but they wanted to come.

We had a captured Jap fishing vessel, sixty-five-feet long. Deck was rotten. Had a diesel motor that had to be started with a blow torch. We had natives to run it. We could bring a couple of hundred men in it. God, they were packed in the doggone thing! The stench that came up! One hundred and thirty degrees in the hold where the Japs had their storage for fish. I don't see how the governments let me go on a recruiting trip in a boat like that, but I was expendable.

That wasn't any doctor that checked them, it was me. I took two or three I know I shouldn't. I've taken some older men that wanted to bring some grandchild. They couldn't have danced on my ship, the deck would have fallen in.

We paid in invasion money. We wanted to pay $1 per day but the French raised such Hail Columbia that we cut back to $.25 per day. Paid them monthly. After two or three months I'd take them back and recruit another bunch. My whole effort was not to offend. I let them take back Army and Navy clothes, tobacco, rice, calico for Maria. The Army was not supposed to let the natives have clothes, but I would get a call saying they would survey clothes and leave them where we could pick them up. I'd send natives up to get them on the pretext they were for me, otherwise the Army never would have released them. Only thing that worried me was that they'd get shoes. They shouldn't wear shoes.

The main thing was . . . I just looked upon them as young children. When anything came up that the natives thought was wrong I went to bat for them. I would get them tobacco, that dark tobacco, about one sixth of an inch thick and twelve inches long. They would break it off, cut it off, roll it in the hands and put it in the pipe. I got them cigarettes for five cents the pack, calico for ten cents the yard to take back. I treated them as I would like to be treated. I held sick call. I was doctor, lawyer, father confessor, everything.

They were taken advantage of all the time by the colonials. When a native would sell the whites a thousand feet of seashore, the French and the British would claim land back to the mountains, maybe a couple of miles. They were supposed to get £1 British a year, about $3.25, and many Frenchmen wouldn't pay even that. We paid two bits a day. Some would goof off, maybe a few. I wouldn't want to pay them, and then I would say, what the hell . . .

I almost had a riot one time, before we set up the last native village. The natives had accumulated some Army and Navy clothes and some stuff they had brought from Vila. This sergeant was drunk and remembered the natives weren't supposed to wear GI clothes and he opened up their small packages. I got the boss boy (from every village we had one boy in charge), I said, "Let that guy do what he wants, just leave him do what he wants. Pack up your things and hide them in the bush."

They have been bamboozled for one hundred and sixty years. I wish I could tell them something that would give them hope. They are a million years behind the niggers in our own country. (I wonder how the niggers who stayed are making out. Some of our own boys took off into the jungle. The MP's would go after them but they couldn't always tell one of ours if he kept his mouth shut.)

One of the worst things that happened was that the Tonkinese were indentured servants. Supposed to go back to Indo-China but they wouldn't return and started to give trouble. This was right before the war. So the French set up a guillotine and executed six of these boys and got everybody from miles around to see. The white women fainted and it was a miserable affair.

No cannibals left on Tanna then, but a lot of these natives had their teeth filed, especially the Malekula boys. On Malekula the Big Nambas ate the British resident's child, six, seven, eight years old, three or four years before we got down there. The natives didn't eat a white man out of hunger or spite but to get the white man's spirit.

They used to talk about John Frum . . . ["Do you know about him?" Tom asks me.] John, from the native standpoint, was an American. He came out to the islands before we got there. We think—that is the Army, Navy, French and the English—that he was a Jap who had come from the States. I imagine John

Frum is operating down there now, because the native never changes.

John Frum. F-R-O-M-M-E was the Australian spelling. Could have been three or four men put off a Japanese sub. No question about Frum being Japanese. Everything points to that. John Frum would not have advised the native to sit down and stop working, he didn't have to do that.

He said a ship would appear and take all the natives off and the island would do a flip-flop and the natives would go back. I heard that so many times from intelligent natives. It wasn't a secret. The ship would stand off Lenakel, and the island would physically turn over. But we assumed that "flip-flop" meant the Japanese or Germans would take charge and there'd be a change of government.

In my opinion John Frum did not do as much harm as the authorities thought he was doing. He did not cause us any trouble. I slept on Tanna many nights. I never had a gun or carried a gun. About that airstrip on Tanna, I think that may have been John Frum's idea. I don't know. The authorities rounded up as many of the natives as were involved in building the airstrip and took them to Vila. George Riser, my immediate authority, got them back to Tanna. George H. Riser. Captain at that time, later major. He saw things as I saw them. He's dead now.

The natives thought hell was in the volcano, and heaven too. (You're the center of the universe for yourself, and I for myself.) They all believe in John Frum. They all think he was an American but maybe a Japanese-American. He was a legendary figure. There was too much evidence that he was operating down there to doubt there was such a person. But I actually believe that there might have been more than one John Frum over a period of years. The Japanese could bring a sub up and take a guy off. But John Frum was only on Tanna. I don't think the other islands comprehended John Frum at all.

The club. When the Marines were going into Bougainville, they made a dry landing at Vila. Fifteen hundred Marines on Efate. A correspondent said the Marines went crazy over the way I treated the natives. I was everything to them. They wanted a souvenir: I gave them the club. The Malekulans had given me a cane. Made of an ox prick. Carried the penis around. It was dried and twisted, as hard as a dad-gum piece of steel. You could kill a man with it. The club I got on Tanna was about one and a half inches by eighteen. A finely done composition. I had a foot locker full of native objects and when it got to the Philippines there was nothing in it but a pea coat. Everything I had was stolen by the other Americans. Every memento was taken. Most of my officers were just a bunch of punks. They thought I had stolen government property and they broke open my foot locker. I don't know who, but.

The dead. Lord have mercy. I kept track of them. There was a certain group assigned to the Army, another to the Navy. I would write a note saying who passed away. I must have treated one hundred and fifty of them. Eighty Army, eighty Navy. Army surpassed the Navy. They died of fear and noise. Of course, a lot of them had malaria and yaws. One of the things you had to be particular about, some of the natives were afraid to go to the hospital. They'd hide under their beds. Sometimes when a native would die, I'd have the grandest funerals. I gave them a surveyed Army blanket to wrap the corpse in. They appreciated it. Weeping and gnashing of teeth until the sun set.

Americans also died. Sixteen thousand nigger troops, combat troops, and the general wouldn't let them do any work. All the time fighting among themselves. The whole thing was the Marine Corps, they were sent to make the initial landing in the Solomons. Sixteen thousand nigra combat troops on Efate, about three thousand Seabees and Marines. But Santo had a bigger base.

The nigras got in there and told them about the United States.

There was only one car on Tanna, Nicol's Land Rover. A Mrs. Eddy at Lenakel had the concession to sell the natives goods from Australia. Canned meats, especially corned beef. Raised the price one thousand per cent. About one hundred and fifty whites on Tanna in forty-two. Maybe three hundred.

The French hospital had a Boston girl. Became a nun, was sent to the New Hebrides, forgot English.

The Army recommended me for the Legion of Merit, but I didn't get anywhere. Some of those officers didn't think much of me because I was as independent as a hawg on ice. I was under instructions to give all the officers a reasonable amount of natives and send the rest to the Army storage area. But if an officer was giving me a hard time . . . he wouldn't get his natives that day.

"We will meet again." They got that from MacArthur. Everybody was discussing him. I thought after ten or fifteen years I would like to go back. Now I haven't any desire. What can one man do? I don't like flying. I won't even go to Florida.

*

Under my urging, Tom Navy wrote a letter to John Kalate. He said the club had been stolen. Then he added something about how the Tannese must have patience and should trust in Jesus. I remarked that under the circumstances it wasn't a great idea to send them "Christian" messages. Tom looked hurt. So I said, "It's your letter, you can say what you want." But I felt that preaching resignation was a very harmful idea. I was rather annoyed at the situation, at Tom for not seeing the turn of events at Tanna and at myself for not making them clear. Anyway, the letter was mailed. I'm sorry I didn't make a copy.

JOHN KALATE: II
On the meeting of Tanna and America

John Frum came first and mentioned to Jack Kohu, "I have
a son."
Jack Kohu told him to name his son after Jake Kratis (his name
Jesus Christ for missionaries).
After he named Jake Kratis as his son and went away, Jake
Kratis stayed behind looking, and John Frum went away.
God is there and his son Jake Kratis is doing everything.
Jake and Nakua both leading but if people believe in Nakua
when the day comes, his father, that is, John Frum, will stay
behind and let Nakua win.
But if people follow Jake Kratis he will fight for them on the
Judgment Day here. Similar to what Jesus do.
Jake pointed to people and said, "I'm preparing a place for
you but if you disobey my will and follow Nakua, you'll be
sorry, you won't be allowed to get in." Today we cannot say
that John is doing anything, but his son Jake Kratis is with
the people as mentioned in the Bible.

*

What is a man? John came as a person, his son is a spirit, but
when we see Jake it is the end of everything. That is, death,
when we go to Jake.
Through our Custom the people are following both Nakua
and John. Iolu Abbil follows Nakua and not John. For
example, John said, "Have gardens, have only little enough."
Nakua said, "You must have big gardens." John: "Work and
rest." Nakua: "Keep on going."
John: "Work only a little, rest, think of me, talk about me to
your neighbors and your friends. If you have friends, I'm in
the center." Nakua didn't think this way; he said: "Go
ahead." And if you keep going ahead you hurt people.
And in the language of Tanna, Nakua also means Frenchman.

*

If you think carefully you will remember John's word, that he will change Tanna. Tanna has everything. It is the bank, the treasury of all the world.

So far nothing has happened, and this is because of the Europeans. John said: "Let me drop everything, hold myself back, let it develop from the European side."

As John is the first person, the second is America. Tom tried to help but was stopped by the Condominium.

From the beginning until today God is here, Custom was there. God is sitting on His Custom. Through our Custom we love, but the Europeans are blocking us from reaching America. Law has many sides, nail point so sharp it hurts. From the

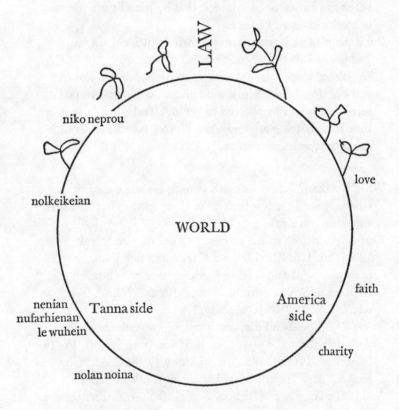

JOHN KALATE'S "WORLD"
The vines (or ropes) are trying to reach each
other over the law. (Law = Europeans)

beginning John came from Love. He reaches Law. It is hard. Law is putting people in jail.

Nolan noina is charity.

Neinian nuparhienan le Wuhein is faith.

Nolkeikeian is love.

Nikou neprou has everything, like a ship, like a kingdom. This kingdom wants to cut across, to contact America, to be equal in peace, love, charity.

It's free. From the king it was.

John came through the same thing, to come to be equal, to find the way through the Law from the European side.

He came and he stood watching. It's hard, because of the French, because of the British. America is the only place.

While he's at *Nikou neprou* he's with everything. Through Custom he's trying to reach across.

America can help him to break through.

As John Frum pointed out to John Kalate, not to chase the Europeans away but to try to find a peaceful way for his kingdom to reach the American kingdom, with the ropes that are trying to tie us together.

We cannot see John now, but if this end, American can smash the LAW, wash it out as it was in the beginning then there will be no law and men will be free.

In the beginning was the Creator. John was there. John has faith, love, charity. He loves everybody (as you can see at the bottom of the circle). He told the people: "While I'm here, to love everybody—every color, every nation—and seeing that there are two sides, to become equal and live together. If anyone wants to go back to his own country, all right, but he cannot be chased away."

And now he's a witness from the beginning as it stands through Custom nowaday while you are living in a proper state of love.

If someone spoils things by causing hurricanes, turn your cheek.

Don't hurt people by keeping things from them.

Don't go to the store and buy things. All should be free. This does not mean all New Hebrides but Tanna only.

John told us, the people are here, that people living in a poor

state, having no riches as in Europe, and he wanted them
to do this thing to help people but the Europeans came to say,
"No." So he left everything on the Europeans' side and
promised if they are there, there are many things and share in
the poorest, then he can leave everything to go right—he can
hide himself for a while—and then appear the second time and
finalize everything.
This is what I have taken from Tom in Vila.

        *

What John suggests will come from the American side.
The only place John will come is Lenakel beach.
At Sulphur Bay they speak his name: they mean Lenakel.
John assured the world, "Do God's word." Through the lower
states he felt that this must be the true thing. The world must
come together again.
In 1972 the show was held at Leminuh [the sacred place] for
the first time since the missionaries came. The Presbyterians—
that is, Nakua—kept the people from using that place to meet
in. No Custom has been allowed there.
As John Frum appeared and went away, "Through days and
nights . . ."
"Days will come, nights will come without talking about me.
Then will bring the right time to form up the ants through
Leminuh." This means John will go but will return.

John Kalate in meditation

My kaha told me death and finish
    but John witnessed the Bible
    that there is a Paradise
can go follow spirits by slightly different

What John mentioned was people can be changed
    (like insects, etc.)
    no death at all
    everlasting life

Those who died will be raised through the Resurrection
which is still stand
but people (especially from this island)
would not see
   but men like you, Tom (etc.) KNEW

I am sorry that during the war and when it ceased, those buried
in Vila were dug and brought back to America
   except Mine—100—men who are still buried there

This makes me feel sad, but I stand by my faith
as told by John
to see this before separation comes
otherwise we'll be changed as creeping things

If John told me lies
   then we'll see
but I wish if Tom could visit us if possible . . .
as you heard around Tanna
people announcing
         AMERICA
through words and songs

Myth-dream from Sulphur Bay

We have lived so long in poverty
O John star from the East
Give us the good things of the world
in nineteen seventy-four!

AFTERWORD: SECOND THOUGHTS ABOUT SECOND COMINGS

Everything in the preceding pages is true, if you accept what people believe in their own heads as truth to be "true."

The historical facts are also true as much as they can be verified.

What I have put down on paper is a state of mind, a way of life, a mythology, a mythos, a "myth-dream," as it has been called.

Europeans cannot accept the fact of John's appearances, and as you have read, they dismiss him as a fantasy of the native mind or as a hoax, this being their own kind of fantasy, that the white man is "civilized" and the native ignorant, childish, uneducated, primitive, for whatever list of derogatory and pejorative words the European uses to put down those he is exploiting physically, economically and psychologically, whether they are people of another race or nation, or even his own wife, children, friends and employees.

But John Frum exists. He lives, comes and goes, and returns. To the Tannese he is *alive* as Jesus was to the Christians, early and late. There were several times in the past when the Second Coming of Christ was expected, notably at the year One Thousand—the Millennium—when the world was physically readied, churches freshly painted white and people put on white to greet Him. Jesus did not come. Does that make Him any less real for the Christians, who were then forced to readjust their thinking and expectations and rephrase the theology of the Second Coming in other, less-worldly terms? As the Tannese remark to whites who needle them about John's failure to return, "You have waited two thousand years for Christ, so we can wait for John." Western rationalists have "proved" that Jesus never existed. Does that make Christ any less real for the convinced Christian? I think that a fairly concrete case can be and has been made of the irrationality of believing in Christ (and of God the Father), which is why the various Christian churches say that in the long run Christian belief comes down to a matter of faith alone. I won't extend the analogy to John Frum, having brought it up only to make the point that what Christians ridicule in others they accept without questioning in their own faith.

*

Cargo is now being analyzed over and over by westerners, often with great perception (cf. the books by Burridge, Lawrence and Worsley). However, they talk about Cargo and cargo messiahs in earthly terms. The messiah is a man, and nothing but a man, though he may claim some divine attributes such as perpetual life, indestructability, rebirth. The typical cargo messiah is only human not a god or God. However, John Frum is believed to be God or the Son of God (in Christian theology the distinction between the two is explained as a Mystery). The leaders who interpreted John, and through whom they claimed he spoke, were and are all completely human. None of them claim any divine touch, not even that of an Old Testament prophet, nor did I learn of any such rumors about them. Only John partakes of the Divine.

Cargo cults are invariably based on Christian teachings— Christianity as it has been given to the indigenous people, a Christianity as they have been able to understand it. (Worsley: "The greatest single agency for the world-wide spreading of millenarianism has been the Christian mission.") Many of the missions have been fundamentalist in their approach, taking a literal and narrow view of Christianity, of sin, grace and human destiny. We have seen the destructive results of the Scottish Presbyterian Church on Tanna, perhaps an extreme example, but it happened. Other islands, from Hawaii to New Caledonia, have also suffered fundamentalist Protestant theology. The teachings of the Seventh-Day Adventists, at least as far as the Tannese are concerned, seem to have a great influence on the development of John Frum, even though the church itself had only a small number of members; but they were willing proselytes, not coerced converts, as with the Presbyterians. Thus the S.D.A.'s chiliastic view of the world echoes through the Tanna jungles.

Even the very small Roman Catholic mission, hampered by the Presbyterian-imposed prejudice against anything "French," carries millennial currents; witness, for one very simple example, the very chiliastic gospels of the last Sunday of the liturgical year and of the first Sunday of the new year, which begins with Advent, both bearing a message that John might have proclaimed himself.

And then there is that often noted discrepancy between what the missionary teaches, how he often fails to live up to it himself, how badly the planter, trader and government official (ostensibly Christian because white like the reverends) all live and act. I wonder too if even the most convinced Christian does not have certain reservations continually in the back of his head, for no matter how often he may preach that "The Lord will provide," he doesn't believe it or act it. But the native, once he is convinced, accepts God's provenance as a fact until proven otherwise.

What this boils down to is that the white introduces a way of life, a belief, a hope of a transcendent future that he himself is quite incapable of accepting and following. He puts ashore a shipload of high explosives, and when it blows up in his face he is both confused and angry. Not at himself but at the native. These are all clichés and truisms I have been stating, but they must be constantly brought to light again, to emphasize that "native" behavior is not so irrational, not so extreme in the face of the facts. The one reality that stands out above all is that the white makes no effort to see his own behavior in objective terms, either in the light of his own teaching and preaching as a missionary or his rule as a government official, or in the final and most glaring light, of how the native thinks, believes and acts.

The final irony, after a devastation of Third World life from one end of the map to the other, is the conviction that white ways are the best. This is not a nineteenth-century aberration (which, incidentally was challenged by such people as Melville, Stevenson, Trollope and Loti) but a common conviction held as strongly today as in the past. Throughout my entire South Pacific journey (I visited other islands besides the New Hebrides) I heard the white-is-superior (smarter, better, etc.) view over and over. This means the white male, as white women and children are inferior, but not as inferior as the native, the "boy." A certain J. K. McCarthy, who served for some twenty years as a District Officer in New Guinea, presents a wonderfully concise and naïve expression of the white point of view in his foreward to Lawrence's *Road Belong Cargo*. "From long years spent in New Guinea," writes the District Agent, "I can vouch for the native peoples' skill in playing white man against white man," proving again that spears are stronger than guns, magic better than reason. Cargo is not easy to overcome, he says, "Yet overcome it must be for, while a sympathetic appreciation is required in its handling, this does not mean the cults should be condoned. Bluntly, cargo cult is one of the great barriers that impede the advancement of the people. It must go if progress is to be achieved." But native resistance to progress continues: "The very thinking of the people may be the main obstacle in the path of their development. That this is a fact is shown in the several 'dissentient' groups that have continued to resist the Administration's efforts to bring them into Local Government Councils. The so-called 'Submarine Men' of Kokopo—a cult that had its genesis in the cargo cult belief—is an example of how a group, sophisticated and economically well off, preferred magical and religious ritual to the white man's ways in their endeavour to find betterment."

The Tragedy is that "Once more the Administration has been confronted with the age-old beliefs of the people it is trying to develop." In conclusion District Agent McCarthy makes twin points: one, the white must understand Cargo because it is "a highly integrated belief system so widely held that it is entitled to be regarded as a philosophy in its own right" and not "a mere series of isolated superstitions." Therefore he recommends its destruction. His second point is a wish that the people of New Guinea might read the Lawrence book, because it "would do much to teach them how the white man thinks."

Of course, the native knows how the white man thinks. That is why he is angry, hurt, frantic, rebellious, becoming neurotic and psychotic from frustration and murder by whites. Mr. McCarthy and all those nice white administrators are going to kill him for his own good.

*

We might consider some random observations about Cargo.

The white man never works, yet he has things the native hadn't known about and now can only dream of possessing. He sits on the verandah of the bungalow he has bullied and threatened the natives into building for him, sipping his scotch (forbidden to the native, for who can stand a drunken native?).

The native works on the copra plantations, the docks, in the mines, the hotels, the forests. "Climb that tree, boy, and shake down those nuts!" Hard work all same but no got money like white man. White man he no work got plenty money.

A puzzle.

No one has seen the production of the white's goods. Yet they exist and appear when needed.

Virtually everything the native does is accomplished with the aid of magic. Better crops, good health, the weather for good or bad. *Magic works.* The right incantation means a better pig with handsome tusks. Bad magic brings bad health, death.

If the white man finds you using magic he may put you in jail, even though he says magic is a hoax. Bad magic discovered (like someone's death) is sure to mean jail or at least an investigation.

If the black man employs magic for what he gets, is it not a likely corollary that the white man also employs magic?

But the white man's magic is so much more powerful!

Therefore we must find the secret of the white man's magic.

The white man says: "It all comes from hard work."

But the white man never works.

Therefore the white man is a liar, a fact we have known from the first meeting.

So the white man is hiding the secret of his magic. He gives us Bibles with the magic pages missing [a fact: there are very few Bibles with the full text anywhere in the world for any "native" group].[1] We must find that secret, turn it to our own use, be rich, successful, happy like the white man.

We may even be the same color by and by.

Europeans constantly complain that the native is lazy. He won't work. What this means is that he hates doing the European's work for him. It has been very difficult for the white to get the (local) native to work; he is forced to import Tannese to Australia, Tonkinese to the New Hebrides, etc.

*

A few more observations about John Frum. The continued arrest and jailing of Tannese over a seventeen-year period was religious persecution in the vilest sense. These men were arrested because they *believed* in John Frum, a personage anathema to the ruling church on Tanna, which used the government as its secular arm. The government could, and did at times, state secular reasons for the arrests, but the true reason is that the Tannese were arrested for their religious beliefs. In trying to justify the arrests (and lack of trials) a Condominium official remarked to me that the Tannese were picked up because the government feared a Japanese invasion.

John Frum is strictly an oral tradition. No writings on the Tannese are known except Joe Nalpin's letter and one or two minor documents. Any writing about John Frum is by white hostile observers. At best they are "neutral," as was Guiart. Whites act as if this is something the Tannese (like others) will pass through, a stage in growing up to be white men. And so on . . .

*

As for the final question, Does the author believe in John Frum? . . . Are we not all ephemeral? Do I not believe in you, reader? or myself?

You answer.

Who *is* John Frum?

So far we have seen John from a variety of views, yet the question must be asked: "Who is John Frum?" We have not yet grappled with his identity in any tangible manner. It would be easy to dismiss the question with a facile answer, like, "John is whoever you believe him to be," but that does not solve the basic physical, psychological, or supernatural queries. John is Tannese, American, both, or none. During World War II he was believed—by many whites, as we have seen in Tom Navy's discourse—to be a Japanese agent, if not Japanese-American.

Yet, again: "Who is John Frum?" When John was first noticed on Tanna by Mr. James Nicol, the District Agent, it seemed clear that he was a tangible person and one who was causing trouble. Solution: arrest him. So one Manehevi was arrested, tied to a tree as an example, and then sent to prison in Port Vila, along with Jack Kohu. But (as the Tannese allowed) Manehevi was *not* John Frum. Mr. Nicol was quite worked up over the affair and it consumed much of his time, because Anglo-Presbyterian rule, which once seemed so stable, so enduring, was now falling to pieces. A second John Frum was arrested, and then a third and a fourth, along with many of John's followers. All of the arrested men were jailed and exiled without due process of law, some of the sentences being for periods of years. In most cases no definite crime was ascribed to them other than that they were vaguely, indefinably, against "law and order." If pressed, the British might have justified detention under a general regulation—18-B, I think it was—which allowed them to round up undesirables and potential saboteurs and spies. But the most precisely defined "crimes" were "adultery" or "incest," catch-all charges against unruly natives.

There are several possible explanations for the phenomenon of John and we will work our way through them, beginning with the easiest, which was outlined years before John's appearance by R. H. Codrington, D.D., a member of the Melanesian Mission. Codrington was a pioneer anthropologist in the South Pacific, doing his researches in the years 1863 to 1887, publishing the results in *The Melanesians* (The Clarendon Press, Oxford, 1891). Codrington, so a note in the Dover reprint (New York, 1972) says, had "the unparalleled opportunity to study a virgin field of primitive peoples: the natives of the Melanesian Islands, before acculturation had set in." At the mission station on Norfolk Island, where young Melanesians were brought for study and training, Codrington questioned them at length about their backgrounds; he also made several field trips into the various island groups. "It has been my purpose to set forth as much as possible what the natives say about themselves, not what the Europeans say about them," was his very sensible guideline for himself.

The following passage appears to give a clue to John: "There is certainly nothing more characteristic of Melanesian life than the presence of Societies which celebrate Mysteries strictly concealed from the uninitiated and from all females. A dress, with a mask or a hat, disguises the members if they appear in open day; they have strange cries and sounds by which they make their presence known when they are unseen." So is not some Tannese disguised as an American, in his hat, sunglasses, talcumed face, brass-buttoned jacket, speaking in a falsetto? But there is more, on a deeper level. "The Melanesian mind is entirely possessed by the belief in a supernatural power or influence, called almost universally *mana*. This is what works to effect everything which is beyond the ordinary power of men, outside the common processes of nature; it is present in the atmosphere of life, attaches itself to persons and to things, and is manifested by results which can only be ascribed to its operation. . . . This power, though impersonal, is always connected with some person who directs it; all spirits have it, ghosts generally, some men."[2]

To be concise: "The Melanesians believe in the existence of beings personal, intelligent, full of *mana*, with a certain bodily form which is visible but not fleshly like the bodies of men. These they think to be more or less actively concerned in the affairs of men, and they invoke and otherwise approach them. These may be called spirits, but it is most important to distinguish between spirits who are beings of an order higher than mankind, and the disembodied spirits of men, which have become in the vulgar sense of the word ghosts. . . . It is plain that the natives of the southern islands of the New Hebrides, though they are said to worship 'gods,' believe in the existence and power of spirits other than the disembodied spirits of the dead, as well as of the ghosts

238

of men." Thus, under this definition, John—for the Tannese—could be a spirit. But for the white this definition presents difficulties, for it is virtually an axiom of faith among us that such a notion is on the one hand unscientific, and on the other, un-Christian. Therefore we dismiss John as higher spirit out of hand, those old bugaboos, white obtuseness, chauvinism, insensitivity and pride being in the ascendancy.

Yet, practically speaking, we must hold on to some vestige of this partial answer drawn from Codrington, as we must from the first simple clue that he supplied, which at least fits the surface aspects of John's appearances. To go further we must turn to Carl Gustav Jung, weirdo shrink, eccentric outsider, mystic, misfit—not for explanation, for no one can explain John but must experience him—but to shed some light on our question.

In his autobiography, *Memories, Dreams, Reflections* (New York, 1961), Jung devotes quite some space to his "Confrontation with the Unconscious." Here we are told—for the first time—about the various figures who inhabited his subconscious: a white bird which is transformed into a little girl about eight years of age, with pretty blond hair; twelve dead people who symbolize many different facets of the Unconscious; a dwarf with leathery skin; a youthful corpse with blond hair and a wound in the head, floating in an underground stream; a scarab; jewels; blood; a red newborn sun; and so on. One might give special notice to a long dream in which Jung is accompanied by an unknown, small, brown-skinned savage, who helps Jung kill the blond Siegfried, symbol of Germanic mastery over others. The small, brown-skinned savage, Jung realizes is "an embodiment of the primitive shadow." In another encounter, Jung meets an unusual couple: "Near the steep slope of a rock I caught sight of two figures, an old man with a white beard and a beautiful young girl. I summoned up my courage and approached them as though they were real people, and listened attentively to what they told me. The old man explained that he was Elijah, and that gave me a shock. But the girl staggered me even more, for she called herself Salome! She was blind." Soon after this fantasy comes Philemon, a pagan of Egypto-Hellenic origin with Gnostic coloration. Philemon is "a winged being sailing across the sky." Jung writes: "I saw that it was an old man with the horns of a bull. He held a bunch of four keys, one of which he clutched as if he were about to open a lock. He had the wings of the kingfisher with its characteristic colours." Jung begins to paint this figure, and a few days later finds on the lake shore where he lives the body of a dead kingfisher.

Jung has extensive conversations with Philemon, and the role of these figures gradually becomes clear. "Philemon and other figures of my fantasies brought home to me the crucial insight that there are things in the psyche which I do not produce, but which produce themselves and have their own life. Philemon represented a force which was not myself. In my fantasies I held conversations with him, and he said things I had not consciously thought. For I observed clearly that it was he who spoke, not I. . . . It was he who taught me psychic objectivity, the reality of the psyche. Through him the distinction was clarified between myself and the object of my thought. He confronted me in an objective manner, and I understood that there is something in me which can say things I do not know and do not intend, things which may even be directed against me.

"Psychologically, Philemon represented superior insight. He was a mysterious figure to me. At times he seemed to me quite real, as if he were a living personality. I went walking up and down the garden with him, and to me he was what the Indians call a guru."

This is extremely dangerous psychic material that Jung has been dealing with. I will not retrace his analysis of the figures, and of the anima that he also found present in his subconscious (the reader is referred to the autobiography), but a final point must be included. Jung states that while such material is the stuff of psychosis and might be found in the insane, it is also "the matrix of a mythopoeic imagination which has vanished from our rational age. Though such imagination is present everywhere, it is both tabooed and dreaded, so that it even appears to be a risky experiment or a questionable adventure to entrust oneself to the uncertain path that leads into the depths of the unconscious. It is considered the path of error, of equivocation and misunderstanding."

Consequently, we may admit that in the mythopoeic imagination which has vanished from our rational age, John is the embodiment of our primitive shadow, though for the Tannese, of course, he is not ephemeral but real. This dreaded, tabooed intruder invades our unconscious, which is why whites have so feared Cargo whenever they have encountered it, in the Pacific or elsewhere. Now, to continue our inquiry into John's identity. I will turn to the late Christo-Buddhist mystic Thomas Merton, who lost his life during such a search as that which John represents. Merton had been deeply interested in Cargo, and shortly before his death drafted a long essay on the subject, which, however rudimentary and unfinished it might be, still offers some insights into the problem of Cargo and, by extension, of John.[3] Merton wrote: "Our communication with primitives and with a primitive society demands an ability to communicate with something deeper in ourselves, something with which we are out of touch. This is our primitive self which has become alien, hostile and strange."

Now we go off on a tangent, on a path virtually unconnected with the others, and find ourselves, so to speak, in a kava clearing amidst dense jungle, where John appears in another form. Now we see John as avatar. Here we are on shaky ground, rationally speaking, and might as well be clutching the trembling slopes of windy Yasur with our toes buried deep in volcanic ash while Kalbapen and Karaparamum—both aspects of John—raise hell with the Richter scale.

John as avatar

It is a truism among many mystics that God has many messengers, nabis, prophets, manifestations: Abraham, Moses, Buddha, Christ, Muhammad, the nine avatars of Vishnu, messengers without count. What we are not prepared for is a messenger who is black, who appears among men who beat their wives and get intoxicated every evening on a narcotic, hallucinogenic root, who spend their lives on the edge of the Stone Age.

The suggestion that John may be an avatar is not likely to be received with wild enthusiasm by anthropologists, sociologists, Districts Agents, missionaries, etc. On the other hand, people who accept the notion of the avatar in history should find no serious objections. The idea is "irrational" only if a false sense of the rational rules your life.

But what kind of avatar is John? If the British District Agents are to be believed, John was nothing but a series of Tannese impersonators. However, aside from Manehevi, the first man to be arrested, the District Agents were never sure if they were arresting John. And, of course, Manehevi was immediately disclaimed by the Tannese as John. Thus, the British arrested "John" but not John. That John—or "John"—appeared frequently on Tanna is not a matter of dispute, as both Mr. Nicol and the Tannese testified; John was common knowledge among foreigners, like Tom Beatty. And then John manifested himself regularly to the prisoners at Vila in 1942. Mellis's claim to see John often in the 1970s is open to doubt, but I have no way of disproving him, and he cannot, or will not, prove it (or John will not let him).

The point I am leading up to is that John lives in the hearts and minds and souls of the Tannese. Whether or not he is physically present, he is very much a spiritual and psychic reality. To deny this would be to deny life itself.

John as Parousia

John is alive. With us is his "presence"—the Greek theological term is *Parousia.* He is the ever-coming, who has already come to his people on Tanna and Vila.

"By doing all of these things you have grasped all of me," John has said in a phrase that echoes the Christian Gospels. But the fact that certain concepts, themes, phrases may have appeared earlier in both Christianity and in Judaism does not nullify John.

We cannot ignore the fact that John appeared, Mr. Nicol being as valid a witness as the Tannese. Whether or not Mr. Nicol arrested "John" or someone else is irrelevant. One cannot imprison a Parousia, a presence.

John is deeply rooted in the past, Melanesian, Judaeo-Christian, and world, but he is also Present and Future.

Though he may seem simple and unsophisticated, we have no reason to ignore him. Complexity and a multifaceted surface need not be a virtue. John is trying to tell us as westerners to disconnect our minds from the American computer, to turn off the air-conditioned nightmare, to float with the mighty currents that sweep through the rest of the world, Africa, Asia, the Pacific.

John has come to transcend our limitations as westerners and whites, as educated people who see others as "primitives, illiterates, unsophisticated, unskilled, *dark*."

He has come to turn us inward to that primitive self, now become alien, hostile and strange, with which we have lost touch.

For, look within, and you will find John.

His Parousia, his Second Coming, is constant.

*

[*Thomas Merton*] I am trying to figure out some way I can get nationalized as a Negro as I am tired of belonging to the humiliating white race. One wants at times the comfort of belonging to a race that one can like and respect. This unfortunately has been concluded beforehand for everyone . . . I am going to write to the Govt. about resigning from the human race. Or at least the white part, which is not by all accounts the most human.

*

"How did you like the South Pacific, Captain?"

"Oh, you know, it's all the same, nothing but palm trees and natives."

NOTES

Introduction

1 Kanakas. Peter Lawrence (in *Road Belong Cargo,* Melbourne University Press, 1964) says that "Kanaka is a Pidgin English term of contempt for the unsophisticated native." Nevertheless the term is widely used and is probably not as offensive as common alternatives down there, like coon and nigger.

2 Lawrence, op. cit.

3 Peter Worsley, *The Trumpet Shall Sound,* Schocken Books, New York, 1962.

4 Public transportation. Never mind the jokes about *our* public transportation.

5 Margaret Mead, *Growing Up in New Guinea,* Penguin, 1942.

6 Jean Guiart, *Un Siècle et demi de Contacts Culturels à Tanna,* Publications de la Société des Océanistes, No. 5, Musée de l'Homme, Paris, 1956.

Jesus Christ He no come

1 This and the following section are based largely on Guiart and the Government Diary (see Appendix), and personal interviews.

White shadows on the South Seas

1 Guns. It wasn't until the 1880s, when the rapid-loading, single-shot cartridge rifle was introduced, that white firepower had the advantage in overcoming native resistance.

2 The *Santa Isabel.* Current speculation by Pacific scholars is that the ship reached the island of San Cristobel in the Solomons. Little good it did, as the evidence is that the crew was killed and eaten.

3 The name of Tanna. Nearby islanders call the place Ipari.

4 In fairness to these particular missionaries, they were very much opposed to such punitive acts.

5 The smell of the white man. Based on several passages in Daisy Bates's *The Passing of the Aborigines,* Frederic A. Praeger, 1967. Monnup, the last of the dingo-totems of the experiment, died in 1913.

[6] Kennelm Burridge, *Mambu,* Harper Torchbook, 1970.

[7] Dealing with a native. From W. F. Alder, *The Isle of Vanishing Men,* The Century Company, New York, 1922.

[8] A good boy. Quoted by Osa Johnson in *Bride in the Solomons,* Houghton Mifflin Company, Boston, 1944.

[9] To balance the record, Gauguin also worked for a notorious pro-planter newspaper when he lived in Tahiti in order to support himself and made a number of inexcusable statements justifying colonialism and missionaries, both of which he otherwise opposed. As Gauguin lay ill in the Marquesas a senior investigator, one Andre Salles, on a trip of inspection from France, denounced Gauguin as "a sick painter of the Impressionist school," and when Gauguin died shortly afterwards, Bishop Joseph Martin wrote home that he was "a contemptible individual." For Gauguin, alive, defended "all native vices."

[10] Tom Harrisson, *Savage Civilization,* Alfred A. Knopf, New York, 1937.

[11] Paton also wrote about Northern Ireland. "No man, however dissevered from the party politics of the day, can see and live amongst the Irish of the North, without having forced on his soul the conviction that the Protestant faith and life, with its grit and backbone and self-dependence, has made them what they are. Romanism, on the other hand, with its blind faith and its peculiar type of life, has been at least *one,* if not the main, degrading influence amongst the Irish of the South and West, who are naturally a warm-hearted and generous and gifted people. Ireland needs the pure and true Gospel, proclaimed, taught and received, in the South as it is now in the North. Jesus holds the Key to all problems, in this as in every land."

[12] Tahiti is a good example of the disastrous effects of white influence. When the island was discovered in 1767, it had an estimated 150,000 inhabitants; thirty years later there were only 15,000, and by 1827, 8,000, which figure remained stationary for many decades. To return to the New Hebrides: A. Bernard Deacon, in *Malekula, a Vanishing People in the New Hebrides,* writes of the year 1926: "While I have been here there has been a flu epidemic beginning apparently in Santo, and spreading like a scourge through all the islands. The death rate has been ghastly. Here, in one village of twenty people, nine died in one week. To my knowledge, in Telag district, where I am working, with a population of about 250, twenty-two men died." Deacon himself died soon afterwards of blackwater fever and his notes were edited and published by someone else.

Now Cargo come

[1] A large part of Fiji's troubles developed from a run-in with the States, following the destruction of American property in 1853 and 1855, when

Levuka was burned in antiwhite demonstrations. America demanded $45,000 in compensation. Thombaku, the king, knew damn well that one had to pay, American warships being just as short-tempered as British. In 1858, with the support of the local white residents, he offered the islands to England, on the theory that England would be bound by the debt. But England's hands-off policy continued until 1874, when the islands were formally accepted. Meanwhile an Australian company was formed which paid off the American debt, getting in return choice pieces of land. And then Mother England reimbursed the Aussies.

[2] Brewster, in order to provide an alternate outlet for the energies of the young Fijians, established cricket clubs, which, he learned later, more or less followed the structure of the Tuka Army and were merely a screen for the continuation of the Water Babies. So much for white naïveté.

[3] Do you really think those gas chambers and the ovens were merely an effing aberration?

[4] The Bank Cult. Reported in *The Pacific Islands Monthly*, January 1968.

Some story long New Hebrides

[1] New Hebrides Biennial Report. Issued 1969 and 1970 by the Anglo-French Condominium. Selected and edited as needed. The report changes glacially in each edition, merely bringing pertinent facts up-to-date. The Tourist Office is a lot livelier, with monthly publicity releases, which make the islands sound as if they were really swinging. All a dream!

[2] Same fellows who got the land?

[3] NaGriemel, from the nagaria and namele plants, which were taken to symbolize custom law.

[4] Kalkoa, quoted in *The Journal of Pacific History*, Volume Seven, Oxford University Press, 1972.

Tanna stories

[1] The Ark of Tanna. Told by Lauhman Teni. Later a European added that some of the nearby trees bear bullet holes from the time when Noah fired his musket.

[2] On top of Old Smokey. Also narrated by Lauhman Teni.

White man he muck up John Frum

[1] This same westerner, a most sensible man, tells me that he used to have some kind of arthritis until he tied a cotton cord—not nylon—around his waist. Previously he couldn't bend to work on his jeep. Now he's not bothered in the least.

An aside on the Stoned Age

[1] Austin Coates, *Western Pacific Islands,* Her Majesty's Stationery Office, London, 1970.
[2] The John Frum file. But see the Appendix, page 251.

John Frum he come

[1] Mr. Tacuma adds the aside that a black fowl is known as Kalpaben's fowl.
[2] That man. The reporter from *The New York Times,* who wrote the article on John Frum.
[3] Various voices. Tom, Henry, Joe, John, Fred, Jimmy, etc.

Afterword

[1] Bibles. There are very few complete Bibles in the "minor" languages of the world. Most translations comprise primarily the Gospels, first, then the Epistles, Acts, perhaps the Psalms. It is natural for the native to wonder why the white man has not translated the entire Bible for him. Are there not secrets the white man does not want the native to learn?
[2] Codrington has also defined *mana* as follows: "The religion of the Melanesians consists, as far as belief goes, in the persuasion that there is a supernatural power about belonging to the region of the unseen; and, as far as practice goes, in the use of getting this power turned to their own benefit. The notion of a Supreme Being is altogether foreign to them, or indeed of any being occupying a very elevated place in their world . . . There is a belief in a force altogether distinct from physical power, which acts in all kinds of ways for good and evil, and which it is of the greatest advantage to possess or control. This is Mana."
[3] Thomas Merton, in a draft of a work which was to be revised and expanded. Merton covered some of the same ground in letters to friends and in conversations with this author.

APPENDIX
"John Frum Cult—Diary of Events"

Phase I

27.11.40 Enquiry held by B.D.A. at Lenakel over killing of goats by natives of Green Point to feed the followers of J.F.

    KAHU and KARUA admitted J.F. had a house in their village and came to talk to them at night.

    Assessors sent to examine came back staunch J.F. supporters. KARUA subsequently ran away after questioning. J.F. then went "underground."

29. 4.41 A rush takes place in the stores. By 16.5.41 over £1000 had been taken over store counters and many bullocks and pigs killed. Dances held nearly every night, and excessive kava drinking.

12. 5.41 Telegram from BDA Tanna B.R.C. reporting that J.F. gave orders to spend all money. Casual labour withdrawn from Europeans. Nonattendance at church.

21. 5.41 B.D.A. to B.R.C.—giving background of present J.F. activities, mentioning particularly KAHU AND KARUAU, also NAKO, Chief of Lenakel. (This information later embodied in report to both R. Crs. on 6th June, and amplified.)

26. 5.41 B.R.C. to B.D.A. / Advises police leaving for Tanna.

1. 6.41 POLICE arrested 11 J.F.s, including person impersonating J.F. (MANEHEVI)

7. 6.41 B.D.A. to B.R.C. / Report on J.F. movement to date, enclosing statements KARNUA. KAHU, KAMTI. MOKEKS, NOKLAM. Also advising head men had offered to pay £100 to Government in respect of the trouble caused through the masquerade.

9. 6.41 Police, prisoners, report and £100 cash arrive in Vila. (MANEHEVI, KARAUA)

7. 7.41 Two children of J.F., ISAAC and JACOB, reported to be in Sulphur Bay.

11. 7.41 9 more Tannese sent Vila. KAMTI, KAINILLAGA, KOKUES, KAHU, NOKLAM, NANUIO, *NAMPAS*, MIKIAU, *NAROSAKA*.

23. 8.41	£100 acknowledged by Government.
15. 9.41	B.R.C. to A.M.C. / Because of case to date implicating KAHU (C. of P.'s draft). Interesting point that MANEH-EVI and his collaborator KARAUA do not appear to have any personal profit from the affair.

Phase II

23. 9.41	B.D.A. to B.R.C. / Letter seized from Pte. NALPIN instructing NAKO to build house for J.F. at Lenakel, also two letters from prisoners in Vila gaol.
29. 9.41	B.D.A. to B.R.C. / 6 letters arrive per "Morinda" on 12/9 from Joe NALPIN. Person who saw J.F.'s sons land from plane on Siwi, taking them to Sulphur Bay to hide is MAILES.
7.10.41	3 prisoners sent Vila. SEMANA, KISAR, MAILES.
17.10.41	B.H.C. to B.R.C. / Agrees to MANEHEVI and KARAUA 5 years banishment.
24.10.41	Report based on remarks made by Mrs. Bell re J.F. policy and continued activity.
5.11.41	C. of P. to B.R.C. / Report on Joe NALPIN's letters, recommending NALPIN to 6 months' detention for issuing subversive correspondence.
15.11.41	B.D.A. to B.R.C. / Enclosing statement of NGUIA on children of J.F.
17.11.41	10 prisoners arrive Vila. MALAKE, NAUKE, NAKO, SOMO, FORMAN, TANI, NATOGO, IO (Kava instigator), IARUELLI, SIAKA POITA, YALITAN.
24.11.41	B.D.A. to B.R.C. / Recommends 5 years for SOMO, IO and Natogo, remainder 1 year.
14.12.41	B.D.A. to B.R.C. / Advises J.F. still very active and wishes to defer leave. Dances less frequent, kava drinking diminished, but still taking place. Reports anti-British feeling on island, and continued reports of J.F.'s half-caste children.
6. 1.42	B.D.A. to B.R.C. / Report on current situation, including another (and differing) translation of NALPIN's letter to SOMO, and pointing out danger of this person.
28. 2.42	Joe NALPIN banished for 5 years plus 6 months.

7. 8.42	One of the Tannese, NATOGO, dies in British hospital (abdom. trouble).

2. 3.42   B.D.A. to B.R.C.
IARUEL, LAHUA, KAPAIU and INIUA to be sent to Vila, advise one year's detention. LAHUA responsible for burst of spending in January. Children of J.F. still going strong in Sulphur Bay. Pro-Japanese talk. Traders threatened. J.F. reported to have warship and recommended licentious behaviour between young people. Young girls involved in affair of "ISAAC" impersonating J.F. / ISAAC confesses impersonation.

21. 4.42   B.D.A. to B.R.C. / An old man of Futuna says he is J.F. / All quiet otherwise.

29. 6.42   B.R.C. to F.R.C. / Recommends 4 men kept in gaol.

10. 7.42   F.R.C. to B.R.C. / Thinks they should be repatriated.

29. 7.42   B.R.C. to F.R.C.
After seeking advice from Tanna advisers 4 men should not be sent back.

5. 8.42   F.R.C. to B.R.C.
Says he was concerned with LEGAL position in general terms, more than these specific cases. Agrees to send 4 men remaining in Vila.

13. 8.42   B.D.A. to B.R.C.
Reports trouble getting natives to go to Vila to work for U.S. forces stationed there.

24. 9.42   Expiry of detention period of following:
KAMTI
NUNILLANIAGA
NOKNES
KAHU
NOKLAM
NAMPAS
NIKLAM
NAKOMAHA.

2.10.42   Expiry of detention:
MAILES
KISAR
SEMANA.

27.11.42	Expiry of detention period: NAKO, LOFMANTANI, IAURUELLI, SIAKA, MIAKE NAUKA, POITA, IATALITAN.
12.12.42	Joe NALPIN, KARAUA, MANEHEVI banished to Vila for 5 years, and released from detention.
18.11.42	Detainee SIAKA died.
27. 1.43	Balance of returnees returned Tanna, except 3 above mentioned.
16. 2.43	Report that NALPIN and one other returned to Tanna on 14th February illegally.
2. 3.43	Report confirmed. NALPIN, MANEHEVI and KARAUA sent back to Vila from Tanna.
27. 5.43	R.G.A. to B.R.C. / Report of dances and similar activities instigated by *NAMPAS* and NIKIAH.
18. 6.43	B.D.A. arrests NAMPAS and NIKIAU.
26. 7.43	*NAKOMAHA, NAMPAS,* NIKIAU, MAILES sent British Prison Vila from Tanna.
23. 8.43	Ag. B.D.A. to B.R.C. Reports absenteeism from church and school, excessive kava drinking.
30. 9.43	Ag. B.D.A. to B.R.C. Advises return of all J.F. prisoners in Vila to Lenakel prison and gradual discharge and reabsorption into population without celebration.

Phase III

18.10.43	Fresh outbreak of J.F. in Tanna involving person named LOIAG (NELOIG).
19.10.43	B.D.A. to B.R.C. Asks for 100 men as position getting out of hand.
19.10.43	45 members N.H. Defence Force under Lt. Faure Briac and detachment of N.H. Police under Lt. Johnson sail for Tanna in m.v. "Echo."
23.10.43	M.V. "Echo" left Tanna for Vila with 56 prisoners, including instigator NELOIG, who had tried to persuade Tannese to make an aerodrome under threat of shooting.

23.10.43	B.D.A. to B.R.C.
	Advises return of NALPIN, MANEHEVI AND KARAUA to Tanna.
24.10.43	B.D.A. to B.R.C.
	Full report of incident, including address to Tannese given by MAJOR PATTEN.
14.11.43	Major PATTEN's report of the affair.
25.11.43	11 of the 56 Tannese detailed for service with RNZAF at Santo (not including NELOIG, who is considered mad, but the next most important—NALIN, LOPE, KASSO, IAUIAK, LOPESIP, IAUEO, IHI, ALBERT, NOUAL, IATELE, PITA PATA).
1.12.43	B.R.C. to B.H.C. / Full report of incident.
8.12.43	Regulation enacted to provide for temporary control of, possession, and use of firearms.
18.12.43	Further medical report on NELOIG.
8. 3.44	LOPE, one of the RNZAF Tannese, dies of T.B.
7. 9.44	B.D.A. to B.R.C.
	Messages being sent to Tanna, thought to be from *NAKOMAHA* and *NAMPAS*, who were banished for five years at end of 1942.
17. 1.45	B.D.A. to B.R.C.
	Request that NAMPAS and Co. be prevented communicating with Tannese seamen in Vila following upon report of resurrection of J.F. movement in Tanna.
7. 2.45	KENAPKA and MALOUINE charged with assaulting Dr. Armstrong.
24. 2.45	Confining Orders for *NAMPAS, NAKOMAHA,* NIKIAU and MAILES are redefined.
26. 3.45	NELOIG reported to have escaped 30.10.44 (later recaptured).

Phase IV

| 18. 5.45 | 8 J.F. men arrested in Tanna, one eventually tried. |
| 13. 5.46 | NELOIG "banished" from Tanna as first step in regularizing problem of his wife on Tanna, whose undetermined status is causing unrest and revival of J.F. activity. |

24. 5.46	Rev. McLeod recommends the return of certain banished natives to Tanna, because of wives hardship.

29. 5.46   Ag. R.C. to Ag. D.A.
Possibility of wives of *NAMPAS*, NIKIAU, MAILES, NAKOMAHA joining them at Lamap prison. MANUIG and NEMARKA are in different category as they had prison sentences as well as banishment.

13. 9.46   Ag. B.D.A. to B.R.C.
Report on situation in Tanna. Orgiastic dancing, excessive kava drinking, break-down of custom, scattering of communal life and deterioration of sanitation and hygiene, even in villages of close European contact.

29.11.46   Regarding woman KATUA, who went to Vila with Ag. B.D.A. Dr. Johnston, as a servant. She is wife of NELOIG, who is missing, presumed dead. Due to unrest on her behalf in Tanna, she subsequently (31.12.46) confined to Efate.

3. 1.47   B.D.A. to Ag. R.C.
Does not recommend return of *NAMPAS*, NIKIAU, MAILES and NAKOMAHA.

Phase V

11. 4.47   Incident in store in Tanna regarding removal of price tickets. 14 arrests, 3 sentenced to 5 years. IOKAI, NAKOMAHA (? another one), KRASSI JOHNSON, LOWAKA, SAYLAS, KATKINA, JEREMIAH, JOHN TEKNOA, NAWAWINE, KAPEN, NUARAU, NAKAHI, TOM IATA, IATA.

27. 8.47   B.R.C. to B.D.A.
Katua pregnant by IARAMEL in French Police at Vila. Suggests divorce and remarriage to settle this.

1.10.47   Report on contact with LAMAP "Banishees" who are reported to have sent special coconuts to Tanna which were planted in a ceremony at Sulphur Bay. These came by seamen on "Morinda."

26.11.47   Suggestion that the 6 Banishees on Lamap be transferred to Venue.

15.12.47   The Tannese sign an agreement (voluntarily) promising to keep the peace (130 signed). A formal reply sent.

16. 3.48   Decided 6 men should be sent to Malo not Venue (but they don't go yet).

29. 4.48	NELOIG gives himself up, having spent 3 years in the bush in hiding. Further Medical Board on him.
24. 5.48	C. of P. to H.H. Recommends NELOIG as definitely insane and that he should be sent to Nouméa.
19. 8.48	NELOIG sent to Nouméa.
June '48	MALOUINE died in Lamap, Malekula. 5 now remain: NAKOMAHA, NAMPAS, NIKIAU, MAILES, NEMARKA (not transferred to Malo yet).
13.12.48	Suggestion that 12 Tannese detainees in Vila should join PWD sanitary gang.
6. 1.49	Confirming Orders for Malekula detainees expires, with exception of NEMARKA.
14. 1.49	F.R.T. to B.R.C. Suggest all Malekula detainees be sent back except *NAKOMAHA,* who appears unrepentant (though not overtly).
26. 2.49	B.R.C. to F.R.C. Recommends NIAKAU and MAILES to repat. to Tanna, leaving *NIMPAN, NAKOWAHA* and NEMARKATA to go to Malo, and recommends that *NAMPAS* and *NAKAWAHA* whose Confining Orders have expired should be confined for a further year.
26. 2.49	C. of P. to B.R.C. Two prisoners, MALEKUL and KAU imprisoned in Vila—expiry of sentences 20.5.49. The other prisoners are in French prison. (This refers to the 14 arrests made regarding store incident on 11.4.47.)
12. 2.49	B.R.C. to F.R.C. Two prisoners in British prison decline to join PWD. They are released but confined to Efate for 3 years as from 20.1.49. The ten in the French prison are: MUWARAO, YAMA, TOM YATA, TEASA, KATALINNA, KAPEN, LOMANA, NAWAWINE, NAKAHU, SALINAS. (These names vary slightly from list given on 11.4.47.)
30. 4.49	F.R.C. to B.R.C. Ten prisoners in French prison also refuse PWD. At present employed in French hospital. 3 want to join French Police.

13. 5.49	NIKIAU and MAILES ex Lamap return to Tanna on 11.5.49.
13. 6.49	KAU and MALEKUL (released from British prison) decide to start with PWD.
11. 7.49	*NAMPAS, NAKOWAHA* and NEMARKA at last get to Malo on M. Gabriel Bidal's plantation.
30. 6.49	B.D.A. to B.R.C. Return of NIKIAU and MAILES did not cause much excitement on Tanna. They made declaration to be of good behaviour. Noticeable absence of women from Mission churches.
31. 3.50	B.D.A. to B.R.C. Report on situation. Feels that suppression of J.F. has created a vacuum in native life on Tanna and that something is bound to happen, due to breakdown of "Custom," denial of Mission teaching, and reversion to paganism.
10. 5.50	B.R.C. to F.R.C. Recommends repatriation of Vila detainees.
26. 8.50	F.D.A., B.D.A. to F.R.C., B.R.C. Recommend return to Tanna of Malo detainees. Petition against Malo detainees by Malo residents.
11. 5.50	B.R.C. to F.R.C. Regarding petition—recommends *NAMPAS, NAKOHAMA.* NEMARKA held on depot pending inquiry.
17.11.50	F.R.C to B.R.C. Seeks prolongation of banishment order in respect of NAILAK, KAKAHU, WAHAWINE, LOWARA, KAPEN, KATALINA, YEARA, TOM YATA, YATA, NUMAPO.
5.12.51	*NAMPAS, NAKOMAHA,* NEMARKA confined to Malo for further year.
25. 1.51	B.R.C. to F.R.C. Agrees 11 Vila detainees should be returned to Tanna. 3 remaining in French prison.
18. 7.51	B.R.C. to F.R.C. Agrees to repatriate *NAMPAS, NAKOMAHA* and NEMARKA, beginning with the latter.
23. 7.51	F.R.C. to B.R.C. Concurs.

APPENDIX

| 20. 8.51 | Extract from diary of B.D.A. Difficulty in obtaining labour possibly due to loss of influence of chiefs on account of J.F. Feels that some of the Assessors may be personally disliked. |

| 30. 8.51 | C. of P. to H.H. Assessment of above. Does not agree with view regarding Assessors. |

| 3.12.51 | F.R.C. to B.R.C.
As NEMARKA has settled down in Tanna since his repatriation previous July, recommends *NAMPAS* and *NAKOMAHA* to follow. |

| 13.12.52 | *NAMPAS* had in fact returned as a member of crew. Suggests *NAKOMAHA* remains protem. |

| 10. 3.52 | J.F. mentioned in enticement case. Person involved given six months. |

| 28. 5.52 | B.R.C. to B.D.A.
Agrees *NAKOMAHA* should return. |

Phase VI

| 13. 6.52 | B.D.A. to B.R.C.
J.F. activist reported and located. Suggests proposed visit of B.R.C. accelerated. |

| 10. 6.52 | B.D.A. Venan to B.R.C.
Report of trouble on Pentecost. |

| 3. 7.52 | B.R.C. to B.H.C.
Political Activity among bushmen on Santo forestalled by opportune arrival of B.D.A. and F.D.A., R.D., on "Concorde". On Tanna, B.R.C. and F.R.C. were on Eve of Southern District tour when news of unrest came through, and their arrival on Tanna, plus the "Timra" and sailors had a salutary effect on Tannese where there had been disturbances of the peace (Lenakel area). |

| 22. 7.52 | As a result of disturbances, the following were brought to Vila and sentences passed as under:
B.D.A.
3 years
MANGLAM
IATIETAIO
KARAIH
KYEL
SAM TACUMAH
SAGET |

F.D.A.
NACE ITONGA
MAYLES
NAMPAS
POITA
IATAKA
18 months
NEWKA
LIAKA
CHAPLIN KEWWIAH
9 months
YAKAWHA
KATEWA
TAPEAHA
TOETA
NEWIEHA

16. 9.52   B.D.A. to B.R.C.
General drawing away from Mission towards Custom, fore-
shadowing further manifestations.

25.11.52   Rumors circulating in Tanna that prisoners sent to Vila have
been discharged on insufficient evidence and are to be returned.

27.11.52   B.R.C. to B.D.A.
Advises no likelihood of early return—further evidence being
sought.

28. 3.53   5 men returned to be placed under guard: TAKOMA, TA-
PEAHA, KATEWA, TOETA, NEWIEHA (those serving 9
months).

17. 4.53   All sentences reduced to 10 months except *NAMPAS* MACE,
ITONGA, NAGWI, SAM TACUMAH, and CHAPLIN
KEWWIAH.

25. 4.55   MAILES, POITA, IATOKA, MANGLAM, IATIETAIO,
KARAIH, KIEL, NEWKA, LOTAKIA to return.

19. 5.53   WILLIAM IO to be included in list of prisoners. He was
missed out in report.

4. 6.53   F. and B.D.A. to F. and B.R.C.
Concerning *NAKOMAHA,* who has remarried in Vila (As-
sessor Laufmani's daughter).

20. 6.53   F. and B.D.A. to B. and B.R.C.
Advise against return *NAKOMAHA* until either wife NOUA-NOU or wife No. 2 NOTANGI break with him entirely.

26. 6.53   *NAKOMAHA* in gaol Vila for assaulting NOTANGI.

28. 9.53   F. and B.D.A to F. and B.R.C.
Re NAKOMAHA's return, suggest NOTANGI come first and see if there is any trouble between her and NOUANOU.

4.12.53   NAKOMAHA and NEMANIAN to be returned to Tanna, followed by SAM TACUMAH.

13. 1.54   TUKUMAH and MAGEY working in Vila.

23. 1.54   TUKUMAH left for Tanna.

Phase VII

22. 2.54   *NAKOMAHA* remanded on depot by F.D.A. on 20.2.54 as a result of activities on Tanna concerning "Captain World."

4. 3.54   *NAKOMAHA* sent back to Vila.

6. 3.54   Report on "Captain World" hoax involving NAKOMAHA, who concocted a story about a tall mysterious stranger and then impersonated the figure at various gatherings convened by IATIK whom he had primed beforehand. IATIK subsequently confessed, but the stranger's peculiar red-dyed clothes were not found. Offence could not therefore be laid at NAKOMAHA's door, though all evidence pointed to him and he appeared to be intent on subversive activities.

26. 7.54   As a result of NAKOMAHA's activities on Tanna he is banished to Vila for a further 2 years as from 5.3.54.

15.10.55   NAGET, MACE and *NAMPAS* returned to Tanna.

March

1956   NAKOMAHA confined for further 6 months to Vila, as from 5.3.56.

Phase VIII

16. 8.56   Report on revival of J.F. activities on Tanna at Ipekel. Alleged to have been instigated by *NAKOMAHA* in Vila who claims he is confidant of Resident Commissioners and "head of Tannese". Usual manifestations, dances, reported appearance of J.F.

6.11.56   *NAKOMAHA* confined for further 3 months as from 4.1.57.

16. 1.57   *NAKOMAHA* returned to Tanna.

15. 2.57   Red flags hoisted on tall trees and est. 2000 natives visited Sulphur Bay hoping to see J.F. NAKOMAHA mantained flags were to become symbols of Tannese aspirations, etc. (They subsequently turned out to be old American flags.) Wild rumors prevalent re ships, submarines etc. MAIMES, *NAKOMAHA, NAMPAS,* MAILES, POITA KOUKARU involved. However, *natives were friendly and no breaking of law took place.* Government's new policy of non-intervention appeared to have good effect and take a certain amount of wind out of the sails of the ringleaders. B.D.A. addressed about 2000 natives.

17. 5.57   Visit of American ship "Yankee" to Tanna. Speech by Commander pointing out that in America people had to work for what they had, not wait for it to appear by other less certain means!